"It's an extremely rare book that you always want to have within arm's reach. This is one of those rare books. I literally could not put this book down and wanted to have a copy close to keep picking up. This book isn't made up of pages—it's made of what your heart's ever wanted to say to God but couldn't find words for. Not only are Scotty Smith's prayers one of the best gifts to give—the gift of communion with God—this book of cross-saturated prayers is a desperately needed gift to the church."

Ann Voskamp, *New York Times* bestselling author of *One Thousand Gifts* and *The Greatest Gift*

"Scotty has been our pastor and one of our dearest friends for many years, and our journey through deepest valleys and over highest mountains has been lined with the prayers of Scotty Smith. Scotty has a most unique gift of teaching and encouraging even as he leads those he prays with and for into the very presence of God. We are so excited about this new collection of prayers, which give voice to our joy, pains, and longings, and especially to the gospel."

Steven Curtis Chapman, Grammy award–winning recording artist; and **Mary Beth Chapman,** *New York Times* bestselling author of *Choosing to See*

"A book of prayers isn't supposed to make one weep or laugh or feel loved, forgiven, and free. Books of prayers are almost always books of 'religious exercises' whereby one feels more religious. Scotty Smith has walked where I've walked, wept where I've wept, rejoiced where I've rejoiced, worshiped at the altar where I've worshiped, and put words to my life—words that stand up in those places and sing the 'Hallelujah Chorus.' This book will be a devotional anchor for me for the rest of my life."

Steve Brown, broadcaster, founder of Key Life Network; author of *How to Talk So People Will Listen*

"Once again Pastor Scotty Smith has blessed us with a fully orbed, kingdom-bent collection of gospel-centered prayers. Are there really any other? Scotty does not believe so. That's what makes his writing so vital. Never has there been a time when people know so much about so little of importance. Into the fray comes the truly Good News of the gospel of Jesus Christ. Scotty faithfully transcribes the heart of Christ and applies it to the whole of life by way of petition, lament, struggle, and celebration."

Charlie Peacock, professor, Lipscomb University; music producer (Switchfoot, The Civil Wars, Chris Cornell)

"Scotty Smith is a wordsmith smitten by the Word. He lets Scripture form his tongue and shape his prayers to reflect both the depths of the heart and the language of God. These prayers are profound. They provoke me to sing and cry—to know soothing and awakening. You will find yourself gaining greater access to your heart and simultaneously the heart of God."

Dan B. Allender, professor of counseling psychology and founding president, The Seattle School of Theology and Psychology

"The hardest spiritual discipline for me is prayer. I love to lead, to teach, to strategize about how to bring the gospel to the whole world. It is hard to sit and wait on the Lord. It is difficult to have words to say to the Lord. *Every Season Prayers* makes prayer doable and beautiful. Scotty Smith is a person of prayer, and his work will help you be the same."

Darrin Patrick, lead pastor, The Journey, St. Louis; vice president, Acts 29

"*Every Season Prayers* helps us connect the multifaceted grace of God with the complexities of our daily lives. We long for intimacy with God, but we hardly know what to say. As a wise and honest pastor, Scotty helps us, drawing upon his deep knowledge of the gospel and his deep awareness of human need. I wholeheartedly commend this book as an open door for us all into a deeper experience of prayer."

Ray Ortlund, senior pastor, Immanuel Church, Nashville

"We are a weary, disabled people. Life beats us down. We forget God, relegating him to Sunday mornings and selected 'spiritual' moments. Scotty Smith's prayers break God out of the box and bring him into our Cyber Mondays, cranky Tuesdays, selfish Wednesdays, weary

Thursdays, Black Fridays, and lonely Saturdays—giving us a weeklong taste of resurrection Sundays! Scotty's prayers pry open the hidden corners of our lives and invite God in. Enjoy the feast!"

Paul Miller, executive director, seeJesus

"Scotty Smith has been a special friend and mentor since my earliest days in ministry. For nearly twenty years now, he has played the roles of professor, pastor, coach, comforter, counselor, big brother, and cheerleader in my life. Knowing Scotty in each of these ways has given me a unique, up-close access to a marvelous thread that weaves through every part of his life—and that is his life of prayer. It makes such sense that Scotty would write another book on prayer, because Scotty himself is, perhaps more than anything else, a man of prayer. As you read through these pages, you will sense yourself being drawn nearer to the Father, because near to the Father is where Scotty lives his life. Be richly blessed by what is in these pages! I know that you will."

Scott Sauls, senior pastor, Christ Presbyterian Church, Nashville; author of *Jesus Outside the Lines*

"Almost every day for the last four years, my wife and I have eagerly looked forward to receiving the gift of Scotty's prayers by email. It is rare that a prayer is not waiting for us by 6:00 a.m., and so often it eloquently expresses our longings, pain, anxiety, and struggle with life. He then leads us to reminders of God's grace, faithfulness, and love in a passage of Scripture that takes us into our own Bible study and prayer and steadies us and prepares us for the day. Often I will forward the prayer on to a family member, a friend, or a counseling client with a particular need. This new collection of wonderful model prayers teaches us how to speak to God with utter honesty and to allow ourselves to be transformed by marinating in and meditating on biblical truth. They are very helpfully divided into topical sections for particular needs and seasons of the year and of life."

Richard Winter, professor of counseling, Covenant Theological Seminary

"Thank you, Scotty! This is an excellent resource and blessing which can be used in both private devotional and corporate settings. It uses

Scripture well to give words to our hearts and prayers, covering a huge range of themes, emotions, and seasons."

Steve Timmis, executive director, Acts 29 Network Europe

"One of my favorite things about Scotty's life and teaching is his commitment to the holy Scriptures, and this book is no exception. For those of us who fight to keep God's Word and the gospel message at the forefront of our minds each day, this book is a tremendous tool. Thank you, Scotty, for loaning us the words to match what our souls desperately need to pray."

Laura Story Elvington, senior worship leader, Perimeter Church; singer-songwriter; author

"Scotty Smith has given us a great gift in this gospel-saturated book of prayers. There is a place for reading about prayer, but the greater need is to simply pray. This book helps the reader do just that. I found over and over again that Scotty put into words what my heart so often longs to articulate to God but I don't know how to or I fear to. In the spirit of the psalmist, these prayers are dangerously honest yet invite us into the very heart of God, where there is unimaginable hope and healing. I found myself over and over again exploring and expressing the depths of my heart while experiencing God's love afresh. These prayers help the reader know both their own soul and the Triune God in deeper and more revealing ways. As Calvin said, you cannot separate the two. Over the years I have used a number of books to aid my prayers, but I know of none that are as honest, are as vulnerable, and cover as many topics in as many forms (I love the short burst prayers!) as Scotty's book. This will not only be a gift for my personal time with the Lord, but as a pastor and counselor, I will be encouraging others to read and use these prayers for many years to come."

Jason Kovacs, pastor of pastoral care and counseling, Austin Stone Church

Every
Season
Prayers

Every Season Prayers

Gospel-Centered Prayers
for the Whole of Life

SCOTTY SMITH

BakerBooks

a division of Baker Publishing Group
Grand Rapids, Michigan

Published by Baker Books
a division of Baker Publishing Group
P.O. Box 6287, Grand Rapids, MI 49516-6287
www.bakerbooks.com

Printed in the United States of America

Library of Congress Cataloging-in-Publication Data
Names: Smith, Scotty, 1950– author.
Title: Every season prayers : gospel-centered prayers for the whole of life / Scotty
  Smith.
Description: Grand Rapids : Baker Books, 2016.
Identifiers: LCCN 2016009036 | ISBN 9780801014031 (pbk.)
Subjects: LCSH: Prayers.
Classification: LCC BV260 .S57 2016 | DDC 242/.8—dc23
LC record available at http://lccn.loc.gov/2016009036

16 17 18 19 20 21 22   7 6 5 4 3 2 1

Each of the prayers in *Every Season Prayers* was birthed out of relationships—first and foremost, in response to God's incomparable, inexhaustible love for us in Jesus. But many other treasured relationships also provided the fuel and focus and the longings and hope echoed in this volume. They include:

Darlene, my awesome wife of forty-four years
Kristin (my daughter) and my grandson Finn
Scott (my son) and Bayley Smith and my grandson Otis

My local "Gospel Posse"—Carter Crenshaw, Parke Brown, Paul Thomas, Buddy Greene, Steven Curtis Chapman, Scott Sauls, and David Cassidy

My Orlando Centra Care "Gospel Posse"—John Masterfield, Scott Brady, Mark Johnston, Jake Mckelvy, and Rob Paswaters

My aunt Cynthia Ward, Noel Agnew, Rose Marie Miller, Joe Novenson, Bill Fortney, Mark Dalbey, Bob Osborne, Dan and Becky Allender, Kip and Elizabeth Turnage, and Phil and Becky Douglas

The Family of West End Community Church, where I'm honored to serve as teacher in residence

Contents

Foreword

Beloved Christian author George MacDonald wrote that prayer is "the thing we need *first* and *most*." That's an interesting choice of words coming from a man whose words influenced some of the greatest writers of the twentieth century, including C. S. Lewis, G. K. Chesterton, and J. R. R. Tolkien. MacDonald believed that prayer was the most pressing, the most needful activity Christians were called to engage in.

Would you agree? How needful is prayer to you? Is it "first and most" needful? Are those the words that come to mind when you consider it? Perhaps so, but then again, if we were to be brutally honest, those might not be our exact sentiments. For many of us prayer feels more like the obligatory visit to our spinster aunt who demands we sit with her and listen to her criticisms while we stifle yawns and hope our phone will ring so that we can politely excuse ourselves. We all know we should pray; we've heard all the reasons for it and have been guilted into resolving to do better at it every year. And yet . . . it still isn't the "first and most" needful thing in our lives.

I'm just like you. I know that the Lord calls—no, rather, lovingly beckons me to sit and have audience with him at any time, on any day. And I know that when I am in need, I can run freely to the "throne of grace," where I will always find "grace to help in time of need" (Heb 4:16 ESV). Like you, I know these things . . . and yet I find that more times than not I am saying the same things over and over again, day after day, trying to fulfill my obligation, trying to make this time that I've set aside in the morning come to life. Even so, there are many mornings when I just can't seem to frame my words in a way that sparks anything in my heart deeper than the gratification of checking "prayer" off my to-do list for the day. I would like to think that my conversation with the Lord is driven by an impulse greater than the command to pray or even the selfish hope that my day will be blessed because I started it out right. I would like to believe that I'm praying because I'm desperate for the Lord; desperate for his presence, his Word, his grace, his love. MacDonald wrote that prayer is the "supplying of our great, our endless need," our need for "God himself." He continued, "Communion with God is the one need of the soul beyond all other needs; prayer is the beginning of that communion . . . a talking with God, a coming-to-one with Him, which is the sole end of prayer, yea, of existence itself."

And so the question we have to ask and then honestly answer is simply this: "Am I praying because I am desperate for communion with God?" Only you can answer that question. I admit that most of the time my answer is, "No. Sadly, no." I have many motivations for prayer, but being desperate to commune with God usually isn't at the top of that list.

This is where this wonderful book comes in. Once again my dear friend Scotty Smith has gifted the church with more than a typical book about prayer. I'm so very thankful. This book won't tell you how to tap into the power of prayer or how to become some sort of prayer Jedi. No, rather, this is a humble, loving revealing of the heart of a brother who has spent decades in prayer and who gently comes alongside us as we struggle to put words to our faith. As I read the prayers in this book, I sensed that they were written by a man who not only has known desperation for God but also has found him filled with grace and mercy.

In the twelve sections you'll find prayers for every season of your life. Are you in a season of suffering? Use the prayers in the section on lament to shape your language of desperation in this season of trial. Are you having trouble remembering that the gospel really is "Good News" for you? Then pray with Scotty through the section on preaching the gospel to your heart. Are you desperate to hear a word from the Lord? Then listen while Scotty reminds you of God's promises and love through Scriptures that have been spoken to us by our Lord. We are all in different seasons of life, and if our prayer is a reflection of our heart, then our prayer should reflect those seasons. Scotty knows this, and so here you will find prayers crafted with love and learned in the crucible of intense desperation, whispered in gentleness from the heart of a shepherd.

C. S. Lewis wrote of prayer as being an "unveiling" of the heart. *Every Season Prayers* is indeed an unveiling of the heart of Scotty Smith and will lead, if you let it, to the unveiling of your heart before a God who longs to love and comfort you more than you'll ever know. You can unveil your heart before him because he has already declared his unending love for you and his generous welcome of you, and surprisingly—no, shockingly—he actually loves to hear your voice.

I know you'll love this book because you'll love our brother Scotty's heart for prayer. But the best thing about *Every Season Prayers* is that it will help you begin to see prayer as "the thing we need *first* and *most*" because it will help you speak to and hear from the God who is the most necessary Person in the universe. Enjoy.

Elyse Fitzpatrick
Escondido, CA

Introduction

It would be impossible to overstate the joy I have experienced in writing this sequel to *Everyday Prayers: 365 Days to a Gospel-Centered Faith*. I never could have anticipated the response I've received to my first collection of prayers—prayers that were never originally written for publication. Over the course of the past three years, hardly a day has gone by without a note of thanks for one of my prayers showing up in my email box, on my Facebook page, in the form of a tweet, or at one of the websites where my prayers are shared on a daily basis.

Here's a typical response that comes in many forms, from every time zone: "Scotty, thanks for giving me words for what I was feeling but didn't know how to express to God." Few remarks, in my four decades of vocational ministry, have brought me more encouragement, or a greater sense of honoring Jesus and caring for his lambs. But the lambs haven't only given me thanks; they've also given a lot of invaluable feedback.

Quite literally, credit for the form and content of this new book must be given to a myriad of people who not only asked me to continue writing grace-saturated prayers but also made specific recommendations for this second book. The one unanimous suggestion was for a book of new prayers arranged topically, so readers can find a prayer applicable to a particular need, mood, or issue. Speaking of which, I wrote the majority of these new prayers in response to the welcomed and recurring comments, "Scotty, I'm looking for a prayer for . . ." and "Could you write a prayer about . . . ?" It has been a joy to serve a much larger community than I ever envisioned.

I also received great suggestions for different forms, lengths, and voices for the prayers—including from a surprising number of pastors and worship leaders challenging me to write prayers of confession for congregational and family worship. I have synthesized and integrated as many of these requests as possible. The tremendous diversity and rich tapestry of requests compelled me to land on the title, *Every Season Prayers: Gospel-Centered Prayers for the Whole of Life*—as the range and cry of these prayers requires a very big and glorious gospel. Many, many thanks to friends who will remain anonymous but whose imprint is evident throughout this collection of prayers.

As with my first book, my intent with this volume is to equip God's people to pray, not do their praying for them. This is why I've included exercises in this book that will enable you to develop your own voice in prayer as well as cultivate a listening heart.

There's nothing special about my words or prayers. I come to the throne of grace covered in the same righteousness of Christ that is given to every Christian.

I'm a highly ordinary guy who was given the great privilege of being discipled by a remarkable man named Jack Miller, who taught me how to pray the Scriptures back to God through the riches of the gospel in the posture of a humble, joyful, grateful child—beloved of the Father. My goal has been to write and only include prayers "in line with the truth of the gospel" (Gal. 2:14). Where I have succeeded, God be praised! Where I have missed the mark, I rest in Christ's forgiveness and thank you for yours. With all my heart, I continue to affirm: there's nothing more than the gospel, just more of the gospel. *Soli Deo Gloria.*

1

Prayers for All Occasions

A Prayer for Rejoicing
in the Scandalous Goodness of the Gospel

Now to the one who works, wages are not credited as a gift but as an obligation. However, to the one who does not work but trusts God who justifies the ungodly, their faith is credited as righteousness. David says the same thing when he speaks of the blessedness of the one to whom God credits righteousness apart from works: "Blessed are those whose transgressions are forgiven, whose sins are covered. Blessed is the one whose sin the Lord will never count against them." (Rom. 4:4–8)

Dear heavenly Father, this Scripture contradicts *everything* we assume about the way life is "supposed to work." We expect to get what's coming to us. We demand fairness—an honest return for our labor, time, and sweat. But the gospel flies in the face of conventionality, predictability, and normalcy. To which we cry, "Hallelujah!"

Thank you for not being fair with us. Thank you for being outrageously generous, immeasurably kind, and scandalously good. What we could never earn—your perfect righteousness—you have credited to us as a gift. What we fully deserve—to be dealt with according to the wages of our sin—you will never do. What we cannot imagine—that you would justify ungodly people—you have joyfully and legally done.

Because of Jesus' perfect and finished work, our transgressions are forgiven (all of them), our sins are covered (every one of them), and you'll never hold us guilty for them. King David called such people "blessed." Because we are among "such people," we are humbled and grateful, and we are free beyond our wildest imagining.

Thank you for reconciling us to yourself through Jesus, and for placing us in an eternity of your permanent favor. Thank you not only for removing all condemnation for our sins but also for replacing deserved judgment with your exuberant jubilation. Thank you for not just welcoming us but wanting us. Thank you for not just "letting us into heaven one day" but delighting in us fully in this very day!

By the power of the Holy Spirit, drive the gospel, this gospel, deeper and deeper into our hearts, that we might live and love to your glory. We pray in Jesus' trustworthy name. Amen.

A Prayer for Accepting the Changes That Come with Aging

Even to your old age and gray hairs I am he, I am he who will sustain you. I have made you and I will carry you; I will sustain you and I will rescue you. (Isa. 46:4)

The righteous flourish like the palm tree and grow like a cedar in Lebanon. They are planted in the house of the Lord; they flourish in the courts of our God. They still bear fruit in old age; they are ever full of sap and green, to declare that the Lord is upright; he is my rock, and there is no unrighteousness in him. (Ps. 92:12–15 ESV)

Dear heavenly Father, a brief conversation with aging friends yesterday reminded me of the inevitable—we're all getting older. And with the increase of years comes changes over which we have little or no control. Those changes are either going to drive us to you or to denial, self-absorbing sadness, or foolish ways of medicating our pain and fears. I choose option one.

Thank you for your promise to sustain us when our energy is abating; to carry us when we cannot carry as much as we used to or even carry ourselves; and to rescue us when we get entangled in ways of thinking and choosing that contradict your great love for us in Jesus.

Father, thank you for the promise that age doesn't preclude flourishing and fruitfulness. By your Spirit and grace, keep us ever full of "sap and green." You are our Rock and our righteousness—our stability and standing in grace are inviolate.

Though outwardly we are "wasting away," we will not lose heart—in fact, we will thrive in heart, for you will bring to completion the good work you began in us. As our eyesight grows dimmer, let us see the beauty of Jesus with increasingly clarity. As our hearing gets fainter, let us hear your voice louder than ever, declaring us to be your beloved children of grace—in whom you delight and for whom you've prepared an eternity beyond anything we can hope or imagine. We gratefully pray in Jesus' triumphant and tender name. Amen.

A Prayer for Worshiping
and Trusting the God of Hope

May the God of hope fill you with all joy and peace in believing, so that by the power of the Holy Spirit you may abound in hope. (Rom. 15:13 ESV)

Fear not, for I am with you; be not dismayed, for I am your God; I will strengthen you, I will help you, I will uphold you with my righteous right hand. (Isa. 41:10 ESV)

Dear heavenly Father, I begin this day so very thankful for your Word. As I meditate and pray my way through these Scriptures, I'm deeply grateful you chose to reveal yourself to us with words we can understand and trust. Though we don't worship the Bible, we worship you because of the Bible.

Today in particular, I'm thankful to know and worship you as the God of hope. In a world of predictable unpredictabilities; unsettling circumstances; and broken people, places, and things, it is a source of immeasurable joy and peace to know that you love us and are in control of all things. Thank you that you intend for us to abound in hope and not just have enough hope to get by on.

We don't have to be afraid or be dismayed by anything or anyone, for your righteous right hand has a firm hold on us, and your grip is the grip of grace. You are fully with us and you are completely for us. We know this to be true because of your gift of Jesus. You loved us so much you gave your one and only Son, so that instead of perishing, we would have eternal life. Father, thank you that the gospel is true and that you really do love us this much.

Because you have already given us so much grace in Jesus, I choose to obey you and set my hope fully on the grace yet to be given—the even greater grace we receive when Jesus returns. Father, thank you for being so very generous, hope-igniting, and peace-fueling. I pray in Jesus' holy and loving name. Amen.

A Prayer for Healing and Health Concerns

I will restore health to you, and your wounds I will heal, declares the LORD. (Jer. 30:17 ESV)

Dear friend, I pray that you may enjoy good health and that all may go well with you, even as your soul is getting along well. (3 John 2)

We who are living will also be transformed. For our dying bodies must be transformed into bodies that will never die; our mortal bodies must be transformed into immortal bodies. (1 Cor. 15:52–53 NLT)

Dear heavenly Father, my stuffed-up head and slightly sore throat are mere irritants compared to the health crises many of us face as this day begins. How we long for the day of no more cancer, no more dementia, no more heart disease, no more respiratory issues, no more Ebola and AIDS, no more disease of *any* kind—the day of perfect health.

Thank you for the promise of a resurrection body that will never get sick, wear out, or die. Thank you that our life in the new heaven and new earth will not include visits to the ER, health insurance, medical bills, hospitals, nursing homes, palliative care, or funeral homes. Hasten that day, Father; hasten it.

Until then, we will pray for healing—thankful that Jesus' finished work has secured the redemption of our whole being—mind, body, and spirit. Though we'd love for you to answer all of our prayers affirmatively and on our timetable, we will trust and love you when you grant us sufficient grace instead of instant healing (2 Cor. 12:7–10).

Father, we will also seek to take care of these "tents" in which we live (see 2 Cor. 5:1–5). Thank you for good food, opportunities for exercise, the gift of sleep, clean water—gifts you've given us by grace, gifts you intend for us to share with others. Indeed, Father, may our suffering make us more sensitive to the sufferings of others. Even as Jesus joyfully fulfilled the law for us, grant us great joy in fulfilling the law of Christ as we bear one another's burdens (Gal. 6:2). In Jesus' triumphant and tender name we pray. Amen.

A Prayer for Using Our Words to Bring Healing, Not Harm

If you claim to be religious but don't control your tongue, you are fooling yourself, and your religion is worthless. (James 1:26 NLT)

There is one whose rash words are like sword thrusts, but the tongue of the wise brings healing. (Prov. 12:18 ESV)

The mouth speaks what the heart is full of. (Luke 6:45)

Dear heavenly Father, nothing is more daily and revealing than our words—the conversations we carry on in our minds and the communications we share with one another. That is both sobering and encouraging to me as I begin this day.

It's sobering for obvious reasons. I don't want to contradict my love for you by an irresponsible use of my words. I don't want to speak like a man thrusting a sword; I want my words to bring healing and grace.

That's where the encouragement comes in. That which fills my heart will shape my words. So before I have my first interaction with anyone else today, Father, I want to set my mind, heart, and affection on you. Before I speak, I want to listen to what you are constantly saying to us, your beloved children. I want my heart to be so full of your grace that it will be difficult not to speak with grace-seasoned words today.

Father, thank you that it was with everlasting love and tenderness you drew us to yourself. Thank you that it was your kindness that led us to repentance. Thank you for giving Jesus on our behalf and for hiding our lives in him. We are now forgiven and righteous, desired and enjoyed, known and secure. Praise your holy and generous name.

Nothing we can do can separate us from your love, cause you to regret saving us, or put you in a bad mood toward us. Your love is the most dependable and unwavering thing in our lives. Nothing can alter your gospelicious plan for our lives or for the entire cosmos. From the overflow of such amazing grace, we will purpose to speak to others today. We pray in Jesus' great and gracious name. Amen.

A Prayer for Those of Us with Loved Ones Impacted by Memory Loss

Can a woman forget her nursing child, that she should have no compassion on the son of her womb? Even these may forget, yet I will not forget you. Behold, I have engraved you on the palms of my hands; your walls are continually before me. (Isa. 49:15–16 ESV)

Dear heavenly Father, though Isaiah used the image somewhat metaphorically, mothers and fathers *do* forget the children they have brought into the world. I know this quite well, having lived through the journey of watching my dad forgetting my name, then my face, then everything about me. The process was very painful, yet you met us time and again with your mercy and grace.

I am so thankful that the gospel is a living hope, not sentimental hype. I am so thankful that long after Dad forgot you, you never forgot him. I am so thankful that Dad's memory has been healed and that he now knows and remembers perfectly. Above all, I am envious that he now knows you perfectly, while I am bound to the world of knowing in part.

As someone who found you to be the Father of compassion and the God of all comfort in a story of dementia and Alzheimer's, it's an honor to pray for others in that same painful journey. Father, grant spouses and children, family members and friends, a profound sense of your presence and the courage to love well.

Grant them freedom to grieve their mounting sense of loss; the grace to accept the changes in their loved one; and power to stay as present as possible when doing so becomes increasingly difficult. Grant them wisdom for each stage of the journey, trustworthy and compassionate medical care, and the necessary financial and emotional resources.

Lastly, Father, I pray you will help all of us impacted by memory loss to treasure being known and remembered by you. If we should forget you in our journey to life in the new heaven and new earth, we will never outlive your love and grace for us. The only things you're not going to remember are our sins against you. Hallelujah, many times over! So very gratefully we pray, in Jesus' strong and loving name. Amen.

A Prayer for Decision-Making Peace

We can make our plans, but the LORD determines our steps. (Prov. 16:9 NLT).

Trust in the LORD with all your heart, and do not lean on your own understanding. In all your ways acknowledge him, and he will make straight your paths. (Prov. 3:5–6 ESV)

Dear heavenly Father, some decisions are "no-brainers," and some require nothing more than sanctified common sense. But there are other decisions in front of us that tie us in knots, rob us of sleep, and keep us second-guessing. Today I'm praying for myself and friends who find themselves in that third category. We need your peace to rule in our hearts as we seek to choose wisely (Col. 3:15).

It's incomparably comforting to know that you are the God who determines our steps, even as we nervously punch an address on the GPS of our hearts. This doesn't mean we are to be passive in our decision making but means we must realize that you are very present—opening doors we cannot shut and shutting doors we cannot open. We praise and bless you for your sovereign, comprehensive, and constant engagement in our lives.

We certainly have every reason to trust you with all of our hearts, Father, because you loved us with all of your heart when you sent Jesus into the world to be our Savior. Since you've given Jesus to us and for us, we can depend on you to give us everything else we need (Rom. 8:32). So leaning away from our own understanding, we now lean fully upon your heart and hands.

Father, make our ways straight as we seek to honor you with decisions that concern our children; decisions about employment and financial matters; decisions about health care for ourselves and those we love; decisions required in messy and broken relationships; decisions generated by unexpected circumstances and fresh heartache; decisions with a deadline staring us in the eyes.

Father, thank you for teaching us that life is not primarily about making the right decisions but about trusting the right Lord—and that would be you. Your name is Redeemer, and you do all things well. We pray in Jesus' merciful and mighty name. Amen.

A Prayer for Days
When We're Feeling Discontented

Godliness with contentment is great gain, for we brought nothing into the world, and we cannot take anything out of the world. But if we have food and clothing, with these we will be content. (1 Tim. 6:6–8 ESV)

Keep your life free from love of money, and be content with what you have, for he has said, "I will never leave you nor forsake you." (Heb. 13:5 ESV)

Dear heavenly Father, I assume that until the day you either take me home or send Jesus back to finish making all things new, I'm going to be both a whiner and a worshiper. Some days, *nothing* feels like it's enough—people, places, or things. Other days, your love, grace, and presence are more real and satisfying than anything else or all things combined.

I want more of those days, Father—more of the days when your love is better than life, your grace is more than sufficient, and your presence is sweeter than honey. But until the day of no more whining, discontent, and grumbling, free me, Father, to more fully delight myself in you. Not to get the desires of my heart, but that you may be the primary delight of my heart. I cannot imagine a freer posture in life.

Help me know the difference between redemptive discontent and destructive ingratitude. To remind us that we're not "home" yet, you've placed a limit on how much satisfaction anything or anyone can give us. Thank you, Father, for doing so. This means our idols will always fail us eventually.

Father, I can claim "godliness" unto contentment only because you have hidden my life in Christ—who is my righteousness and sanctification and redemption (1 Cor. 1:30). May this profoundly good news impact the way I enjoy my food, put on my clothes, and relate to other people. In Jesus' wonderful and merciful name I pray. Amen.

A Prayer for When I Wake Up with a Low-Grade Irritability

If I speak in the tongues of men and of angels, but have not love, I am a noisy gong or a clanging cymbal. And if I have prophetic powers, and understand all mysteries and all knowledge, and if

I have all faith, so as to remove mountains, but have not love, I am nothing. If I give away all I have, and if I deliver up my body to be burned, but have not love, I gain nothing. Love is patient and kind; love does not envy or boast; it is not arrogant or rude. It does not insist on its own way; it is not irritable or resentful. (1 Cor. 13:1–5 ESV)

Dear heavenly Father, though there's a lot more in this remarkable passage about love, I chose to stop this morning with Paul's couplet about love not being "irritable or resentful," because I woke up with a measure of each vying for my day. I need your grace, even before the sun comes up. So I come to you—I run to you, thankful for your welcome and new mercies.

Father, I don't want this to be a bad-attitude day, and as tempting as it is to blame and make excuses for my low-grade irritability, I'm not gonna do it. I am canceling my plans for a pity party, and I relinquish my elder-brother attitude of condescension, withdrawal, and judgment. Our feelings are to be taken seriously, but our feelings aren't lord—that would be Jesus.

So, Father, by your grace, settle me, center me, and gentle me for the day. I am grateful for your steadfast love, inexhaustible patience, and perpetual kindness. I want to walk in your Spirit today, a whole lot more than I want to "cop an attitude." May I forgive as you've forgiven me; accept as you have accepted me in Christ; and encourage others increasingly as the great day of Jesus' return approaches.

Once again, I trust you for thick skin and a big heart. Free me to love to your glory, all day long. In Jesus' great and grace-full name I pray. Amen.

A Prayer for Remaining Grateful When Life Is Messy

Give thanks in all circumstances; for this is the will of God in Christ Jesus for you. (1 Thess. 5:18 ESV)

Fear not, for I am with you; be not dismayed, for I am your God; I will strengthen you, I will help you, I will uphold you with my righteous right hand. (Isa. 41:10 ESV)

Dear heavenly Father, there are some days when it's good (and important) to remember that you call us to offer thanks *in*, not *for*, all circumstances. The gospel isn't about magical thinking or make-believe living, spiritual anesthesia or circumstantial amnesia. In fact, the gospel is the only place in the universe where we don't have to pretend about anything. That's one of the many reasons we love you and are grateful to be your children.

Father, strengthen, help, and uphold us with your righteous right hand, in stories that are recipes for dismay.

For those of us for whom holidays highlight the brokenness of our family system—grant us grace and freedom to love well in the chaos.

For those of us bearing the weight of health concerns for ourselves or those we love—grant us grace, peace, and the assurance of your nearness.

For those of us weighed down by some combination of the six o'clock news, financial pressures, vocational issues, and relational heartache—grant us grace and a vision of the occupied throne of heaven.

For those of us who hear the condemning whispers of Satan louder than the consoling voice of Jesus, grant us grace and fresh assurance that nothing can separate us from your love—that Jesus plus nothing is our righteousness, period.

Father, in these and other scenarios of difficult circumstances, reassure us that you are very much at work, for your glory and our good. For you have called us—you have subpoenaed us to an eternal life of intimacy with yourself. You want us, you have us, and you love us. Hallelujah, now and forever we are yours. In Jesus' merciful and mighty name we pray. Amen.

A Prayer for Reaffirming That God Is in Control of Everything

Remember the former things, those of long ago; I am God, and there is no other; I am God, and there is none like me. I make known the end from the beginning, from ancient times, what is still to come. I say, "My purpose will stand, and I will do all that I please." (Isa. 46:9–10)

Dear heavenly Father, though there are days when I, the clay, presume to tell you, the Potter, what to create next; and though there are stories where I, the character, want to dictate to you, the Author, how the plot should change; and though there are circumstances about which I, your subject, want to order you, my King, into action—no, I really don't. Not really. A thousand times over, not really!

I am so thankful that you are God and I am not. I am so thankful that you are the Alpha and the Omega and every other Greek letter in between. I am so thankful you know the beginning and the ending and every other moment as well. I am so thankful that you don't answer all my prayers with a resounding "Yes!" I am so thankful that you don't cater to my fancies, give in to my whining, or share your throne with me—even for a nanosecond.

I am so thankful that you do as you please, even when your pleasure requires my displeasure. I am so thankful that you're not codependent on me in any way, shape, or form, and that I'm absolutely dependent on you—even when I "kick against the goads" (Acts 26:14), get frustrated with your sense of timing, or, in my moments of temporary insanity, question your goodness.

Father, I am so thankful you are God and the gospel is true, period. In Jesus' triumphant and tender name I pray. Amen.

A Prayer for the Peace of Jesus to Reign in Our Relationships

He brought this Good News of peace to you Gentiles who were far away from him, and peace to the Jews who were near. Now all of us can come to the Father through the same Holy Spirit because of what Christ has done for us. (Eph. 2:17–18 NLT)

Dear Lord Jesus, this Scripture is so encouraging and hope-fueling. By your life, death, and resurrection, you have become the ultimate Peacemaker, and now you ever live to preach peace to our hearts through the gospel. We praise you for being the hostility-destroying, enemy-reconciling, relationship-healing Savior.

First and foremost, we bless you for securing us in a perfect relationship with God. Because of your finished work, we no longer live with fear and doubt about what God thinks about us. We now not only enjoy unbroken access to our Father but also are assured of his great delight, perpetual rejoicing, and constant pursuit of us. Even when he must discipline us, our Father does so with a heart of love, not disgust or aggravation. There is no peace like peace with God.

Though we sometimes offer you resistance, Lord, we're also grateful that you preach peace to us as those who participate in a wide array of broken relationships. You're committed to destroying all kinds of hostilities and reconciling all kinds of people—in the body of Christ, in our families, in our communities, and even with our enemies. Forgive us when we choose resentment over reconciliation, nursing grudges over building bridges, and rehearsing our hurts quicker than we remember the gospel.

Glorious Prince of Peace, one day you will reconcile wolves and lambs, leopards and goats, calves and lions. Until that day, give us the desire, humility, and power to live as a people of peace. For your glory and by your grace, free us to live as agents of your reconciling love. Life is just too short to get and stay mad. Melt our hearts; heal our relationships. We pray in your peerless and peace-full name. Amen.

A Prayer for Extending the Kindness of God

But when the goodness and loving kindness of God our Savior appeared, he saved us, not because of works done by us in righteousness, but according to his own mercy, by the washing of regeneration and renewal of the Holy Spirit, whom he poured out on us richly through Jesus Christ our Savior. (Titus 3:4–6 ESV)

Or do you think lightly of the riches of His kindness and tolerance and patience, not knowing that the kindness of God leads you to repentance? (Rom. 2:4 NASB)

Dear heavenly Father, I praise you for being so kind, gentle, and patient with me. When I consider the difference between how much I know and how well I love, I am compelled to worship you for the truth and riches of the gospel. You don't love me to the degree I love others; you love me to the degree you have hidden my life in Christ, which is completely. This Good News is my peace, hope, and joy.

It's also the basis, and rocket fuel, of my repentance. Even as your kindness continues to lead me to repentance and to more of Jesus, so I repent, Father. I repent of nourishing lingering resentments. I repent of holding on to a few hurts a little tighter than others. I repent of not being as quick to forgive, heal, and move on as you intend.

I acknowledge what you already know to be true: I've enjoyed the role of victim a little more than I've relished the thought of being a peacemaker. Avoidance has been easier than hoping. But, Father, I now crave freedom more than I "need" justice. The only justice I need has been meted out at the cross, where Jesus died for my sin and you reconciled me to yourself.

So, Father, as I reach for the garments of grace—compassion, kindness, humility, gentleness, and patience—I trust you for strength to extend to others the same loving-kindness you have poured on me richly in Jesus. Bring glory to yourself. I bring my convicted and grateful heart to you. I pray in Jesus' tender and loving name. Amen.

A Prayer for Remembering
God's Steadfast Love during a Busy Day

This I call to mind, and therefore I have hope: The steadfast love of the LORD never ceases; his mercies never come to an end; they are new every morning; great is your faithfulness. "The LORD is my portion," says my soul, "therefore I will hope in him." (Lam. 3:21–24 ESV)

You keep him in perfect peace whose mind is stayed on you, because he trusts in you. (Isa. 26:3 ESV)

Dear heavenly Father, I woke up today with all kinds of random thoughts competing for my attention and energy. My "to-do list" has more demands than there are hours in this day. That's what makes this Scripture so precious and timely. Even before the sun comes up, I want to remember what matters and Who matters. Even before I fix my breakfast, I choose to feast on your new mercies.

So, Father, I bless you for your steadfast, irrepressible, life-defining love. Life isn't about getting everything done but is about knowing you, walking with you, and enjoying you. I won't add a day or hour to my life by stress and worry. Far better to do a few things well, as a man of peace and kindness, than to rush through my list and run over people. Help me to remember, all day long, that the only thing that counts is faith expressing itself in love (Gal. 5:6).

Father, you are my "portion"—that is, my joy, peace, and inheritance. So I will hope in you today—not in people's approval, a demand-free life, or pride of accomplishment. I have a pretty good plan for the day, but I trust you to order my steps (Prov. 16:9). I pray in Jesus' peace-giving, heart-centering name. Amen.

A Prayer for a Mary Heart in a Martha World

As Jesus and the disciples continued on their way to Jerusalem, they came to a certain village where a woman named Martha welcomed him into her home. Her sister, Mary, sat at the Lord's feet, listening to what he taught. But Martha was distracted by the big dinner she was preparing. She came to Jesus and said, "Lord, doesn't it seem unfair to you that my sister just sits here while I do all the work? Tell her to come and help me." But the Lord said to her, "My dear Martha, you are worried and upset over all these details! There is only one thing worth being concerned about. Mary has discovered it, and it will not be taken away from her." (Luke 10:38–42 NLT)

Dear Lord Jesus, first of all, thank you for being so welcoming and desirous of our fellowship. Not only do we have access to your throne of grace 24/7, it's *you* who greets us there. We're never a bother, are never put on hold, never have to take a number and wait. We'll never meet a tired and frustrated you, because you're *always* the Bridegroom who delights in and rejoices over his Bride. Hallelujah, we cry, many times over!

We're the ones who get tired and frustrated. We live in a "Martha" world of many distractions, never-ending demands, and overstimulation. Lord Jesus, help us—help me cultivate a Mary heart in a Martha world. My problem isn't the world I inhabit but the heart that inhabits me. I make King David's prayer mine, Jesus: "Give me an undivided heart that I may live in awe of your name" (see Ps. 86:11). You are the "one thing worth being concerned about"; you are the "one thing" that will never be taken from us.

My "must get done list" isn't going to go away, but as you refresh and deepen my communion with you, I'm certain I can live with a quieter, gentler, kinder heart. By the compelling wonder of your beauty and the relentless power of grace, I trust you for that work in my heart. In the gospel I hear you say, "Come away, my beloved; my desire is for you." To which I respond gladly, Lord Jesus. I pray in your compassionate and welcoming name. Amen.

A Prayer When Feeling Fearful and Angry in a World of Evil

Be still before the LORD and wait patiently for him; fret not yourself over the one who prospers in his way, over the man who carries out evil devices! Refrain from anger, and forsake wrath! Fret not yourself; it tends only to evil. For the evildoers shall be cut off, but those who wait for the LORD shall inherit the land. In just a little while, the wicked will be no more; though you look carefully at his place, he will not be there. But the meek shall inherit the land and delight themselves in abundant peace. (Ps. 37:7–11 ESV)

Dear heavenly Father, it's beginning to feel like it's always another day, another story of terror-making, evildoing, life-taking madness. How long, O Lord, how long before you send Jesus back to eradicate all evil? How long before the wicked will be no more? How much longer is "just a little while"?

It's hard not to fret. It's hard not to feel fearful and angry when women, children, and the elderly are slaughtered in African villages; when the streets and markets of Paris become the venue for the perversion of religion and the murder of your image bearers; when your church and children are being subjected to unconscionable persecution.

Father, I offer my prayer not as an arrogant man judging the sins of others to be more reprehensible than my own but as a longing man, so ready for the fulfillment of your promises for a world of shalom—an eternity of abundant peace in the new heaven and new earth. Until that day, grant me grace not to be a man of anger and revenge but to be a man of peace and prayer. Vengeance belongs to you, not to me.

Grant me wisdom to know what loving mercy, doing justice, and walking humbly with you looks like in my community. Replace my frets and fears with faith and trust, and my anger and wrath with patience and courage. In Jesus' triumphant and grace-full name I pray. Amen.

A Prayer for Parenting by Grace, Faith, and Love

Unless the LORD builds the house, those who build it labor in vain. Unless the LORD watches over the city, the watchman stays awake in vain. It is in vain that you rise up early and go late to rest, eating the bread of anxious toil; for he gives to his beloved sleep. Behold, children are a heritage from the LORD, the fruit of the womb a reward. (Ps. 127:1–3 ESV)

Dear heavenly Father, yet again we turn to you as the designer and builder of all things, including the lives of our children and grandchildren. Thank you for reminding us that our children are a gift, not a project.

At times you've had to use a gospel wrecking ball on my parenting style in order to build something more lasting and

41

beautiful. That process continues. But even when I'm over-bearing or underbelieving, disengaged or too enmeshed, I am thankful to know that you remain faithful and loving.

Continue to rescue me from relational "laboring in vain"—assuming a burden you never intended parents to bear. Father, only you can reveal the glory and grace of Jesus to our children. Only you can give anyone a new heart. You've called us to parent as an act of worship—to parent "as unto you," not as a way of saving face, making a name for ourselves, or proving our worth.

It's the height of arrogance to think our "good parenting" accounts for the best of what we see in the lives of our children, and it's a lie from hell to assume that our "bad parenting" is the sole reason for the things that break our hearts. Free us, Father; free us and forgive us. Oh, the undue pressure our children must feel when we parent more out of our fear and pride than by your love and grace.

Since our kids are your inheritance, Father, teach us how to care for them as humble stewards, not as anxious owners. More than anything else, show us how to parent and grand-parent in a way that best reveals the unsearchable riches of Christ. Give us quick repentances and observable kindnesses. Father, we want to love and serve our children "in line with the truth of the gospel" (Gal. 2:14). We pray in Jesus' faithful and powerful name. Amen.

A Prayer of Longing for Our Resurrection Body

Therefore we do not lose heart. Though outwardly we are wasting away, yet inwardly we are being renewed day by day. For our light and momentary troubles are achieving for us an eternal glory that far outweighs them all. So we fix our eyes not on what is seen, but on what is unseen, since what is seen is temporary, but what is unseen is eternal. (2 Cor. 4:16–18)

For we know that when this earthly tent we live in is taken down (that is, when we die and leave this earthly body), we will have a house in heaven, an eternal body made for us by God himself and not by human hands. We grow weary in our present bodies, and we long to put on our heavenly bodies like new clothing. (2 Cor. 5:1–2 NLT)

Dear heavenly Father, the current aches and pains in my body give me an unavoidable opportunity either to whine or to worship. Since I know where my whining usually takes me, I think I'll stay with worshiping you. But first of all, thank you for giving us the important gift of lament. I've learned the hard way that if we're unwilling to grieve our losses, then our compassion for others will be significantly stunted. I don't like pain, but if it tunes my heart to care for others, grant me grace, Father, to rejoice in suffering.

That being said, I do rejoice in the hope of the new body we will receive when Jesus returns. Our healing will be complete. Father, thank you that Jesus secured not only the perfection of our spirits but also the resurrection of our bodies. Even as Jesus was raised, so shall we be. We groan now but will be whole forever. Hallelujah! These "light and momentary troubles" are incredibly inconvenient and bothersome, but our rejoicing will be eternal.

Until that day, Father, I will seek to take care of myself and will trust you for healing and health. By the power of the gospel, please help me be someone in whom the weak, weary, and broken find understanding and encouragement. In Jesus' tender and triumphant name I pray. Amen.

A Prayer for Days When You're Feeling Weary

Come to me, all who labor and are heavy laden, and I will give you rest. Take my yoke upon you, and learn from me, for I am gentle and lowly in heart, and you will find rest for your souls. (Matt. 11:28–29 ESV)

He will not crush the weakest reed or put out a flickering candle. (Isa. 42:3 NLT)

Dear Lord Jesus, we praise you for occupying the throne of grace with so much joy, gentleness, and burden-bearing love. When we feel our weakest—when we feel like "flickering candles"—you don't critique us, but you shower us with compassion. You promise a rest you alone can give, and we are ready to receive.

We bring you the weariness that comes from seeking to love well. No aspect of our lives is more delightful and more depleting than our relationships. As parents, spouses, and friends, grant us grace, wisdom, and strength, Lord Jesus. Give us thick skin and big hearts for staying present and engaged.

We bring you the exhaustion we feel from having longer to-do lists than there are hours in the day. Sometimes the sheer "demandingness" of life makes us want to get a one-way ticket to a faraway place. But since that would solve nothing, we ask for grace to choose between the critical things and the less important things immediately in front of us. Jesus, please grant us the gift of good, deep, restorative sleep, and free us from our reliance on the stimulants of caffeine and sugar, activity, and the approval of people.

We bring you our fatigue born from our stories of grief and loss. Jesus, help us to accept the reality of our emotional depletion and mental tiredness. Grant us grace, friends, and strength for the healing journey in front of us. We pray in your kind and trustworthy name. Amen.

A Prayer for Perspective When Suffering

Do not fear, for I have redeemed you; I have summoned you by name; you are mine. When you pass through the waters, I will be with you; and when you pass through the rivers, they will not sweep over you. (Isa. 43:1–2)

And after you have suffered a little while, the God of all grace, who has called you to his eternal glory in Christ, will himself restore, confirm, strengthen, and establish you. (1 Pet. 5:10 ESV)

Dear heavenly Father, thank you so many times over for the way you come to us in your Word. You don't merely give us "verses to claim," but you reveal yourself as a Father to know—a Father who loves and cares for us, so much more than we realize.

Today, in particular, thank you for validating our sufferings and for pledging yourself to us in our hard places and broken stories. There is no name that you call us that is any more precious to us than "Mine." We are honored to be yours and relish everything that belonging to you implies.

Father, you say to us that not if but when we pass through deep waters and rushing rivers, you will be with us. Thank you for being up front about life between the resurrection and return of Jesus. There will be, and there are, difficult seasons and all types of suffering in this life.

Grant us the perspective Peter had. No matter how many years you give us in this world, sufferings in this life are for "a little while." In the big scheme of things, it's only going to hurt for "a little while." Thank you for your promise to restore, confirm, strengthen, and establish us—in, through, and after our suffering.

And grant us Paul's perspective as well—his sense of redemptive math. The things you have prepared for us in the future do far, far, far outvalue the present sufferings we are called to endure now. Father, grant us the grace we need to suffer to your glory, the strength to trust you in the hardships and with our heartaches, and the wisdom and kindness to care for our fellow sufferers. In Jesus' tender and triumphant name we pray. Amen.

A Prayer for Resting in the Sovereignty of God

After this time had passed, I, Nebuchadnezzar, looked up to heaven. My sanity returned, and I praised and worshiped the Most High and honored the one who lives forever. His rule is everlasting, and his kingdom is eternal. All the people of the earth are nothing compared to him. He does as he pleases among the angels of heaven and among the people of the earth. No one can stop him or say to him, "What do you mean by doing these things?" (Dan. 4:34–35 NLT)

Dear heavenly Father, like Nebuchadnezzar, I am never more sane than when I am worshiping you and acknowledging your sovereignty. I am so very thankful that you are God and I am not. Forgive me when I think less of you and otherwise of me.

I am grateful that you do as you please and not as we often beg you to do. Indeed, Father, I've lived long enough to praise you for some of the "no's" I've received to prayers for which I desperately wanted a "yes." You do all things well—not easy—but in time, you will make all things beautiful. Give me grace to wait for that day, Father.

Help me to trust your heart when I cannot see your hand at work. Forgive me for thinking I need to draw certain international crises and personal situations to your attention, as though you're not aware, or worse, as though you don't care. Thank you, Father, for your kindness and patience when I'm anxious and demanding.

So as this day begins and continues, I'm grateful to affirm that Jesus has the hearts of all kings in his hand; that you care not only for birds and fields but also for me and the people I love; and that nothing can happen or will happen apart from your sovereign will. Forgive me when I doubt your faithfulness, and grant me grace when I struggle with your ways. In Jesus' trustworthy and worship-worthy name I pray. Amen.

A Prayer for Being Still and Trusting God to Fight for Us

"Didn't we say to you in Egypt, 'Leave us alone; let us serve the Egyptians'? It would have been better for us to serve the Egyptians than to die in the desert!" Moses answered the people, "Do not be afraid. Stand firm and you will see the deliverance the Lord will bring you today. The Egyptians you see today you will never see again. The LORD will fight for you; you need only to be still." (Exod. 14:12–14)

Dear heavenly Father, fear and anxiety can really do a number on us. I totally get how your children could prefer returning to a life of slavery in Egypt over trusting you in the wilderness of the unknown. I've often felt a similar temptation to choose a known brokenness over the promise of unseen beauty. Help my unbelief as I face different battles and skirmishes in life. Help me to be still and trust that you will fight for me.

Father, I'm not facing the threat of Egyptian soldiers (thankfully). Often my biggest battles are within my own heart. You tell me of your great love for me in Jesus—which I really believe is true—yet too often I look to people to validate me, as though your delight in me is not enough. Continue to free me from my love of the approval of man.

Many times I battle with trusting you with the hearts of others—people I love. I resort to ineffective ways of manipulating, spiritualizing, or trying to "fix" people. It never works, never. Help me to love others as Jesus loves me. Help me to extend your welcoming heart, your acceptance, and your grace. I throw down my weapons of trying to be the fourth member of the Trinity in the lives of others.

You've always been faithful, generous, and present. I choose stillness and trust over fear and worry. I pray in Jesus' tender and triumphant name. Amen.

A Prayer for Accepting God's Plans over Our Druthers

I know the plans I have for you, declares the Lord, plans for welfare and not for evil, to give you a future and a hope. (Jer. 29:11 ESV)

Dear heavenly Father, this well-known, beloved verse simultaneously confronts us and comforts us. It confronts that part of us that wishes you would simply "baptize" the plans we make for ourselves. We'd write stories that include as little disruption and change as possible, few surprises and no suffering, tons of familiarity and predictability, and very little actual need for faith and waiting. In essence, we'd love for you to be more of a sugar daddy than Abba Father. Thank you for your kindness and patience with us.

In our heart of hearts, that's not what we really want. We don't really want you to be the clay and us the potter—not really. We trust you; we love you, Father. You gave Jesus to us and for us; of course you'll give us everything else we actually need (Rom. 8:32).

It's just that sometimes your plan includes things that in the moment don't really feel like they're for our welfare at all. You call our favorite pastors to new places; you send our kids to college ten states away, rather than only one; you give us new neighbors who are loud and boorish and take the ones with whom we could weep and laugh.

There are stretches when it seems like you answer our prayers with a disproportionate amount of "no's" to "yeses." Healing doesn't come quick enough and funds run out too quick. Instead of grace upon grace, sometimes life feels like disappointment upon disappointment.

And yet, and so very yet, Father, we know better. So grant us fresh grace to wait upon you for the future and hope to which you have called us—temporally and eternally. Turn our whines into worship, our daily carping into carpe diem, and our frets into faith. In Jesus' beautiful and grace-full name we pray. Amen.

A Prayer for Resting in God's Faithfulness and Timing

> But do not overlook this one fact, beloved, that with the Lord one day is as a thousand years, and a thousand years as one day. The Lord is not slow to fulfill his promise as some count slowness, but is patient toward you. (2 Pet. 3:8–9 ESV)

Dear heavenly Father, thank you for being patient with our impatience. You've never been late for anything. "Swiss timing" is tardiness compared to the precision of your faithfulness. You *will* send Jesus back at just the right time to finish making all things new. That grand day will happen, not a day early and not a day late.

And how we long for that day! No more death, pain, or mourning; no more knowing in part or loving in part; no more goodbyes or good riddances; no more disappointing others or being disappointed; no more betrayals or rejections; no more broken hearts or broken anything; no more heartaches or even heartburn.

But Father, your faithfulness isn't just tied to the timing of the second coming but tied to everything else you've promised as well. Indeed, there's no panic or second-guessing in heaven today. You're not distracted or perplexed about anything—that would be us, not you. Though it's hard to imagine why you haven't answered certain prayers we've offered with a quick and big "Yes," nevertheless, you do all things well. You gave Jesus for our sins; certainly we can trust you to give us everything else we really need.

So grant us grace in our waiting, strength in our weariness, and wisdom in our bewilderment. And in the meantime, help us to be more attentive to the needs of others. Fill our hearts with kindness and gentleness as we bear one another's burdens. We pray in Jesus' compassionate and grace-full name. Amen.

A Prayer for Trusting God with Things We Can't Control

That is why I tell you not to worry about everyday life—whether you have enough food and drink, or enough clothes to wear. Isn't life more than food, and your body more than clothing? Look at the birds. They don't plant or harvest or store food in barns, for your heavenly Father feeds them. And aren't you far more valuable to him than they are? Can all your worries add a single moment to your life? (Matt. 6:25–27 NLT)

Dear Lord Jesus, whenever we're tempted to wonder about our value to the Father, all we have to do is consider the astonishing sacrifice you made for us. By your life, death, and resurrection, we are clothed with the very righteousness of God and have been given a steady, free diet of bread from heaven and living water. We praise, bless, and adore you. The birds of the air have nothing on us!

Nevertheless, our weakness persists, our anxieties flare up, and our worries often get the best of us. So we run to you, confident of your welcome, compassion, and grace. Please help us with the things we'd love to control but can't. It's not so much that we're anxious to add a single hour to our lives; it's more that we don't want our loved ones to suffer unnecessarily.

Jesus, please reveal more of your beauty and love to our children. If we could give our kids and grandkids anything, it would be to know and love you and to find safe and welcome haven in your heart. Keep them restless until they rest in you.

For our friends and family members facing vocational crises, health issues, and relationship challenges, Jesus, lift the weight of our worries as you give us the assurance of your engagement. Show us how to love well, without meddling and manipulating. It's hard not to want to be dispensers of anesthetics on demand, relieving pain at will. But our biggest need isn't for relief but for more of you.

Jesus, we will trust you—not horses, chariots, or our devices. Grant us grace, fuel our hope, and give us peace. We pray in your loving and strong name. Amen.

A Prayer for Keeping Our Sufferings in Perspective

After you have suffered a little while, the God of all grace, who has called you to his eternal glory in Christ, will himself restore, confirm, strengthen, and establish you. To him be the dominion forever and ever. Amen. (1 Pet. 5:10–11 ESV)

For I consider that the sufferings of this present time are not worth comparing with the glory that is to be revealed to us. (Rom. 8:18 ESV)

Dear heavenly Father, thank you for the weariness-validating, heart-liberating voice of the Scriptures. Your Word brings us the encouragement we need at just the right time. Today I'm grateful for both Peter and Paul's words about the sufferings we experience in this world. Both of these men were quite familiar with suffering, and both of them were even more familiar with your sovereign might and endless mercies.

I sometimes forget that until Jesus returns, suffering will be more the norm than the exception. Everything and everyone is broken, so to suffer is to be human and alive. The day of no more "death, mourning, crying, or pain" is coming (see Rev. 21:4), but that day is not yet. But until that day, there is you and all the grace we will need to suffer to your glory.

In the bigger scheme, as Peter said, all suffering is just for "a little while," though sometimes it feels like forever. Father, when life hurts the most, remind us in our heart of hearts that you are the "God of all grace"—the one who has called us to "eternal glory"—and that you will most definitely "restore, confirm, strengthen, and establish" us. Make your Word more real than our pain. Make your grace more substantive than our sufferings.

Grant us, like Paul, the joyful assurance that "the glory that will be revealed to us" will make all the sufferings of our brief journey in this world seem like feathers compared to the weight of eternal goodness that will be lavished on us when Jesus returns. Hallelujah! Until that day, grant us grace to steward our pain as a gift, making us more compassionate and merciful to others. We pray in Jesus' faithful and beautiful name. Amen.

A Prayer for Healing from Our Grace Allergies

Soon a Samaritan woman came to draw water, and Jesus said to her, "Please give me a drink." He was alone at the time because his disciples had gone into the village to buy some food. The woman was surprised, for Jews refuse to have anything to do with Samaritans. She said to Jesus, "You are a Jew, and I am a Samaritan woman. Why are you asking me for a drink?" Jesus replied, "If you only knew the gift God has for you and who you are speaking to, you would ask me, and I would give you living water." (John 4:7–10 NLT)

Dear Lord Jesus, what a great story—you often disrupt our lives, but it's always that we might finally find our delight in you. The more this woman played hide-and-seek with you, the more you played seek-and-catch. She'd been on a quest to fill her emptiness in the arms of men, many men, and it left her even more empty. She ran; you pursued. She danced around; you stopped the music. How I praise you that you came to seek and save the lost, not just broadcast an offer from the distance.

Though the details of our stories are different from this nameless Samaritan woman's, we often resort to the same foolish strategy—hiding from true love, ignoring your daily mercies, resisting your great compassion.

Jesus, deliver us from our grace allergies—living with an aversion to the gospel. That we choose broken cisterns, dumb idols, and self-help over your love is sheer madness. Grace is for sinners, not for pretenders, posers, and performers. You intend to heal us, not harm us; embrace us, not embarrass us; shower us with compassion, not shame us with contempt.

Jesus, we're tired of wasting our thirst on water that does not satisfy. We're tired of digging our own wells. We're tired of sitting under dry spigots. We're tired of being tired. Once again, we bring our thirst to you. We bring our grace-avoidance to you. We bring our excuse making, unbelief, pride, and self-righteousness.

We ask, and because you do not lie, we shall receive living water—copious amounts of living water—sufficient grace for our insufficient selves. Thank you, Jesus, for not giving up on us. In your kind and powerful name we pray. Amen.

A Prayer for Reveling in the Ultimate Romance

I am my beloved's, and his desire is for me. (Song of Sol. 7:10 ESV)

And Jesus said to them, "The sons of this age marry and are given in marriage, but those who are considered worthy to attain to that age and to the resurrection from the dead neither marry nor are given in marriage." (Luke 20:34–35 ESV)

Dear Lord Jesus, in our culture, it's called Valentine's Day, but on the calendar of grace, it's just another day for coming alive to the only love that is better than life—the only love that answers the longing of our hearts for inviolate love and perfect intimacy.

Indeed, no human being (or any number of them), no human romance story, no torrid love affair can possibly fill the vacuum inside of us that is uniquely reserved for you. Every dating relationship or marriage brings together two broken people, two redeemed sinners who ultimately will not be enough for the other. Even the best marriages are just a hint and whisper of what belonging to you actually means and gives us.

Jesus, grant us grace to grow a deeper and richer experience of belonging to you, for you are the ultimate Spouse, the one we always wanted—the one with whom we will enjoy perfect intimacy, bliss, and joy forever. Make this Good News more than our theology; make it our doxology—our song, passion, and über-delight. We believe; help our unbelief.

When we get disconnected from your pursuit of us, love for us, and delight in us, we grow vulnerable. Temptation looms, discontent festers, and roaming hearts become foolish hearts. Whether we are single or married, Jesus, meet us in our brokenness, weakness, and desires.

Until the day our betrothal becomes the day of great banqueting (Rev. 19)—the day we long for more than any other—take us further up and further into relationship with you. And help us—free us for loving others as you love us, Jesus. We pray in your tender and tenacious name. Amen.

A Prayer for Pondering Our Father's Love and Hearing the Spirit's Voice

For you did not receive the spirit of slavery to fall back into fear, but you have received the Spirit of adoption as sons, by whom we cry, "Abba! Father!" The Spirit himself bears witness with our spirit that we are children of God, and if children, then heirs—heirs of God and fellow heirs with Christ, provided we suffer with him in order that we may also be glorified with him. (Rom. 8:15–17 ESV)

Dear heavenly Father, we praise, bless, and adore you for the privilege of knowing you as "Abba Father." We were slaves to sin and death, selfishness and fear, when you saved us by your grace and adopted us as your beloved daughters and sons. And now your Holy Spirit is constantly telling us how much you love us and delight in us.

Father, please turn up the volume of the Spirit's voice, because so many other voices are vying for our attention. There's the voice of Satan, who still tries to condemn us for sins you've already forgiven. There's the voice of our vain regrets, haunting us about our past failures and hounding us about missed opportunities. There's the voice of our fears, pestering us about our insecurities and inadequacies.

But then there's your blessed voice, Father. By the Spirit we hear you say, "I have loved you with an everlasting love and with cords of kindness I have bound you to my heart. I have given Jesus as your righteousness and have sealed you with my Spirit. Nothing will separate you from my love—nothing. Don't be afraid to suffer, for I am with you and I am for you. I won't give you more than you can endure, but I will give you more of my grace. Your past is forgiven, your present is in my hands, and your future is beyond all you could ask or imagine. Trust me."

Abba Father, thank you for loving us—not as we will be or ought to be but as we actually are. We begin this day, and will continue in it, heeding your voice. We pray in Jesus' glorious and grace-full name. Amen.

A Prayer for Rejoicing in Jesus' Once and for All Sacrifice for Our Sins

Under the old covenant, the priest stands and ministers before the altar day after day, offering the same sacrifices again and

again, which can never take away sins. But our High Priest offered himself to God as a single sacrifice for sins, good for all
time. Then he sat down in the place of honor at God's right
hand. There he waits until his enemies are humbled and made a
footstool under his feet. For by that one offering he forever made
perfect those who are being made holy. (Heb. 10:11–14 NLT)

Dear Lord Jesus, I cannot hear it too much. I cannot believe
it too deeply. I cannot rejoice in it too fully. By your death
on the cross, you have taken away our sins, *once and for
all.* Nothing is left undone. Nothing more needs to happen.
Nothing else could have met our need. Nothing else must be
our cry but "We have been made righteous in Christ forever!
Blessed be the name of our God and Savior, Jesus—the Lamb
of God who has taken away our sin; the Lord of all, who
is making all things new; the Lamp of the New Jerusalem,
whose glory will shine eternally!"

And now, having completely justified us by your finished
work, you are perfecting us by your glorious gospel. It's all
of grace, from beginning to end. We who have been declared
perfectly righteous will be made perfectly holy—O blessed
and happy hope. One day we will be as lovely and as loving
as you, Lord Jesus. There is no greater longing, no greater
joy, and no greater future—none.

Even as we rest in your finished work, so we rejoice in your
present reign, Lord Jesus. Atoned-for sin will be abolished
sin; defeated evil will be eradicated evil; vanquished enemies
will be eliminated enemies. May the joy of this Good News
buckle our knees in humble adoration and empower our
hands for neighbor edification.

As we are loved, so let us love; as we have been served, so
let us serve; as we are encouraged, so let us encourage one

another, as we long for the day. We pray in your holy and loving name. Amen.

A Prayer for Lamenting Evil and Longing for Its Demise

The reason the Son of God appeared was to destroy the devil's work. (1 John 3:8)

He disarmed the rulers and authorities and put them to open shame, by triumphing over them in him. (Col. 2:15 ESV)

Dear Lord Jesus, I am so thankful for the hope we have of a world and eternity completely devoid of all sin, evil, and brokenness. Though it will require your second coming, nonetheless, I am grateful for that day and long for it more than ever.

The day of no more beheadings, or even kidnappings; no more human trafficking or even bad traffic; no more greed or any form of need; no more harming in any form, just blessing in every form; no more vengeance or retaliation, just peace and reconciliation; no more broken people, places, or things; just beauty, in everyone in every place.

Thank you, Jesus, for destroying the devil's work by your work on the cross. His crushed head, broken dominion, and sure demise are sweetness to our souls, peace in our storms, and power for our mission. Through your shame you shamed evil and by your defeat you defeated darkness. Terror is now terrified of you. Though the devil is filled with fury, he is on a leash, knowing his time is short (Rev. 12:12).

We will not shrink back; we will not cower; we will not fear. You have won the war, and you will win the remaining battles. As full as the world is with evil and devils, it will be filled thousands of times over with beauty and with you. As surely as you spoke the world into existence, you will speak the one word that will ultimately fell the devil and spell the end to all his deadly doings. Hallelujah. Hallelujah. Hallelujah!

Lord Jesus, we praise, bless, and adore you for so great a salvation and so trustworthy a hope. For your glory, we will live this day in light of that day. In your exalted and majestic name we pray. Amen.

A Prayer for Relearning the Secret of Contentment

I have learned in whatever situation I am to be content. I know how to be brought low, and I know how to abound. In any and every circumstance, I have learned the secret of facing plenty and hunger, abundance and need. (Phil. 4:11–12 ESV)

Keep your life free from love of money, and be content with what you have, for he has said, "I will never leave you nor forsake you." (Heb. 13:5 ESV)

Dear heavenly Father, there are some aspects of this life of grace for which I seem to need constant refresher courses. Contentment is one of them. I know you're not calling me to kill desire, demonize ambition, or decry enjoyment. And yet at the same time I totally "get" your warnings about complaining, ingratitude, and discontent.

So I come to you, Father, once again acknowledging a need you alone can meet. Grant me the grace of contentment. Whether I have a little or a lot; am well known or forgotten; live in a palace or a garage apartment; feast on filet mignon or yesterday's mac and cheese. Whether I feel included or left out, celebrated or underappreciated; have discretionary funds for splurging or literally have to pray for daily bread. Whether my relationships are "rocking" or are rocky; whether I have really good health or chronic maladies. Father, I want to be content, not passive; not in denial, but truly grateful; not immune to pain, but alive in Jesus.

So, by your Holy Spirit, convict me when I default too easily to murmuring and complaining, which usually segues into whining and blaming. Heal me of gospel amnesia—too easily forgetting every good thing we have in Christ. Open the eyes of my heart as I begin (and continue) this day. Let me see a little more of Jesus—actually, a lot more. That's all I need; that's all I really need. I pray in Jesus' all glorious and grace-full name. Amen.

A Prayer for the Imprisoned and Persecuted Christians

And the LORD said, "You pity the plant, for which you did not labor, nor did you make it grow, which came into being in a night and perished in a night. And should not I pity Nineveh, that great city, in which there are more than 120,000 persons who do not know their right hand from their left, and also much cattle?" (Jon. 4:10–11 ESV)

> Continue to remember those in prison as if you were together with them in prison, and those who are mistreated as if you yourselves were suffering. (Heb. 13:3)

Dear heavenly Father, we run to your throne of grace today on behalf of our Assyrian brothers and sisters, imprisoned for no other reason than because they are followers of Christ. Their fear must be great, as their threat is quite real. We especially think of the women and the elderly held captive by this act of terror. Have mercy, O Lord; have mercy.

Hold them tighter than their captives, Father. May the grasp of your grace be more real to these Assyrian Christians than the grip of the darkness. Such a request of you is no vain thing, Father, for centuries ago you brought your saving love to Assyria through Jonah. Though he was a reluctant prophet, you are a generous Redeemer. You showered great mercy on Nineveh, the capital of Assyria. Why not again, why not in this chapter of their story? May your name be great among the nations, now and forever.

Father, these one hundred fifty imprisoned Christians are the ones most obvious to us today, but there are thousands like them held in various places of the world. You have called us to remember them as though we ourselves are imprisoned and to identify with the persecuted church as though we too are suffering great mistreatment. By the power of your grace, grant us this measure of compassion and concern, Father. May the threat of evil fuel our passion to share the gospel all the more.

Having been freed for eternity by the riches of the gospel, we long for the day when all captivities will be crushed; all persecutions will be pulverized; all terror will be defanged, tamed, and gone forever. Hasten that day, O holy and sovereign Father; hasten that day. We pray in Jesus' triumphant and tender name. Amen.

A Prayer for Letting Go of the Desire for Revenge

> Dear friends, never take revenge. Leave that to the righteous anger of God. For the Scriptures say, "I will take revenge; I will pay them back," says the LORD. (Rom.12:19 NLT)
>
> "It is mine to avenge; I will repay. In due time their foot will slip; their day of disaster is near and their doom rushes upon them." (Deut. 32:35)
>
> The God of peace will soon crush Satan under your feet. The grace of our Lord Jesus be with you. (Rom. 16:20)

Dear heavenly Father, in view of the increase of kidnappings and human trafficking, the proliferation of pornography and the spirit of jihad, I find myself growing angrier and angrier. I find myself craving revenge and relishing the thought of harming the purveyors of terror and evil. So I'm *desperate* for you to apply these Scriptures to my heart this morning. I need fresh and specific grace. It's one thing for me to long for justice but an altogether different thing to want to repay harm for harm, evil for evil, beheading for beheading.

Father, thank you for your commitment to avenge and annihilate all evil. Thank you for your commitment to wipe all tears, put all things right, to make all things new. Just as in the "fullness of time" you sent Jesus to be our Savior (Gal. 4:4 ESV), so in "due time," the day of disaster and doom will come upon the kingdom of darkness. I praise, bless, and adore you for your promise to crush Satan under our feet "soon." May soon be very soon.

Until then, Father, help me to be more aware of the advancing of your kingdom than the exploits of evil. May the beauty and present reign of Jesus be more real to me than the ugly and sinister deeds of darkness. Father, show me my place in your story, with your communities, in my city.

Instead of wasting energy on fretting evil, help me use that same energy on loving my neighbors and pushing back the effects of the Fall in my community. Instead of chatting up the latest menacing story, help me to be more ready to share the gospel and speak of the hope you have given us in Jesus. In Jesus' loving and triumphant name I pray. Amen.

A Prayer for Greater Release from Our Shame

Fear not; you will no longer live in shame. Don't be afraid; there is no more disgrace for you. You will no longer remember the shame of your youth and the sorrows of widowhood. For your Creator will be your husband; the Lord of Heaven's Armies is his name! He is your Redeemer, the Holy One of Israel, the God of all the earth. (Isa. 54:4–5 NLT)

Dear heavenly Father, you come to us so faithfully in your Word, giving welcome to the exiled, balm for the broken, and grace for the disgraced. Thank you for your tenacious tenderness, inexhaustible patience, and heart-healing kindness. Thank you that I don't have to be ashamed of my lingering battle with shame. Thank you for the promise that one day I will be completely free, healthy, and whole.

Until that day, I will blast my heart with the Good News—the true news. You are not ashamed of me, Father. In fact, you delight in me—as hard as that is to believe at times. Your gaze is the gaze of grace. When you look at me, you not only see the righteousness of Jesus, with which you've clothed me, but you see me and desire me.

There's nothing about me you don't know. There's nothing left to discover, shock, or disappoint you. You don't love me as I should be or will be but as I am right now—your beloved child, en route to becoming more like Jesus. Thank you, Father, thank you—words that come easily, but words that feel woefully inadequate to express my sense of gratitude, relief, and peace.

As this day begins and will end, I bless you that there's no more disgrace for me and that I no longer have to live in shame; that Jesus is my Spouse and the armies of heaven are marshaled against all the lies of the enemy; that your name is Redeemer and my name is beloved. In Jesus' merciful and mighty name I pray. Amen.

A Prayer for Trusting and Resting in God's Prayers for Us

Therefore he [Jesus] is able, once and forever, to save those who come to God through him. He lives forever to intercede with God on their behalf. (Heb. 7:25 NLT)

Likewise the Spirit helps us in our weakness. For we do not know what to pray for as we ought, but the Spirit himself intercedes for us with groanings too deep for words. (Rom. 8:26 ESV)

> My intercessor is my friend as my eyes pour out tears to God;
> on behalf of a man he pleads with God as one pleads for a
> friend. (Job 16:20–21)

Dear heavenly Father, as I meditate on the multiple ways you love and care for your children, few things create a deeper sigh of relief, sense of peace, and smile of joy than knowing the whole Trinity is praying for us—for me.

Father, nothing or no one can sabotage your sovereignty, warp your will, divert your decrees for your children and your world. Thus, when we cry out to you, it's actually you at work in our hearts both to will and do the things that honor you (Phil. 2:13). We don't have to get your attention, make a case, or convince you of anything. We don't have to gussy up, buck up, or ramp up our spirituality when we come before you. But as children with a loving Father and real people with real tears, we come.

Lord Jesus, because you ever live to pray for us, may we ever more abandon ourselves to you. Certainly, anything and everything you pray for will come to pass. Your advocacy is our assurance; your intercession is our liberation; your prayers are our peace.

And Holy Spirit, thank you for so faithfully praying inside of us—especially in those moments and seasons when we don't know what to pray or even have little desire to pray. As we cry out to God—with many words of desperation or joy, or in the silence of our sadness and confusion—heal our prayers as we wing them heavenward. We rest more in the groaning of your work than in the rightness of our words. In Jesus' merciful and grace-full name we pray. Amen.

A Prayer for Stewarding
Our Theological Differences with Others

For the entire law is fulfilled in keeping this one command: "Love your neighbor as yourself." If you bite and devour each other, watch out or you will be destroyed by each other. (Gal. 5:14–15)

For we know in part and we prophesy in part, but when the perfect comes, the partial will pass away. (1 Cor. 13:9–10 ESV)

Dear heavenly Father, there are so many reasons I'm looking forward to life in the new heaven and new earth. And though it's not at the top of my list, perfected theological understanding among your children is going to be awesome. When your sons and daughters "bite and devour" one another because of doctrinal differences, no one could possibly grieve over it more than you. Have mercy on us, Lord; have mercy on me.

Oh, for the day when we will no longer know in part or love in part—the day when we will no longer label, dismiss, or marginalize one another over our differing biblical and theological understandings. When I think about it, Father, it's rather absurd (and worse) that we who have been saved by your grace from beginning to end should ever resort to condescending, judgmental, dismissive attitudes with fellow brothers and sisters in Jesus.

Father, I can only speak for myself today about this matter. Please forgive me for leading with my rightness over my kindness, and for loving my theological tribe more readily and fully than those in other tribes. Forgive me for defending sovereign grace ungraciously; forgive me for thinking to myself, "I get the gospel so much more than they do"; forgive me for using biblical knowledge to put up walls rather than build bridges. Forgive me and free me for living and loving to your glory, this very day. I pray in Jesus' tender and triumphant name. Amen.

A Prayer for Bringing Others to Jesus

Some men came carrying a paralyzed man on a sleeping mat. They tried to take him inside to Jesus, but they couldn't reach him because of the crowd. So they went up to the roof and took off some tiles. Then they lowered the sick man on his mat down into the crowd, right in front of Jesus. Seeing their faith, Jesus said to the man, "Young man, your sins are forgiven." (Luke 5:18–20 NLT)

Dear Lord Jesus, thank you for the all-weather friends you've given us—those who have stood with us in every season of life, through thick and thin, rapture and rupture, merriment and misery. Today we return the favor. Though there are many ways to be a good friend, certainly one of the most important ones is faithfully to bring our friends to you. Thankful we don't have to lift tiles, we run now to your occupied throne of grace. Hear our pleas, O wonderful, merciful Savior.

We bring you our friends who are suffering spiritual disconnect and crises of faith. Lord of the heart, please restore our friends to the joy of your salvation for them—to their first love, settled peace, and certain hope that you are enough. You've won us for eternity, but the battle for our hearts remains until the final day.

We bring you our friends who are suffering in broken and messy relationships. Few things make us more vulnerable to emotional anguish, poor choices, and deep regrets. Jesus, center them with your peace and wisdom. Send grace in the shape of the real issues, and send us as listeners and warriors of the heart.

We bring you our friends who are suffering physical illness and chronic pain. Jesus, there are some stories over which we wish we could be sovereign for a moment and fix the seemingly unfixable. Have mercy, O Lord; have mercy. We unabashedly ask for healing. We will not rely on ourselves but wait on the God who raises the dead.

For these friends and others, Jesus, show us how to love well, stay present, and extend grace. In your tender and triumphant name we pray. Amen.

A Prayer for Trusting God in Seemingly Impossible Situations

Jesus replied, "What is impossible with man is possible with God." (Luke 18:27)

Dear heavenly Father, we praise you for your promises of steadfast love, daily mercies, and doing the impossible, for we need all three. Because of your steadfast love for us in Jesus, we have incomparable peace. Because of your daily mercies, we have the freedom to be vulnerable. Because nothing is impossible for you, we can trust you with our hardest situations and most broken stories.

Father, some of us run to your throne of grace today primed for a miracle; some of us are making our way very slowly, under the weight of shame and emotional exhaustion; and some of us are stuck on the mercy road, not sure we can risk the pain of hoping again. Thank you that you meet us where we are, just as we are, because you are always running towards us in the gospel.

Father, for those of us who ache with the pain of betrayal, loss, and rejection, hold us close to your heart, tightly. We want you close, yet we are inclined to stay away from you. We want you to bring healing, yet some days we want justice much more than we want mercy. Help us, Lord.

Father, for those of us who feel the burden of our guilt, the consequences of our failure, and the shame of our foolishness, help us leave our agenda for putting things right with you and simply come home to you as Abba. You must script our repentance and renewal. We're tired of being our own savior.

Father, for those of us who are ready to trust you with failing health, limited finances, unexpected reversals, big and little decisions, spiritual malaise (ours and others'), job situations, children who are all over the map, and any of a number of other situations, with palms up we praise you and surrender to you—the God who does all things well and who makes all things beautiful, in your time. In Jesus' loving and powerful name we pray. Amen.

A Prayer for Affirming the Lord to Be Our Most Treasured Inheritance

I said to the LORD, "You are my Master! Every good thing I have comes from you." The godly people in the land are my true heroes! I take pleasure in them. Troubles multiply for those who chase after other gods. I will not take part in their sacrifices of blood or even speak the names of their gods. Lord, you alone ·are my inheritance, my cup of blessing. (Ps. 16:2–5 NLT)

Dear heavenly Father, as I meditate on these words of David, my response is simply, "Amen, amen, and amen." You are my Master; thankfully *you* are, and not sin or death, my whims or lusts, or a multitude of other empty gods. And what a Master you are—you created us for life in a garden paradise and intimacy with yourself, and you have redeemed us for an eternal life beyond our greatest imagining.

Indeed, every good thing I have comes from you—the fountain of pleasure and delights, the wellspring of joy and satisfaction, the God from whom all blessings flow, not drip or trickle! You give cheerfully, not begrudgingly; you love lavishly, not reservedly; you redeem fully, not partially. In your time and in your way, you will make all things new and all things beautiful.

Of all the inheritances my temptable, wandering heart might run after, you alone are to be desired and treasured. Compared to you, all other gold is fool's gold, all other currencies are counterfeit, all other riches are rubbish, and all other treasures are trash. By the grace and truth of the gospel, you have changed all the price tags in my life. Life is Christ, death is gain; boasting in weakness is freedom, posing and pretending are slavery; humility is the way up, pride is the way down.

Because of the cup you gave Jesus to drink, our cup is now a bottomless cup of grace. Hallelujah, what a Savior! Hallelujah, what a salvation. We pray in Jesus' wonderful and merciful name. Amen.

A Prayer for Freedom
from Our People-Pleasing Ways

When Cephas came to Antioch, I opposed him to his face, because he stood condemned. For before certain men came from James, he used to eat with the Gentiles. But when they arrived, he began to draw back and separate himself from the Gentiles because he was afraid of those who belonged to the circumcision group. The other Jews joined him in his hypocrisy, so that by their hypocrisy even Barnabas was led astray. When I saw that they were not acting in line with the truth of the gospel, I said to Cephas in front of them all, "You are a Jew, yet you live like a Gentile and not like a Jew. How is it, then, that you force Gentiles to follow Jewish customs?" (Gal. 2:11–14)

Dear heavenly Father, I am so thankful this story has been captured in your Word, for it deals with a struggle we all face, people-pleasing; and it reveals the way of freedom—living in line with the truth of the gospel. Cephas's (Peter's) weakness is one I'm all too familiar with.

Father, I confess there are times when what people think about me has more functional power over my day than what you think about me. When I'm not living in rich fellowship with you, disapproval and criticism, or being left out or not being appreciated, can impact me way more than it should. Likewise, being included, affirmed, and celebrated (all good things) can feel too good, and I can fall into being an affirmation junkie.

Father, help me to increasingly live "in line with the truth of the gospel"—that is, more consistently with the riches of grace and the freedoms you've given us in Christ. May your desire for me and delight in me free me to be a servant of all and a slave to none.

Free me to be far more concerned about welcoming others than hurt when I'm left out. Free me to accept criticism humbly, without becoming defensive or going to self-contempt. Help me to take back the power I've given some people to either make me or break me with their praise of me or their indifference toward me. Free me to love others as Jesus loves me. I pray in his holy and heart-liberating name. Amen.

A Prayer for Knowing and Resting in the New Names Jesus Gives Us

He who has an ear, let him hear what the Spirit says to the churches. To the one who conquers I will give some of the hidden manna, and I will give him a white stone, with a new name written on the stone that no one knows except the one who receives it. (Rev. 2:17 ESV)

Dear Lord Jesus, this Scripture reminds me that *nothing* is more central to our identity than the names by which we live. And often our most formative name isn't the one on our birth certificate. Some of us have been branded with names that have shamed and wounded us deeply, and some of us have greatly harmed others by the things we have called them. All of us stand in need of your mercy and grace, which you readily and freely give.

Jesus, whether or not there's literally a new name you'll give us in heaven, I'm not sure. But it is enough that you look at me today and address me as "Mine," "Beloved," and "Desired." I am so grateful for the power of the gospel to rename, renew, and release us from old destructive labels—the ones others have given us and the ones we've given ourselves.

But as much as I love my new name, Lord Jesus, your name is the name I love to hear more than any other. It's by your name that I'm fully forgiven and declared righteous, being healed of every disease and being freed from every bondage. And it's at your name, Jesus, that one day I will gladly bow my knees with everyone in heaven, on earth, and under the earth (Phil. 2:9–11). Hasten that blessed day!

Lord Jesus, it's only because you overcame sin and death for us that I dare call myself an "overcomer." It's only because you drank the cup of our judgment that I'll get to feast on the "hidden manna" of eternity. Continue to free me to live by the names you've given me. I pray in your exalted and all-glorious name. Amen.

A Prayer for Extending Mercy in Normal and Difficult Relationships

Be merciful, just as your Father is merciful. (Luke 6:36)

Speak and so act as those who are to be judged under the law of liberty. For judgment is without mercy to one who has shown no mercy. Mercy triumphs over judgment. (James 2:12–13 ESV)

Dear heavenly Father, we praise you for being the Father of mercies and God of all comfort—the God of limitless patience, inexhaustible forbearance, and incomparable compassion. Instead of giving us what we deserve, you have given us Jesus—who is our perfect righteousness, everlasting peace, and greatest joy. We want your mercy to trump our judgmental attitudes. We want to live more fully by the law of liberty, instead of by the toxin of criticism. Only the gospel can free us to live and love this way.

Father, we lament and repent for being too easily irritated, offended, and impatient. We confess to you what you already know: we keep records of the ways people hurt, fail, and disappoint us, more readily than we remain committed to overlooking, forbearing, and forgiving. Thank you for the full forgiveness we have in Christ and for grace to repent and change. Father, to whatever degree it is possible for redeemed sinners, we want to be merciful with others as you are merciful with us.

For our more complex relationships, Father, we appeal to you for wisdom and strength. Show us what mercy looks like when we feel like we are being exploited, manipulated, and "played." We know you're not calling us to be doormats, but you are calling us to wash the feet of repeat offenders like ourselves. Our cry is, "Help, Abba, help!"

Teach us about healthy boundaries, severe mercy, and extraordinary grace. Free us for loving in the broken places, as Jesus loves us. Fill us with your Spirit, empower us by the gospel, and bring the right people into our lives who can help us navigate some of these more soul-depleting relationships. Father, thank you for your promise and provision of daily mercies. In Jesus' kind and powerful name we pray. Amen.

A Prayer for Humbling Ourselves When We'd Rather Not

Humble yourselves before the Lord, and he will lift you up. (James 4:10)

Be completely humble and gentle; be patient, bearing with one another in love. (Eph. 4:2)

Dear heavenly Father, being right is so much more fun than being humbled; remaining defensive is so much easier than offering kindness; getting even is more instinctive than getting low. Alas, I find myself again in need of fresh grace as this day begins. Thank you for convicting me without condemning me.

I know you resist the proud but give grace to the humble—and the last thing in the world I want is to experience your resistance, so, Father, I humble myself before you today. Bring glory to yourself as you bring me back to the ways of the gospel.

Forgive me for trying to justify my haughtiness, coolness, and withdrawal. Nobody's failure to love well can excuse my own. Forgive me for investing more energy in propping up my reputation than in working towards peace and reconciliation. Forgive me for confusing the self-righteous monologue I've been carrying on in my head with prayer. I've been talking to myself, not to you.

Forgive me for relishing the thought of being right, when there's been everything wrong with my attitude. Forgive me for "processing" the broken situation with others when it's really been closer to gossip. Forgive me for being passive in the face of a potential messy confrontation rather than active as a peacemaker.

Have mercy on me, gracious Father; have mercy. As the day unfolds, please grant me humility, kindness, and courage to move toward the situation. Bring glory to yourself, gentleness to my heart, and a good gospel outcome. In Jesus' wonderful and merciful name I pray. Amen.

A Prayer for Acknowledging
Our Performance-ism and Perfectionism

When I first came to you, dear brothers and sisters, I didn't use lofty words and impressive wisdom to tell you God's secret plan. For I decided that while I was with you I would forget everything except Jesus Christ, the one who was crucified. I came to you in weakness—timid and trembling. And my message and my preaching were very plain. Rather than using clever and persuasive speeches, I relied only on the power of the Holy Spirit. (1 Cor. 2:1–4 NLT)

Dear heavenly Father, how I need this Scripture today. Paul's model of relying on the Spirit—and nothing in himself—is both indicting and inviting. By your grace, Paul was *so* over himself. These verses are indicting because they expose the performer and perfectionist in me. I still get "sucked into" trying to gain and maintain people's approval by what I do. Likewise, I often consider a day good or bad, based on the quality and quantity of my production. Rather than boasting in Christ alone, alas, I want to find something boast-worthy in me.

That's where this Scripture moves from indicting me to inviting me to a better, more beautiful way. Father, thank you for intending, and securing, our freedom by Jesus' performance. Perfection can only be found in one place—in Christ. Your approval is all that really matters, and you've already given that to us fully in Jesus.

Of course, what others think about us—and how we think of ourselves—is going to impact us. We're human, not robotic. But you've given us the same gospel and the same Spirit you gave Paul. Thank you, Father. So, owning my weakness, I'll seek to rely on the Holy Spirit all day long today, and forsaking all scorecards, I'll seek to make Jesus my primary boast.

Father, I'm trusting you to help me be really present with people today. Grant me quick repentances, good listening, and words for building others up—according to their needs. I pray in Jesus' loving and powerful name. Amen.

A Prayer for Days When You're Feeling a Mild Case of the Blahs

Have you not known? Have you not heard? The LORD is the everlasting God, the Creator of the ends of the earth. He does not faint or grow weary; his understanding is unsearchable. He gives power to the faint, and to him who has no might he increases strength. Even youths shall faint and be weary, and young men shall fall exhausted; but they who wait for the LORD shall renew their strength; they shall mount up with wings like eagles; they shall run and not be weary; they shall walk and not faint. (Isa. 40:28–31 ESV)

Dear heavenly Father, there's nothing major going on—no foreboding issues in front of me or recent disappointments dogging me. I'm just feeling a bit tired and "blah-ish" as this day begins. So this Scripture comforts me on many levels. First of all, I'm glad to be reminded that even youths get faint and weary and young men get exhausted, because I'm neither a youth nor a young man. So thanks for the freedom to accept my limitations and humanity—a freedom I need to access more regularly.

But more importantly, Father, I'm thankful for what this passage reminds me about you. You are tireless in your care, everlasting in your mercies, and generous with your grace. You anticipate our weakness and meet us right there. When we get worn out, you don't roll your eyes and call us "couch potatoes," but you call us beloved children.

Father, thanks for your promise to renew our strength. Thanks for the calling to wait on you and not simply get up and get busy. Since you have perfect understanding, I will quiet myself before you and let you refresh my heart and replenish my resources. With the gospel at my core, I don't feel any condemnation or guilt, just the need for a less busy, quieter, distraction-less stretch of a few days. I pray in Jesus' kind and powerful name. Amen.

A Prayer for Relying on the God of Resurrection for Our Hardest Stories

We think you ought to know, dear brothers and sisters, about the trouble we went through in the province of Asia. We were crushed and overwhelmed beyond our ability to endure, and we thought we would never live through it. In fact, we expected to die. But as a result, we stopped relying on ourselves and learned to rely only on God, who raises the dead. (2 Cor. 1:8–9 NLT)

Dear heavenly Father, what a joy it is to call you the God of Resurrection, for that is who you are. Death died and evil received a mortal wound the day you raised Jesus from the grave. On your time schedule, everything sad will come untrue and everything broken will be made new; resplendent beauty will replace forms of ugly; everlasting symphony will silence all cacophony. This is our peace, joy, and hope.

Father, it is because of your mercy and grace for us in Jesus that we freely bring to you the things that have the power to overwhelm and crush us. Though the details differ from Paul's story, we too know what it feels like to question our ability to endure much longer. So, forsaking all self-reliance, we collapse on Jesus today and ask you to bring life and light into these stories of death and darkness. We bring our friends, and ourselves, to your throne of grace.

Father, we pray for the persecuted church throughout the world. We live in a day in which martyrdom is becoming normative rather than episodic. Father, grant heroic grace and peace and supernatural protection, especially for children in the crosshairs of evil. Our cry is, "How long, O Lord?"

Father, we pray for marriages that are already four feet down into a six-foot-deep grave. May the toxins of hurt and anger give way to a season of truce, then humility, wisdom, and healing. Whoever and whatever you choose to use, replace the growing stench of death with the aroma of grace and life.

Father, we pray for families marked by mental and emotional illness. Whether the cause is genetic, demonic, trauma-based, or something else, we pray for sufferers and caregivers alike. Bring glory to yourself by bringing the power of Jesus' resurrection to bear.

Most gracious and sovereign Father, bring other stories to mind and heart as our day unfolds. Empower us for praying without ceasing, hoping without doubting, and loving without fearing. In Jesus' triumphant and tender name we pray. Amen.

A Prayer for Avoiding the Deadly Toxins of Bitterness and Resentment

Look after each other so that none of you fails to receive the grace of God. Watch out that no poisonous root of bitterness grows up to trouble you, corrupting many. (Heb. 12:15 NLT)

Resentment kills a fool. (Job 5:2)

Dear heavenly Father, these Scriptures cut to the chase and bring conviction to our hearts. We are your beloved daughters and sons, but today we are also your "busted" daughters and sons, for resentment comes to us as quickly as someone steals our parking place, or eats the saran-wrapped piece of cake we hid in the fridge, or fails to include us in some social event. It's amazing how quickly a little slight can launch us into a big spite. Have mercy on us, Lord, and grant us fresh grace, thicker skin, and bigger hearts.

Father, being slighted is one thing, but being assaulted by the betrayals and failures, deceit and lies, attacks and abuse of others is an altogether different matter. These aren't things to shake off but deep wounds, broken hearts, and incredible pain to bring to your throne of grace. You're not calling us to denial but to yourself. Have mercy on us, Lord—have big mercy—and grant us wisdom, strength, and tons of grace.

Father, through the power of your Holy Spirit, the truth of the gospel, and the gift of community, don't let our appropriate anger morph into destructive revenge. Don't let our raw hurts become a band of vigilante marauders, bent not just on getting even but on upping the ante—repaying harm for harm, evil for evil, and death for death.

Don't let our vulnerable hearts become gardens for the planting of roots of resentment and bushes of bitterness, and keep us from medicating our pain foolishly. Father, as Jesus has forgiven us, so help us to want to forgive others. Write stories of redemption and restoration with the ink of our hurt and your grace. We pray in Jesus' tender and triumphant name. Amen.

A Prayer for Hours, Days, or Weeks When Temptation Is Raging

No temptation has overtaken you except what is common to mankind. And God is faithful; he will not let you be tempted beyond what you can bear. But when you are tempted, he will also provide a way out so that you can endure it. (1 Cor. 10:13)

The thief comes only to steal and kill and destroy. I came that they may have life and have it abundantly. (John 10:10 ESV)

Dear Lord Jesus, I praise you for the dailyness of your warnings, and the persistence of your wooings. Every day, sometimes every hour, we have life-and-death choices set before us. Satan intends to steal, kill, and destroy us, but you give limitless mercy, abounding grace, and abundant life. The very fact that we often pause between these two choices underscores our weakness and vulnerability and just how much we need you as this day begins and will continue.

Jesus, some of us are highly temptable right now. Grab us and grace us. Temptation is raging, and it looks pretty appealing. Whether from weariness in well-doing or the exhaustion of difficult relationships; the ache of unfulfilled longings or the pain of living in craziness; the quest for new adventure or the lure of old memories; a plan to out-hurt those who have hurt us or unguarded moments of carelessness—we are weak and we need you.

Thank you for your promise that with every temptation we face in life—every one of them—you will always provide a way out and grace to endure. Show us what that looks like today—especially when our cry for relief is much stronger than our cry for a changed heart. Like for Esau, sometimes a bowl of hot oatmeal in hand looks a lot more satisfying to us than the promise of a future inheritance.

Help us make redemptive choices today—choices that celebrate the abundant life you freely give us. Help us, Lord Jesus, for your honor, glory, and praise. In your powerful and precious name we pray. Amen.

A Prayer for Jesus to Tear Down Walls and Bring Peace between Us

For he himself [Jesus] is our peace, who has made the two groups one and has destroyed the barrier, the dividing wall of hostility, by setting aside in his flesh the law with its commands and regulations. His purpose was to create in himself one new humanity out of the two, thus making peace, and in one body to reconcile both of them to God through the cross, by which he put to death their hostility. He came and preached peace to you who were far away and peace to those who were near. For through him we both have access to the Father by one Spirit. (Eph. 2:14–18)

Dear Lord Jesus, we praise, bless, and adore you for making peace between God and us. Through your finished work, we haven't "just" been reconciled to God but have become objects of his affection and children of his delight—a people upon whom Abba's favor rests and for whom heaven is prepared. Hallelujah, many times over!

We praise you, Lord Jesus, for tearing down the wall of hostility between Gentiles and Jews. It was always your plan to do so—to make enemies into friends and replace hostility with hospitality, enmity with empathy, and loathing with loving. Indeed, in you, Jesus, distinctions are no longer barriers that exclude but bridges that unite. Diversity becomes a bouquet of beauty when the gospel is in play. Nothing is impossible for you.

So, Lord Jesus, we earnestly ask you to do this same enmity-destroying, heart-gentling peacemaking in our most broken relationships. Where high dividing walls (with barbed wire and shards of glass on top) have been built between husbands and wives, between children and parents, in friendships and churches—thick walls made with bricks of pain and pride, betrayals and busyness, abuse and neglect—come and tear down our walls, Jesus. You alone are Redeemer and Reconciler, our peace and Peacemaker.

One day we will love perfectly as you love us, Jesus. May we in this day give concrete evidence of that sure and coming day. In your merciful and mighty name we pray. Amen.

A Prayer for Those Days When We Need a Little Perspective Adjustment

We can rejoice, too, when we run into problems and trials, for we know that they help us develop endurance. And endurance develops strength of character, and character strengthens our confident hope of salvation. And this hope will not lead to disappointment. For we know how dearly God loves us, because he has given us the Holy Spirit to fill our hearts with his love. (Rom. 5:3–5 NLT)

Dear heavenly Father, multiple difficulties plus waiting is an equation that often results in wrong thinking and poor choices. My heart goes out today to friends whose trials seem to be increasing in both frequency and intensity. When this happens, it's hard not to conclude either something is wrong with us, for which it's "cosmic payback time," or something is wrong with you—you're choosing not to be merciful and mighty on our behalf.

Thus these words from Paul come as mind balm and heart salve. Just when we start heading into a downward cycle of either self-contempt or heavenward railing, you send your Word and grant us much needed perspective. Thank you, Father; thank you. Though you don't promise to explain the reasons for our extended seasons of problems and trials, you do promise us a hope that will not disappoint us and a greater experience of your love.

Father, it seems to me that it's your love that makes this hope palpable, so I beseech you: please pour fresh and copious amounts of your love into the hearts of my friends who are tired and weary, spent and used up, vulnerable and easy targets for the lies of the enemy. By your Holy Spirit, give them a supernatural sense of your hand and heart at work. Instead of feeling abandoned, may they sense their adoption—the reality of their being your beloved children. Turn their cries of "Why me, Lord?" into "Abba Father."

I'm enough of a rescuer, Father, that if you gave me a magic wand, I'd simply try to relieve the pain and change their circumstances. But you're promising something much better than relief; you have promised yourself. May it be, Lord; may it be. I pray in Jesus' merciful and grace-full name. Amen.

A Prayer for Once Again Boasting in Our Weaknesses

Each time he said, "My grace is all you need. My power works best in weakness." So now I am glad to boast about my weaknesses, so that the power of Christ can work through me. (2 Cor. 12:9 NLT)

We ourselves are like fragile clay jars containing this great treasure. This makes it clear that our great power is from God, not from ourselves. (2 Cor. 4:7 NLT)

Dear heavenly Father, I wish I didn't have to keep learning this same lesson over and over and over: that your grace is all I need and Christ's power is released through my weakness. This way of life is so counterintuitive and paradoxical, and at the same time so wondrously glorious and freeing.

Oh, to be done with the foolish quest for competency and control, self-sufficiency and self-anything. I know that day is coming, but well before the second coming of Jesus, Father, free me to boast in, not bemoan about, my weaknesses. Father, grant me grace to accept my limitations and quirks, my body pains and heart wounds.

Free me to be more excited with being a fragile jar of clay, releasing the aroma of grace, as opposed to being a swaggering vessel of togetherness, dispensing impressive insights. Free me from comparing myself to anybody, by intensifying my awe of the beauty and magnificence of Jesus. May Jesus increasingly become my treasure; the gospel my delight; and grace my sufficiency.

For this one day, Father, I trust you for the freedom to be invisible and irrelevant and given over to the needs of my neighbors and strangers. Thank you for your endless patience, your inexhaustible forbearance, and your great delight in us, your children. May your love be the most compelling and transforming influence in my life today. In Jesus' merciful and mighty name I pray. Amen.

A Prayer for Those Days When We're Feeling a Bit Scattered

And this is the plan: At the right time he [God] will bring everything together under the authority of Christ—everything in heaven and on earth. (Eph. 1:10 NLT)

Since, then, you have been raised with Christ, set your hearts on things above, where Christ is, seated at the right hand of God. Set your minds on things above, not on earthly things. (Col. 3:1–2)

Dear heavenly Father, I awoke today feeling scattered, unfocused, and pulled in many directions. There's nothing heavy on my heart, major on the horizon, or haunting me from the past. I just feel the need to settle and center. I want to live today in light of the great day when everything will be summed up and united in Christ.

What a blessed day that will be! No more divided self, but a united heart; no more fractures in anything, but the unity of all things; no more much-ness and many-ness, but the order and ardor of your peaceful kingdom; no more rush, but the hush of a centered world; no more schedules to keep, but a Triune God to love with everything we have and are. I cannot wait.

So today, Father, in this very moment, I choose to set my heart and thinking on Jesus—the Author and Perfecter of my faith, the Lamb of God and Lord of all things, alone worthy of my affection, adoration, and allegiance. The more I center on Jesus, the more clearly I will see my way through the unsettledness and disquiet I'm feeling as this day begins.

Indeed, Father, every care we have, you ask us to cast on you. Lord Jesus, you have commanded us to bring our weary selves and heavy-ladenness to you. Holy Spirit, you are committed to witnessing to our sonship and belovedness, all day long. O blessed Triune God, I praise you for the overabundance of grace you will lavish upon us this very day. Thank you, thank you, thank you. In Jesus' loving and powerful name I pray. Amen.

A Prayer for Grace to Love Hard-to-Love People

If you love those who love you, what benefit is that to you? For even sinners love those who love them. And if you do good to those who do good to you, what benefit is that to you? For even sinners do the same. And if you lend to those from whom you expect to receive, what credit is that to you? Even sinners lend to sinners, to get back the same amount. But love your enemies, and do good, and lend, expecting nothing in return, and your reward will be great, and you will be sons of the Most High, for he is kind to the ungrateful and the evil. Be merciful, even as your Father is merciful. (Luke 6:32–36 ESV)

Dear Lord Jesus, I need to meditate on this Scripture regularly, because there are few portions of the Word that are more "daily" and necessary than this one. First and foremost, I'm stunned by what I already know to be true: "God is kind to the ungrateful and evil." I know this to be true because God is über-kind to me—every day, in every way. My ingratitude confronts me on a daily basis—about every good thing I have in you and for all the creature comforts I take for granted.

And my evil thoughts (no exaggeration) show up in the form of envy about what others have and are; pride over who I think I am and what I deserve; revenge towards others who have "dissed" or hurt me; lust for pleasure and comfort outside your will and provision. I throw no stones today at anyone. I just throw myself upon the mountain of your mercy.

Jesus, help me love the ungrateful and fellow evil people in my world. Grant me quick repentances when I judge others harshly; plenty of mercy to share, the kind lavished on me in the gospel; more awe of your love for me than irritation and anger over the ways people fail me; and compassion rather than reaction towards fellow sinners like myself. You are my reward, Jesus. Help me to love well in this one day the way you love us every day. I pray in your kind and exalted name. Amen.

A Prayer for Those of Us in "Wait on the Lord" Mode

I waited patiently for the LORD to help me, and he turned to me and heard my cry. He lifted me out of the pit of despair, out of the mud and the mire. He set my feet on solid ground and steadied me as I walked along. He has given me a new song to sing, a hymn of praise to our God. Many will see what he has done and be amazed. They will put their trust in the LORD. Oh, the joys of those who trust the LORD. (Ps. 40:1–4 NLT)

Dear heavenly Father, we look forward to the day when our weary cry of "How long, O Lord?" becomes an exuberant shout of, "Now, O Lord!" We come before you, many of us, with sighs, though preferring to come before you with songs. Thank you, Father, for meeting us exactly where we are and for taking us where you alone can.

We praise you for King David's story, recorded in this psalm, and we will trust you for a similar outcome. Though our "muddy, miry pits" differ from his, we are familiar with feelings of exhaustion, exasperation, resignation—even degrees of despair—as we wait upon you.

Some of us are mired in parenting stories, wondering when, or if, our children will ever rest in your grace, love, and peace. Grant us endurance, hope, and great compassion for our kids—no matter their age, no matter the issues.

Some of us are in the pit of difficult marriages, wondering where the kindness and connection went. Father, you are the God who raises the dead. Bring the resurrection power of Jesus to our marriages. Bring repentance and forgiveness, courage and gentleness, healing and hope.

Some of us are covered in the mud of our own poor choices, the consequence of unguarded hearts and soul drift. Like prodigals in a faraway country, we remember home with you but aren't certain we will be welcome again. Father, help us hope; bring us home. We grieve our sin, blame no one, make no excuses, and throw ourselves on Jesus—the only Rock, our only righteousness.

Still others of us are in pits of failing health or exhausted finances, church messes or vocational challenges, fresh betrayals or old wounds. Father, turn our sighs of unbelief into songs of praise. Grant us a measure of joy even before you grant us stories of relief. Bring glory to your name by bringing us to yourself. We pray in Jesus' trustworthy and worship-worthy name. Amen.

A Prayer for Grace
When Things Are Actually Going Well

Two things I ask of you, LORD; do not refuse me before I die. Keep falsehood and lies far from me; give me neither poverty nor riches, but give me only my daily bread. Otherwise, I may have too much and disown you and say, "Who is the LORD?" Or I may become poor and steal, and so dishonor the name of my God. (Prov. 30:7–9)

Dear heavenly Father, this portion of your Word carries a warning that's both well founded and timely. Of late, things for the most part have been going really well. I've been in a steady stretch of encouragement, joy, and hope. It's not that I'm doing anything differently or that I've deserved a break; it just seems like I've been enjoying a little more of the "already" than the "not yet" of our life in Christ. And I hasten to say, thank you, Lord! It's been great.

But this stretch of oasis-like ease has underscored the sanity of a prayer like this one offered by Agur: "Lord, don't give me riches, lest I have too much, disown you, or live as though I don't need you." Father, that prayer can only be prayed by somebody really secure in your love—somebody who has probably learned the hard way about the destructively seductive, soul-desensitizing, heart-deceiving power of money and stuff.

Father, by your providence, I happen to live in a culture and community of abundance, one in which you can easily become a spiritual add-on—an important add-on, but not as essential or vital as to most of your children in the world, who don't just say the Lord's Prayer but actually pray for daily bread.

So by your Holy Spirit, please keep me humble, stunned with gratitude, and increasing in generosity. May the gospel continue to change and reset the price tags in my life, Father. Grant me quick repentances from every expression of entitlement and presumption, any spoiledness, or an unhealthy dependence on creature comforts. I pray in Jesus' exalted and treasure-worthy name. Amen.

A Prayer for Remembering Our Most Glorious and Eternal Marriage

I will make you my wife forever, showing you righteousness and justice, unfailing love and compassion. (Hosea 2:19 NLT)

As a bridegroom rejoices over his bride, so will your God rejoice over you. (Isa. 62:5)

Dear Lord Jesus, our oldest ache, deepest longing, greatest delight can only be understood (and satisfied) in light of these Scriptures. We crave intimacy because you wrote it into our DNA. We're love-hungry because you've made us for yourself, and we will remain restless and foolish until we rest in *your* love. We're wired for hope because you have secured a future for us that immeasurably exceeds everything we could ask or imagine.

Hallelujah, hallelujah, hallelujah! Jesus, you are the Spouse we always wanted, the Savior we always needed, and the Sovereign who reigns forever. By the power of the Holy Spirit, we ask you to take us "further up and further in"—take us deeper and deeper into the wonders of your love, the ocean of your grace, the vastness of your delight.

Free us from the heart-dulling limitations of our doubts and disbelief. Forgive us for ever thinking, looking, or hoping for some human being, some horizontal relationship that could possibly give us what we can only find in you.

For those of us who are married, liberate us from underbelieving the riches of the gospel and over-expecting our marriages to give us what they were never meant to deliver. Free us, as spouses, to love each other as you—our ultimate Spouse—love us. For those of us who are single, make it palpably and profoundly real that indeed, we are married . . . to you and for eternity.

Jesus, we praise, bless, and adore you for so great a salvation, so marvelous a story, and so eternal a joy. We pray, in your great and grace-full name. Amen.

A Prayer for Families Impacted by Stories of Addiction

For we do not want you to be unaware, brothers, of the affliction we experienced in Asia. For we were so utterly burdened beyond our strength that we despaired of life itself. Indeed, we felt that we had received the sentence of death. But that was to make us rely not on ourselves but on God who raises the dead. He delivered us from such a deadly peril, and he will deliver us. On him we have set our hope that he will deliver us again. You also must help us by prayer. (2 Cor. 1:8–11 ESV)

Dear heavenly Father, with track shoes on I run to the throne of grace today on behalf of families called to love and care for an addicted family member. Few stories hold more potential for exhaustion and exasperation, discouragement and despair, giving in and giving up. Even more so, few stories represent such an opportunity, for you—the God who raises the dead—to bring the resurrection power of Jesus into play.

Father, I pray for the caregivers of the addict. Grant them unity and perseverance in the caregiving plan, heroic grace to love beyond their emotional and physical capacity, and wisdom to withstand the overwhelming pulls and manipulative strategies of their addicted family member. Provide the resources they need to love in the messy places and for the unique challenges of addiction—outside professional help; friends and support groups to offer encouragement and perspective; and funds, Father, as caring for addicts can be so very expensive. Above all, Lord, give them yourself—make your presence, heart, and hand more real than the addiction itself.

For the addicted family member, Father, whether the addiction is alcohol or chemical, pornography or sex, emotional or otherwise—prove yourself to be the God who raises the dead, loves the broken, heals the sick, forgives the prodigal, and rescues the imprisoned. May your mercy and grace, not guilt and shame, have the final word. May Jesus become more alluring and powerful than the addiction and the substance they abuse. Grant them the tenacity and hope to "work the program" of recovery and surrender to whatever stories of redemption you will write.

Father, deliver one and all alike from the deadly peril and despairing power of addiction. In Jesus' triumphant and tender name we pray. Amen.

A Prayer for Releasing the Fragrance of Christ and the Aroma of Grace

But thank God! He has made us his captives and continues to lead us along in Christ's triumphal procession. Now he uses us to spread the knowledge of Christ everywhere, like a sweet perfume. Our lives are a Christ-like fragrance rising up to God. But this fragrance is perceived differently by those who are being saved and by those who are perishing. (2 Cor. 2:14–15 NLT)

But we have this treasure in jars of clay, to show that the surpassing power belongs to God and not to us. (2 Cor. 4:7 ESV)

Dear heavenly Father, these wonderful words tell the story of how I want to live up till either the day Jesus returns or the day you choose to bring me home. May the fragrance of Jesus and the aroma of grace be increasingly released through this fragile jar of clay that I am.

Keep me in the place of humility, brokenness, and dependence, that more of the sweet perfume of the gospel may be released through me, wherever you send me, and waft upward before you as an offering of praise. Father, thank you for making me Christ's captive and a prisoner of hope. Thank you for rescuing me from sin and death, from my guilt and shame, from the illusion of self-sufficiency and the lie of self-righteousness.

Father, free me to love well, wherever I am and whomever I'm with. As these Scriptures remind me, some will experience your grace as life-giving; others will have the opposite response to the gospel. Help me to love one and all alike and not give up on anybody. I truly believe the gospel can change anyone, anytime, anywhere. May the only offensive thing about me be the gospel.

Continue to slay the "approval suck" in me—that part of me that can still treat the approval of others like Christian cocaine. Help me to love to your glory, serve with your joy, and hope with your promise. Thank you, Father, for the über-privilege of being loved by you. I pray in Jesus' wonderful and merciful name. Amen.

A Prayer for a Greater, Gladder, More Spontaneous Generosity

Do not eat the bread of a man who is stingy; do not desire his delicacies, for he is like one who is inwardly calculating. "Eat and drink!" he says to you, but his heart is not with you. (Prov. 23:6–7 ESV)

Each of you should give what you have decided in your heart to give, not reluctantly or under compulsion, for God loves a cheerful giver. (2 Cor. 9:7)

Dear heavenly Father, what a contrast these Scriptures present. I wince at the first and am drawn to the second. I have experienced both and have been both. My longing is to become so much freer, more cheerful, and more spontaneous in being generous with what you have blessed me with, Father—beginning with your mercy and grace.

How my heart needs to hear on a daily basis (even hourly), "As you are loved, love; as you have been forgiven, forgive one another; as God has accepted, so accept others; be merciful just as your Father is merciful." There is no more cheerful giver than you, Father. There is nothing stingy, begrudging, or miserly about you. You are lavish with your love, extravagant with your grace, and limitless with your patience.

The limits I put on being generous with your grace are too often connected to my wounds and pain. But I don't deserve your mercy and grace any more than anyone else. Forgive and free me, Father.

The same is true when it comes to being generous with my money, time, and stuff. Biblically and theologically I affirm that everything I have comes from you, but practically and pragmatically, I can fall into "I worked for it and therefore it's mine" mode. Forgive me and set me free, Father. I don't want to be that stingy person that calculates loss, measures worthiness, and selfishly hoards anything.

Father, you say to us with full-hearted, measureless joy, "Eat and drink!" You give us gospel delicacies in abundance and creature comforts galore. Indeed, you who have given us Jesus, freely give us all things (Rom. 8:32). I praise, bless, and adore you. May your grace and Spirit make me much more cheerful and generous. I pray in Jesus' exalted and loving name. Amen.

A Prayer for Seasons When Jesus Had Better Be "Enough"

Watch out! Sin is crouching at the door, eager to control you. (Gen. 4:7 NLT)

> I say to God, my rock: "Why have you forgotten me? Why do I go mourning because of the oppression of the enemy?" As with a deadly wound in my bones, my adversaries taunt me, while they say to me all the day long, "Where is your God?" Why are you cast down, O my soul, and why are you in turmoil within me? Hope in God; for I shall again praise him, my salvation and my God. (Ps. 42:9–11 ESV)

Dear Lord Jesus, there are times when the emptiness feels like the Grand Canyon on steroids; when the pain feels like it had no beginning and will have no end; when loneliness is magnified to the point we'll welcome any open door or welcoming embrace; when the conflicts of heart and life are so intense, we'll risk anything with anyone for a few moments of oasis and relief. Those are the days, weeks, and seasons when you'd better be enough for our languishing, vulnerable, raw hearts. Otherwise, Jesus, we have no hope.

Jesus, sin isn't just "crouching at our doors" to control us; it's also whispering inside of our hearts to destroy us. We need you and we need each other. We don't need clichés, maxims, or sayings; we need a living Christ for the deadly perils in front of us. Like Cain angry at Abel (Gen. 4); David sighting a Bathsheba (2 Sam. 11); Esau smelling fresh cooking (Gen. 25:29–34); and Asaph envious of the arrogant (Ps. 73), we too have strong longings and opportunities for "relief" that will only lead to destruction.

You've saved us from hell, Jesus; now save us from ourselves. Don't let us outlive our love for you. Don't let us have to learn, yet again, that sin only gives pleasure for a season—a very brief season. Don't let us settle for oatmeal when you give us bread from heaven; don't let us drink from mud puddles when you offer us living water; don't let us look to people for what you alone can give us.

We make David's cry our own: "Why are you cast down, O my soul, and why are you in turmoil within me? Hope in God; for I shall again praise him, my salvation and my God" (Ps. 42:11 ESV). We pray, Jesus, in your powerful and grace-full name. Amen.

A Prayer for Owning Feelings of Vulnerability, Sadness, Anger, and Longing

How long, O Lord, must I call for help? But you do not listen! "Violence is everywhere!" I cry, but you do not come to save. (Hab. 1:2 NLT)

God is our refuge and strength, always ready to help in times of trouble. So we will not fear when earthquakes come and the mountains crumble into the sea. (Ps. 46:1–2 NLT)

Dear heavenly Father, the bandwidth of my emotions this morning is as broad as the Pacific Ocean. I need your audience, perspective, and grace. Looking at scenes of Baltimore burning stirs up my anger and sense of vulnerability. Help me, Lord, to understand why those harmed by injustice would become perpetrators of destruction against their own people, their city, and citizens who have been working to make Baltimore a better place in which to live. It makes no sense to me, Lord.

I understand why you tell us not to be overcome by evil, because right now I relish the thought of repaying evil for evil and harm for harm; so I'm no different from the very people I'm judging in my heart this morning. Have mercy on my critical, resentful soul, Father. Be with those who are seeking to do everything they can to overcome evil with good in Baltimore—today and in the coming weeks and beyond.

Along with that story line, Father, earthquake damage scenes from Nepal also overwhelm me and bring an intense sadness. The poorest of the poor are robbed of the little they have, yet they use their bare hands to try to unearth family members and strangers from tons of concrete rubble. What a contrast, Lord, on a day when Apple tops $700 billion in value.

Father, I am a mess, and I'm glad you love messes. I am so ready for Jesus to come back and make all things new and put all things right. Until that day, grant me quicker repentances, the perspective of eternity, grace for the moment, and hope that will propel me into servant action and away from simply being one more critic and cynic. I pray, in Jesus' merciful and mighty name. Amen.

A Prayer for Bringing Our Annoyed, Irritated Attitude to Jesus

Fools show their annoyance at once. (Prov. 12:16)

Be not quick in your spirit to become angry, for anger lodges in the heart of fools. (Eccles. 7:9 ESV)

Dear Lord Jesus, before this day takes flight, I want to own the annoyed, irritated attitude I feel roaming about my heart. In the last few days, it hasn't taken much to bug me and put me in a bad frame of mind—like lifting an empty milk carton from the fridge when I really wanted a bowl of cereal; someone taking two parking places for their new car when I'm running late for a lunch appointment; the colorful spinning disk on my computer screen saying "I'm not ready to open your file just yet." Or dropped calls and unexpected visitors; eggshells in my omelet and road construction on my route; junk mail in my mailbox and robotic phone calls to my "do not call" registered phone number; delayed flights and deflated bike tires; people who nurse grudges, talk with food in their mouths, and laugh too loud; forgotten passwords, appointments, and names . . . Help me, Jesus!

I don't want to be that fool who shows his annoyance at once or that fool in whose bosom anger lodges like a welcomed guest. Settle me and center me by the grace, truth, and power of the gospel. I make no effort to justify my sinful, self-centered, snarly attitude.

Instead of indulging the ways of my flesh any longer, I surrender to the work of your Spirit in this moment. I repent of not repenting sooner. Thank you for your forgiveness. Jesus, you are my righteousness, peace, and joy. Though I'm no longer condemned for my sins, I want to be convicted about them much sooner and deeper. Humble me, gentle me, and free me, Jesus. I pray in your holy and loving name. Amen.

A Prayer for Seeing and Resting on God's Occupied Throne

Then as I looked, I saw a door standing open in heaven, and the same voice I had heard before spoke to me like a trumpet blast.

The voice said, "Come up here, and I will show you what must happen after this." And instantly I was in the Spirit, and I saw a throne in heaven and someone sitting on it. (Rev. 4:1–2 NLT)

"I know the plans I have for you," says the LORD. "They are plans for good." (Jer. 29:11 NLT)

Dear heavenly Father, on a regular basis you seem to find great joy in reminding me how little control I have over *anything*—over the number of my days and the quality of my health, over circumstances I don't like and people I do love, over the many blessings you do give me and the difficult stories I wish you wouldn't write for me.

And you know what, Father? I'm good with all of that, as long as you keep giving me an unobstructed, undiminished, 20/20 sighting of you sitting on your throne, ruling over all things. I don't really need a timeline of when everything is going to be okay, or a sneak preview of what it's going to look like. All I need to know, in my heart of hearts, is that you are at work for your pleasure in my life and that your plans for me (and all your children) are good—even when in the moment, it might seem otherwise.

Since you have given Jesus for our perfect and full salvation, why would I ever believe that you would withhold anything from me that is central to your will for my life and the outworking of your glory in the world? You promise sufficient grace, not the satisfaction of my agenda. You promise Christlikeness, not a hammock and a cool breeze. You promise full redemption, not immediate relief. Father, I want what you want. In Jesus' kind and glorious name I pray. Amen.

A Prayer for Filling Our Hearts Full of Heaven

I'm torn between two desires: I long to go and be with Christ, which would be far better for me. (Phil. 1:23 NLT)

I consider that our present sufferings are not worth comparing with the glory that will be revealed in us. For the creation waits in eager expectation for the children of God to be revealed. (Rom. 8:18–19)

Dear Lord Jesus, the peace and joy I have pondering our eternal future with you is beyond measure and without comparison. The deepest desires you've written into our DNA; our most intense longings for relationships and intimacy; the insatiable thirst we carry for a perfect world and perfect everything . . . they will *all* find their fulfillment in the life to come. Jesus, thank you for earning heaven for us and for keeping us for heaven.

I agree with the apostle Paul: it would be better by far to depart and be with you right now, Jesus, for you make heaven "heavenly." It's not about streets of gold, angels dancing around singing, or even being freed from all brokenness and pain. Heaven is primarily about being with you, the Father, and the Spirit. Oh, how I crave the unbroken, unfettered, and uninhibited relationship we will enjoy with you forever.

I am a foolish man to think anyone or anything else can fill the void, ease the ache, or satisfy this longing I have for you. Bring me back to gospel sanity quickly when my "light momentary affliction" (2 Cor. 4:17 ESV) feels eternal and heavier than a pack of elephants. Rescue me the very nanosecond my math fails me and I no longer consider the glory to be revealed in us to be greater than the difficulty of our present sufferings in this world.

Don't ever, ever, ever let me settle for a "quick fix" when you have promised eternal wonder. Never let my pain outweigh your praise. Never let me outlive my love for you, Jesus. I pray in your beautiful name. Amen.

A Prayer for Seasons When Certain People Seem Bigger Than God

Fearing people is a dangerous trap, but trusting the LORD means safety. (Prov. 29:25 NLT)

God sits above the circle of the earth. The people below seem like grasshoppers to him! He spreads out the heavens like a curtain and makes his tent from them. (Isa. 40:22 NLT)

Dear heavenly Father, there are days, even long seasons, when people gain more power over our hearts than they deserve or even want. We can feel like grasshoppers in the presence of giants—even when some of those people may be half our height! When this happens, any of a number of broken relational styles results. Thank you that there's grace for every season of life and every expression of "the fear of man." Grant us relational freedom, that we might love well, Father.

Through the power of the gospel, help us take back the power we've given some people to shame us and manipulate us—to make us feel like vulnerable grasshoppers. No one deserves that much power over our hearts. The truth is, if we're going to feel "grasshopper-sized" anywhere in life, it should only be before you. For you are God and people are not. The good news is that in Christ, we are your "beloved grasshoppers"—safe, not threatened; cared for, not used; cherished, not shamed.

Father, also help us take back the power we've given some people to "fill us up" and make us. Whether it's our spouse or our children, friends or strangers, people we work for or people who work for us, those we envy or those we lust after—we can turn anybody into an idol, a substitute god, or a false savior. Father, there is a Jesus-shaped void you have placed in our hearts that only Jesus can fill. Keep us restless until we rest in him . . . or rest in him again. We pray in his glorious and grace-full name. Amen.

A Prayer for Resting in the Lord
When Feeling Stressed and Restless

I will refresh the weary and satisfy the faint. (Jer. 31:25)

And he said, "My presence will go with you, and I will give you rest." (Exod. 33:14 ESV)

It is useless for you to work so hard from early morning until late at night, anxiously working for food to eat; for God gives rest to his loved ones. (Ps. 127:2 NLT)

Dear heavenly Father, all three of these men—Jeremiah, Moses, and King David—experienced overwhelming seasons of stress and restlessness, and your promise to them is still your promise to us: "I am with you and for you. I am your peace and I will give you rest." Such good news for heavyhearted days—really, for any and every day.

Thank you, Father, that you don't roll your eyes when we're "less than conquerors," not exactly in "victorious Christian life" mode or brimming over with faith and confidence. The gospel makes us more, not less, human, and the gospel makes you more, not less, accessible, welcoming, and understanding. Your forbearance is remarkable, your patience is inexhaustible, and your kindness is incalculable.

Father, for those of us just flat-out tired, spent, and exhausted from working too hard, help us make changes in our schedules that need to be made and can be made. Grant us the gifts of relaxation, play, and a few nights' good sleep.

Father, for those of us emotionally exhausted and mentally spent from relational challenges, keep us from either giving up on hope, or giving in to foolish ways of dealing with our pain and longings.

Father, for those of us stressed about health issues or financial pressures, old heart wounds with lingering infection or new heartaches with knee-buckling power, fears about world crises or worries about today's unknowns, give us mercy and grace tailored for the situation. Make it undeniably clear to us that you love us and that you are in control. That's all we need. In Jesus' caring and trustworthy name we pray. Amen.

A Prayer for Wisdom for Loving Well in Complex Story Lines

If you need wisdom, ask our generous God, and he will give it to you. He will not rebuke you for asking. (James 1:5 NLT)

Dear heavenly Father, like every day, I begin this day grateful for your daily mercies, eternal kindness, and measureless generosity. Not only have you given Jesus to us as our perfect righteousness, but you provide us with everything else we need in life. Today I need wisdom, and I trust your promise to give it gladly and freely.

Father, I need wisdom for loving well in complex relationships and broken story lines. Please help me know the difference between overlooking a fault and covering up something that needs to be revealed. When does patience turn into denial, turning the other cheek become enabling, and "trying to be nice" morph into unhealthy conflict avoidance? You must show me, Father; I just don't know.

I know the gospel will always require more of us than I readily give, but grant me wisdom to know what that means when it's just not easy to discern. How do I validate the emotions of others without taking responsibility for those emotions? How do I listen with the goal not of fixing but loving? When should I risk losing a relationship because of a greater commitment to honor you and protect the innocent? What's the line between waiting a little longer and knowing now's the time to act?

Father, help me with my own emotional triggers. Shame, fear, and anger are always lurking around the corner. Continue to reveal and heal the wounds of my heart that remain in need of your grace, surgery, and rehab. Continue to expose old relational patterns I learned (and perfected) in response to abandonment, betrayal, and insecurity.

I so long for the day when I will be made perfect in love and will love perfectly forever. Until that day, I will rest in your love for us, Father, and trust you for all the grace and wisdom that I need on a daily (even hourly) basis. I pray in Jesus' merciful and mighty name. Amen.

A Prayer for Knowing God's Goodness and Nearness in the Storm

But now thus says the LORD, he who created you, O Jacob, he who formed you, O Israel: "Fear not, for I have redeemed you; I have called you by name, you are mine. When you pass through the waters, I will be with you; and through the rivers, they shall not overwhelm you; when you walk through fire you shall not be burned, and the flame shall not consume you. For I am the LORD your God, the Holy One of Israel, your Savior. I give Egypt as your ransom, Cush and Seba in exchange for you. Because you are precious in my eyes, and honored, and I love you, I give men in return for you, peoples in exchange for your life. Fear not, for I am with you." (Isa. 43:1–5 ESV)

Dear heavenly Father, your Word is solace for the sad and ballast for the bewildered, a firm rock for the freshly rocked and bread from heaven for the hungry on earth. This isn't theory, the wisdom of sages, or just true and good theology. It's our reality, and we praise you. You've made promises you alone can keep, and you do not lie. No god is as near or good, merciful or mighty as you—no matter the storm or season.

As you have spoken clearly through Isaiah, you created us and are redeeming us, all for your glory. You summoned us by name, calling us to life in the gospel. You gave us a new name—"Mine." There's no sweeter, more perspective-giving or more peace-generating name you could call us. You never promised we wouldn't experience floods and torrents, fires and flames. But you have promised to be with us. To know your great affection for us and your absolute sovereignty over everything is enough, Father.

Indeed, we know ourselves to be precious, honored, and greatly loved, because you gave Jesus in exchange for us. Though he was rich, yet for our sakes he became poor, so that through his poverty we might become rich (2 Cor. 8:9). We praise you for the indescribable gift of the gospel (2 Cor. 9:15).

And since you didn't spare your own Son, certainly we can trust you to graciously give us everything else we need (Rom. 8:32)—in current storms and future fires. We don't have to be afraid of anything or anyone. You are with us and you are for us. We pray in Jesus' great and grace-full name. Amen.

A Prayer for Seeing Jesus in Painful Moments and Seasons of Life

But Stephen, full of the Holy Spirit, looked up to heaven and saw the glory of God, and Jesus standing at the right hand of God. "Look," he said, "I see heaven open and the Son of Man standing at the right hand of God." (Acts 7:55–56)

Dear Lord Jesus, this vignette from Stephen's life underscores your tender and tenacious engagement, no matter what we are going through. Just before he was stoned for proclaiming your glory and grace, Stephen saw you standing at the Father's right hand—rising for the occasion of his greatest need. Indeed, Jesus, you are our Good Shepherd, faithfully caring for us, your lambs, even from heaven.

Though few of us will be stoned to death as your martyrs, all of us are called to love and serve you in painful chapters and crises of life. Jesus, we too need to see you standing at the Father's right hand for us. In particular, I'm thinking of friends facing difficult seasons in their lives, for which a fresh and clear sighting of you, Jesus, is greatly needed and would be overwhelmingly appreciated.

For friends wearing the label "terminal illness," grant them a profound and palatable sense of your presence, Jesus. Because the gospel is true, "terminal" is really "transitional," for we have already passed from death to life and from judgment for our sin to favor with our God. Hallelujah, so many times over.

For couples in seasons of marital mess that feels very much like death, Jesus, Lord of resurrection and hope, merciful and mighty Savior, I ask you to do exceedingly beyond all we can ask or imagine. Rise for the occasion with healing in your wings and grace in your hands. Humble one, then both spouses. Restore the joy of your salvation and then the tenderness to their marriages.

For friends in church conflicts—oh, how Satan hates your Bride, Jesus. I pray you will be unavoidably large and beautiful. You are the issue, Jesus, whatever other issues may be on the table or under the table. May leaders prove to be chief repenters, and may the gospel be a hundred times more in play than gossip. May guarding the peace and purity of your Bride take precedence over spinning and winning. I pray in your glorious and grace-full name. Amen.

A Prayer for Knowing
the Full Extent of Jesus' Love

Having loved his own who were in the world, he [Jesus] now showed them the full extent of his love. (John 13:1 NIV 1984)

Dear Lord Jesus, I often return to the scene from which this verse is taken, for it's homeroom for my heart—the place I go to settle and center my restless soul. It's the night of your betrayal, the night you would be denied and abandoned, not just by Peter but also by every disciple. You knew the full extent of their weakness, so you showed them the full extent of your love. Washing their feet was a prelude to washing their hearts. Water sufficed for the first; your lifeblood was required for the second.

This is how you love each of us, Jesus—how you love me. Absolutely nothing can separate us from your love or impact the way you love us. You don't love us more when we "get it right," and you don't love us less when we fail you. That doesn't mean you're indifferent; it means you're our Savior, the one who remains committed to showing us the full extent of your love—how wide, long, high, and deep it really is (Eph. 3:18–19).

Only your love, Jesus, can free and change me. Only your love is better than life. Only your love is enough. In my most gospel-sane moments, I know this to be true—my truest truth. Nobody or nothing has to change for me to be at peace and joyful. Continue to rescue me from thinking otherwise. Forgive me for plugging my happy-meter into what people think of me, or how easy or difficult life is, or how much or how little money I have, or how in control or not I am of my circumstances, or anything beyond you.

Jesus, you are my loving Master, not my private masseur. Forgive me when I forget the first and start demanding the second. By the gospel keep washing me, Jesus—bathe me in grace every hour of every day. You are already my perfect righteousness; I long for the day when I will be made perfect

111

in love (1 John 4:18). In your merciful and mighty name I pray. Amen.

A Prayer for the Day of My Surgery

Do not be anxious about anything, but in everything by prayer and supplication with thanksgiving let your requests be made known to God. (Phil. 4:6 ESV)

Heal me, LORD, and I will be healed; save me and I will be saved, for you are the one I praise. (Jer. 17:14)

Dear heavenly Father, I am fearfully and wonderfully made, and am fully and gladly yours. On this morning of my surgery, I am so thankful that you are my God and I am your child. It's a vulnerable feeling to know that pretty soon I will be under anesthesia and without any knowledge of what's going on in my body, but it's a glorious thing to know that you are in control and that I can trust you with *everything*.

I pray for my dear friend and surgeon. Guide his head, hands, and heart. He has incredible skills; now grant him your good providence—not only for me but for others he will serve today as well. I pray for his team and attendants, and I am thankful that we live in a part of the world that affords us incredible medical care.

I pray for my family and friends while I'm in surgery—grateful for their care and prayers. Grant them peace and assurance that all is well. Father, help me to be a good post-surgery patient, following my doctor's orders and doing the work of rehab as prescribed. I can be self-sufficient, pig-headed, and presumptuous. Free me from all three.

112

Lastly, Father, I'm so glad the gospel is true. I won't live one day longer or less than you prescribe. Of this I am absolutely sure: if I should wake up in heaven today, it will be only on the basis of the finished work of Jesus and by the sovereign appointment of you, my loving Father. You do all things well, all the time. I praise, bless, and adore you. I pray in Jesus' merciful and mighty name. Amen.

A Prayer for Celebrating the "How Much More-ness" of the Gospel

But the gift is not like the trespass. For if the many died by the trespass of the one man, how much more did God's grace and the gift that came by the grace of the one man, Jesus Christ, overflow to the many! Nor can the gift of God be compared with the result of one man's sin: The judgment followed one sin and brought condemnation, but the gift followed many trespasses and brought justification. For if, by the trespass of the one man, death reigned through that one man, how much more will those who receive God's abundant provision of grace and of the gift of righteousness reign in life through the one man, Jesus Christ! (Rom. 5:15–17)

Dear heavenly Father, I praise, bless, and adore you today for the hyperabundance, limitless reach, and cosmos-transforming wonders of the grace you've lavished on us in Jesus. Through Adam, we came into the world spiritually dead—willing subjects, co-conspirators, members in good standing in the reign of sin and death. But now, through the work of the second Adam, Jesus, we were born again and now live as objects of your unabated affection and subjects in Jesus' irrepressible kingdom.

As dead as we were in our sins and trespasses, we are much, much more alive in Jesus' forgiveness and righteousness. As distant and disconnected as we were from you because of Adam's sin and our own sin, we are much, much more at peace and intimate with you through the perfect work of Jesus on our behalf. As narcissistic and navel-gazing as we were through our connection to the first Adam, we are becoming much, much more other-centered, loving, and caring through our union with Jesus.

Most generous and loving Father, you are most definitely for us. You didn't spare your own Son but gave him up for us all—how will you not also, along with Jesus, graciously give us all things? You justified us, and there is now no condemnation; you're sanctifying us and will continue to do so until there's no sin left in us; you will glorify us, and on that day we'll be as lovely and as loving as Jesus. Nothing will ever separate us from your love (Rom. 8:31–35).

Indeed, as grave and great as our condition was, the "how much more-ness" of the gospel has trumped it a gazillion times over. I pray in Jesus' great and grace-full name. Amen.

A Prayer for Faith to Keep Hoping When We're Weary of Hoping

Now faith is confidence in what we hope for and assurance about what we do not see. This is what the ancients were commended for. By faith we understand that the universe was formed at God's command, so that what is seen was not made out of what was visible. (Heb. 11:1–3)

Dear heavenly Father, we cannot do relationships well without being aware of the unmet longings, yet-to-be-answered prayers, and fading hopes of good friends—and those we carry in our hearts as well. It's a great comfort to know that the most repeated question in the Bible is "How long, O Lord?"—which means we're in good company. It's an even greater comfort to know you as the Father of mercies and the God of all comfort.

Since you are pleased when we exercise faith, we set our gaze on Jesus as this day begins and will continue, for Jesus is the Author and Perfecter of our faith. When we see Jesus, we have no problem believing you created the seen world out of unseen stuff. Likewise, when we see Jesus, we are emboldened to trust you for the things that don't seem likely or perhaps even possible at this point. Honestly, Father, sometimes it actually feels easier (and safer) not to hope than to hope. But you haven't called us to ease but to yourself—which is better by far.

Father, I pray for parents who quite literally would give their right arm for the assurance of their children's salvation. But it's not about us giving our arms but you giving your Son. O mighty and gracious Redeemer, reveal Jesus to the hearts of our kids.

I pray for spouses who are toast—weary and spent of thinking you can (or will) raise their dead marriage from the dead. Father, you promise to do exceedingly beyond all we can ask or imagine. As you spoke the world into existence, so breathe life into languishing marriages.

Father, I pray for families with health issues, financial challenges, and addicted loved ones; for churches in crisis mode, ministries under attack, and fallen leaders; for missionaries with growing challenges and depleted resources; for those whose guilt and shame seem stronger than your mercy and grace. Meet us where we are and take us where you would, Father, in all of these stories. Grant us faith and renew our hope; in all things, be glorified. We pray in Jesus' triumphant and tender name. Amen.

A Prayer for Remembering
Our True Enemy and Our Best Armor

A final word: Be strong in the Lord and in his mighty power. Put on all of God's armor so that you will be able to stand firm against all strategies of the devil. For we are not fighting against flesh-and-blood enemies, but against evil rulers and authorities of the unseen world, against mighty powers in this dark world, and against evil spirits in the heavenly places. (Eph. 6:10–12 NLT)

But put on the Lord Jesus Christ, and make no provision for the flesh, to gratify its desires. (Rom. 13:14 ESV)

Dear Lord Jesus, foolish me—once again I forgot that our greatest enemies in life are not individual people and groups of men but the devil and his dark minions. Though you crushed his head on the cross, the devil awaits his eradication at your return. Filled with fury because he knows his time is short, he is actively seeking to harm everything you treasure and cherish—your church and beloved Bride; marriages, meant to reveal your gospel and beauty; individuals, made in your image and being remade by your grace; cities, meant to offer a glimpse of the City whose Builder and Maker is God.

Jesus, forgive me for simplistically blaming people for most of the ills in my life and problems in the world. Though we harm one another destructively and inexcusably, there is one who hates all of us collectively. Help us recognize his snarly schemes (2 Cor. 2:11) and prowling ways (1 Pet. 5:8).

My greatest peace, confidence, and hope in the battle is you, Lord Jesus. As surely as I'll dress myself with appropriate clothes for this day, so by faith I choose to dress myself with garments of your grace right now. Jesus, you don't just give us armor, you are our armor—our righteousness, holiness, and redemption. In you, there is no condemnation or fear; by you, we have everything we need, not just to survive but to thrive in life; for you, all things exist; with you, we enter this day dependent, expectant, and ever so grateful. We pray in your triumphant and tender name. Amen.

A Prayer for Those Days and Seasons When We Feel Outnumbered

"Don't be afraid!" Elisha told him. "For there are more on our side than on theirs!" Then Elisha prayed, "O LORD, open his eyes and let him see!" The LORD opened the young man's eyes, and when he looked up, he saw that the hillside around Elisha was filled with horses and chariots of fire. (2 Kings 6:16–17 NLT)

What, then, shall we say in response to these things? If God is for us, who can be against us? (Rom. 8:31)

Dear heavenly Father, sometimes like Elisha, we get overwhelmed at the odds stacked against us in life—whether we're having to deal with a disproportionate amount of broken people, hard story lines, or fresh heartaches; or whether it's a huge school of tiny circumstantial piranha nibbling away at our energy and joy; or whether it's just one big zapping difficulty that's exhausting our resources and actually feels bigger than you. No matter the scenario, you understand, you are with us, and you are for us.

Father, as with Elisha, so with us—open our eyes to see your angels placed all around us; quicken our ears to hear you singing over us with great delight, right in the middle of the chaos; and compel our hearts to know that greater is the One who is in us than the one that is in the world. Indeed, Father, make Jesus the biggest and most beautiful, the most obvious and most unavoidable reality in our lives right now—even if it's a long time before our circumstances change.

Father, help us to steward our vulnerability and weakness well; help us resist evil "carpetbaggers" offering snake-oil remedies and the empty promises of quick relief; help us run to your throne of grace regularly and to the most reliable members of our gospel posses—for some things we simply cannot handle all by ourselves. We praise, bless, and adore you for being our near and grace-full God. You are here; you are in control; and you will win the day. We pray in Jesus' triumphant and tender name. Amen.

A Prayer for Rejoicing in Our Salvation and Encouraging One Another

God has not destined us for wrath, but to obtain salvation through our Lord Jesus Christ, who died for us so that whether we are awake or asleep we might live with him. Therefore encourage one another and build one another up, just as you are doing. (1 Thess. 5:9–11 ESV)

Dear heavenly Father, there are many things over which I don't have any control; many outcomes that remain hidden from me; and many broken stories, broken people, and broken circumstances that may or may not get better this side of heaven. But this I do know: because of the finished work of Jesus, my future contains zero judgment and one hundred percent joyful welcome by you; zero wrath and one hundred percent perfect righteousness in Jesus; zero brokenness and one hundred percent perfect relationship with you. It's *all* gonna be not just okay but magnificent beyond our wildest dreams and hopes.

Until then, Father, make me a genuine encourager and "builder-upper" of my family, gospel posse, and friends. Thank you for the privilege we have of bearing one another's burdens; showing up in one another's stories; holding one another accountable for believing the gospel; and giving each other hope-fueling perspective at low times and life-giving rebukes at wandering times.

Father, thank you that whether we die before Jesus returns or live to see that blessed day, we are your beloved children, now and forever. Nothing can ever separate us from your love, deplete your mercies, or exhaust your grace.

Thank you that the darkest clouds often bring the most refreshing rains; that boasting in our weakness is still the best way to taste your sweetness; and that none of us will ever be beyond the need or reach of your grace. Indeed, Father, make me an encourager with this Good News and living hope, as long as you keep me in this world. In Jesus' tender and triumphant name I pray. Amen.

A Prayer for Those Days You Wish God Would Do Things Differently

Woe to those who quarrel with their Maker, those who are nothing but potsherds among the potsherds on the ground. Does the clay say to the potter, "What are you making?" Does your work say, "The potter has no hands"? (Isa. 45:9)

Dear heavenly Father, even your "woe's" are gifts of grace, for they warn me of the foolishness of my reasoning, the limitations of my perspective, and the self-centeredness of my musings.

Sometimes I think I'd like to be you for fifteen minutes. That'd give me a chance to fix people that need fixing; fund ministries which serve you the best but struggle with finances the most; bring judgment upon those who've got it coming; alleviate the sufferings of friends whose pain is overwhelming; get even with people who've hurt me the deepest and betrayed me the most; put an end to human trafficking; rid the world of annoying politicians, fear-brokers, and pundits; and heal broken marriages of friends.

Alas, Father, I am such a mix of good desires and broken agendas. I look at my list and realize how much I need the gospel—every day and every hour. Of course, you the Potter have hands—big, loving, mighty ones. And not only that, but you have a heart bigger than the universe, wisdom beyond all imaginings, and a timetable that makes Swiss precision seem like laissez-faire laziness.

There is a day coming when you will put all things right and make all things new. Give me patience; increase my gentleness; supersize my mercy; deepen my trust; fill me to overflowing with your grace and hope. And grant me quick repentances when I whine about the way you do your job. I pray in Jesus' mighty and merciful name. Amen.

A Prayer for Growing in the Compassion of Jesus

And Jesus went throughout all the cities and villages, teaching in their synagogues and proclaiming the gospel of the kingdom and healing every disease and every affliction. When he saw the crowds, he had compassion for them, because they were harassed and helpless, like sheep without a shepherd. (Matt. 9:35–36 ESV)

Dear Lord Jesus, there are so many reasons to love you. Today we're particularly thankful for your compassion, greatly convicted by it, and longing to show more of it to others. When you looked at crowds of harassed and helpless people, you didn't ignore them and they didn't irritate you; you made time for them. Sympathy beat within your breast; kindness overflowed. We see this everywhere in the four Gospels. Help us know this is what you feel *for us.*

Jesus, at times our theology outstrips our experience—our doctrine being more certain than our delight. But we long for the Spirit to convince us afresh that as you look upon us right now, it's mercy you feel. We're not necessarily "harassed or helpless," but we want to be certain of your compassion in our current stories of confusion, loss, and disconnect. We know you'll never leave us or forsake us. We know it and really believe it, but would you come and shepherd our hearts today?

Jesus, it really is enough to know that you suffered for us on the cross. We stake our lives and death on this glorious gospel. But it's also comforting to know that you share in our sufferings right now as well. No one understands like you. No one is closer and kinder. You suffered for us, once and for all, and you suffer with us in our sojourning. We are so very, very thankful. We pray in your holy and loving name. Amen.

A Prayer for Receiving God's Promise of Refreshment

I will refresh the weary and satisfy the faint. (Jer. 31:25)

Dear heavenly Father, like a puppy clamoring for morning milk, I'm ready (and grateful) for you to make good on this promise. I'm not close to fainting, but I won't deny my weariness. The combination of the heat, my normally busy schedule, a couple of unexpected providences and unplanned-for "curve balls" have me feeling like I'm pregnant with a bad attitude that's ready to be birthed, and it's a big baby. I'm so thankful that I don't have to pretend around you—to suck it up and get over it. You meet us in our weariness to refresh us as a loving Father, not to reprimand us as a grouchy coach. You meet us with the gospel, not with a scorecard; with grace, not with the law; with a towel to wash our feet, not with a cattle prod to get us going. Thank you.

I'm also a bit weary from grieving the pain friends are carrying. Relationships are so complex, Father. No one knows that better than you. How I long for the day when all brokenness will give way to the perfect blessedness of loving well in the new heaven and new earth. That day cannot come a day too soon.

Indeed, I so look forward to an eternity of no more pettiness or self-pity; no more hard-heartedness or hair-trigger sensitivity; no more communicating in part or using conflict to win; no more passive-aggressiveness or active indifference; no more innuendo or bravado or anything else that hides the beauty of Jesus.

Speaking of which, Lord Jesus, I'm so grateful you still cry out to us in the gospel, with a loud voice, "Anyone who is thirsty may come to me! Anyone who believes in me may come and drink! For the Scriptures declare, 'Rivers of living water will flow from his heart'" (John 7:37–38 NLT). I hear your beckoning, welcoming, gladdening cry, and by faith I come running to you. Fill me to overflowing with the water you alone can give, Jesus. Slake this relentless thirst of mine. I pray in your kind and generous name. Amen.

A Prayer for Days When You're Overwhelmed with Grief and Anger

When my heart was grieved and my spirit embittered, I was senseless and ignorant; I was a brute beast before you. Yet I am always with you; you hold me by my right hand. You guide me with your counsel, and afterward you will take me into glory. Whom have I in heaven but you? And earth has nothing I desire besides you. (Ps. 73:21–23)

Dear heavenly Father, as many times as I've read and prayed, taught and preached Psalm 73, I'm not sure I've ever related to Asaph's anguish more than I do today. I am grieved and heading toward bitterness, feeling beastly and quite capable of thinking senseless, unhelpful thoughts. I pray for myself and others sitting in stories that make our heads spin and our hearts sink. Father of mercy and God of all comfort . . .

Show us how to handle deep disappointment and hurt as redemptively as possible. Show us the difference between appropriate anger and destructive rage.

Show us how to pray down the gospel, lest we try to call down fire.

Show us how to hope when we want to hurl something.

Show us how to keep from importing old wounds into a new wound.

Show us how to listen to you quietly rather than launching our opinions.

Show us how to grieve and lament and not gossip and mock.

Show us the difference between worldly sadness and godly sorrow.

Show us what the gospel looks like in stories that seem to utterly contradict it.

Show us how to be still and know that you are God.

Father, let us palpably feel the grasp of grace right now. You are guiding us in and through the valley of the shadow of death, and you will bring glory to yourself in the most heart-wrecking of stories. Who do we have in heaven or on earth but you? Being with you is what we need more than anything else, in the coming hours and days, weeks and months. We pray in Jesus' merciful and mighty name. Amen.

A Prayer for Getting Still
before God and Living That Way

Be still, and know that I am God! I will be honored by every
nation. I will be honored throughout the world. (Ps. 46:10 NLT)

Dear heavenly Father, I'm staring at a big stack of unopened
mail, a ton of yet-to-be-answered phone calls and emails, and
a gotta-get-done list much longer than my idol of control
will generally tolerate. By your Spirit, settle, center, and free
me to trust you. I want to enter this day and live it at the
pace of grace.

I begin by acknowledging yet again that you are God and
I am not. I don't want my main goal for these next few days
just to be getting a bunch of stuff done. I want my faith in
Jesus to express itself in love to everybody involved. I've
asked it before and I'll ask again, Father: keep my to-love
list more important to me than my to-do list. May you, who
will be honored by every nation and throughout the world,
be honored in my heart, home, and responsibilities.

If I throw my heart into cruise control, I know I'm quite
capable of becoming short and rigid, impatient and pushy,
controlling and obsessive. So I'm not going to do that. With
palms up, I surrender to your peace and presence right now.
Father, by the power of the gospel, I'm getting still before
you, and I want to stay still, even as I take care of many
responsibilities.

What gets done today gets done, and what doesn't isn't of
eternal significance. I cannot add an hour to my life by wor-
rying, but I can surely rob a lot of people with my frenzied
spirit. There's no panic in heaven—no hurrying or scurrying.

Bring heaven to my heart today. In Jesus' reigning and loving name I pray. Amen.

A Prayer for Trusting God with Important Decisions in Front of Us

Trust in the LORD with all your heart, and do not lean on your own understanding. In all your ways acknowledge him, and he will make straight your paths. (Prov. 3:5–6 ESV)

Dear Lord Jesus, many of us are staring big decisions in the face, and we need your help. It's a joy to come before your throne of grace confident of your audience, grateful for your advocacy, and resting in your authority.

Indeed, Jesus, you are an involved Shepherd, not an absentee landlord. Even as we make plans in our hearts, you are actively ordering our steps (Prov. 16:9). This brings us immeasurable peace. You open doors no one can shut (Rev. 3:8), and you shut doors no one can open. Never let us forget that our future is tied not to making the right decisions but to trusting the right Lord.

Because of your great love for us in the gospel, we're learning to trust you with all the stuff in our hearts—with our longings, fears, hurts, and dreams. To acknowledge you in all of our ways is not to make you Lord of anything but to recognize you are Lord of everything. So in surrender to your sovereign heart and hand, we anticipate straight paths as we move ahead into these difficult decisions.

For those of us dealing with job changes and financial stresses, health issues and relationship complexities, show yourself to be both merciful and mighty, Jesus. May your mercy keep us expectant and your might trump our impatience.

For those of us having to make important decisions for the people we love, be huge and present, Jesus. Long-term care for aging parents, the "right" education choices for our kids, the best treatment plan for loved ones battling addictions—make the way clear, Lord. For those of us who feel restless about current life investments and are praying about fresh commitments to missions and ministry, give us clarity of mind and peace in our hearts.

In these coming hours and days, write stories of providence that will reveal your glory, showcase your grace, and leave us reveling in your goodness and timing. We pray in your trustworthy and beautiful name. Amen.

A Prayer for the Renewal of Our Joy

What has happened to all your joy? (Gal. 4:15 NIV 1984)

Will you not revive us again, that your people may rejoice in you? Show us your unfailing love, LORD, and grant us your salvation. (Ps. 85:6–7)

Dear Lord Jesus, we begin our day grateful for your pursuing heart, which is revealed in the questions, wooings, and pleas of the Scriptures. Today we ponder our need for gospel renewal and the restoration of joy. We join the chorus of many who cry out, "Revive us again, Lord, and restore to us the joy of your salvation."

In response to Paul's question to the Galatians, "What has happened to all your joy?" (Gal. 4:15 NIV 1984), there's a wide range of possible answers. Some of us may have fallen back into performance-based spirituality—trusting more in our ongoing feeble works than your perfect and finished work. Some of us may have allowed roots of bitterness to grow deep, infesting our renewed hearts with the toxins of unforgiveness and revenge.

Some of us may be giving greater audience to our fears, worries, and anxieties than to your nearness, sovereignty, and grace. Some of us could very well just be exhausted from life's challenges, bouts with illness, and the price of loving well, and we're just flat-out tired. Some of us are losing sleep and peace because of the condemning accusations of the consummate liar, robber, and joy-murderer—the devil himself.

To every one of these scenarios, the answer is the same: more of you. We need a fresh sighting of and heart-connection with you, Lord Jesus, as our full forgiveness and perfect righteousness, our sovereign King and most loving Bridegroom. Renew, refresh, and restore our hearts in the wonders of your love and sufficiency of your grace.

Jesus, since you are praying for the fullness of your joy to be in us (John 17:13), we will live with anticipation and hope, for your prayers never fail. Fill us afresh with the inexpressible and glorious joy of the salvation you have won for us (1 Pet. 1:8–9). In your trustworthy and triumphant name we pray. Amen.

A Prayer for Trusting in God's Ability to Do Immeasurably More

Now to him who is able to do immeasurably more than all we ask or imagine, according to his power that is at work within us, to him be glory in the church and in Christ Jesus throughout all generations, for ever and ever! Amen. (Eph. 3:20–21)

Dear heavenly Father, I'm so very thankful for your ability to do immeasurably more than all we ask and imagine. Creating the world out of nothing and raising Jesus out of the grave are proof enough. But today my prayer list doesn't contain things beyond the stretch of my imagination, but things very much within its reach and orbit.

I ask you to lift the heaviness of my heart the way you lifted the guilt of my sin. I ask you to open the eyes of a good friend's heart the way you opened the entrance of Jesus' tomb. I ask you to quiet the mouths of cynics, naysayers, and gossips the way you shut the mouths of Nebuchadnezzar's lions. I ask you to comfort the hearts of the disillusioned and disheartened the way your angels comforted the women on the morning of Jesus' resurrection.

I ask you to help me see the legions of angels you've positioned all around difficult stories and broken people. I ask you to help me grieve with hope—even overflow with hope as Paul instructed followers of Jesus. I ask you to lift your robe, run, welcome, and kiss all kinds of prodigals in the coming days, weeks, and months. I ask you to keep me from relying on myself and to help me trust boldly in you—the God who raises the dead. I ask you to bring great glory to yourself in your church, by Jesus, for all to see, now and forever more. I pray in Jesus' mighty and merciful name. Amen.

A Prayer for Letting Go of Trying to Be the Fourth Member of the Trinity

I am the Alpha and the Omega, the First and the Last, the Beginning and the End. (Rev. 22:13)

You will keep in perfect peace all who trust in you, all whose thoughts are fixed on you! (Isa. 26:3 NLT)

Dear heavenly Father, it's time for me to shift my focus from the immediacy of a big disappointment to the permanency of who you are. It's one thing to be lovingly concerned about a matter and another to angrily obsess about it; one thing to pray without ceasing and another to vex without sleeping; one thing to engage sacrificially and another to be enmeshed unhealthily.

So with palms up, I release my burden to you, Lord. I'm not going to shift into a snarly, "I couldn't care less" attitude, but I will care less and trust you more. You are God, and I am very much not so. You've begun a good work in each of your children and in every sphere of your creation, and you're neither AWOL, disinterested, bored, or negligent. You're going to complete your story to your glory, in your time, on your dime, and in your way. Hallelujah!

You are the Alpha and the Omega, the First and the Last, the Beginning and the End, and everything in between. Hallelujah, many times over! You are Father, Son, and Holy Spirit—perfect Trinity, and not looking to make a trio into a quartet. You don't need me; you love me. When the cares of my heart are many, your consolations cheer my soul. When I fix my thoughts on you—as opposed to fixating on messy situations and messy people—your peace centers, settles, and liberates me. So as this day begins and continues, I choose liberation over consternation; I choose to believe the gospel rather than try to be my savior or anybody else's. I pray in Jesus' wonderful and merciful name. Amen.

A Prayer for Friends and Family in Dark, Entangled, Broken Stories

Epaphras, who is one of you and a servant of Christ Jesus, sends greetings. He is always wrestling in prayer for you, that you may stand firm in all the will of God, mature and fully assured. (Col. 4:12)

Likewise the Spirit helps us in our weakness. For we do not know what to pray for as we ought, but the Spirit himself intercedes for us with groanings too deep for words. (Rom. 8:26 ESV)

Dear heavenly Father, sometimes quite literally all we can do is pray for certain family members and friends—people we love who live in the vortex of mental and emotional illness; others who are willing participants and suppliers of their own destructive addictions; still others whose rage, pain, and trauma have more power over their lives than the true Trinity.

Father, help us to know what our limits are in these situations, what loving well in dark brokenness looks like, and what resources are available to us. Teach us how, like Epaphras, to wrestle in prayer for our loved ones without literally wrestling with them one-on-one. Some situations are beyond reason, conventional care, or safe interactions. Help us, Lord; help us.

It's heartbreaking to watch people we love become people we fear. It's unnerving to hear threats of self-destructive behavior and to feel helpless, even hopeless, in the midst of the emotional frenzy, rage-fueled words, and irrational activity. It's paralyzing to feel responsible but incapable of helping. Help us, Lord; help us.

Father, thank you that the Spirit is praying in us and for us when we don't know what to pray, do, or say. As the Spirit prays, Father, I pray for those for whom this prayer is not a memory or a theory but a present reality. Lead my brothers and sisters to the right resources, to the best of gospel wisdom, and to the professional caregivers tailored for their individual stories and struggles. None of us is enough; we need you, Father, and all the grace you will give us. We pray in Jesus' tender and triumphant name. Amen.

A Prayer for Remembering God's Commitment to Complete His Work

And I am certain that God, who began the good work within you, will continue his work until it is finally finished on the day when Christ Jesus returns. (Phil. 1:6 NLT)

Dear heavenly Father, here's a huge understatement: I am so thankful that "salvation is of the Lord," from beginning to end. We were dead in our sins and trespasses when you raised us up to new life in Jesus—granting us complete forgiveness, declaring us righteous in Christ, and sealing and indwelling us with your Spirit. Hallelujah, many times over!

But sometimes I wonder why the process of actually becoming more like Jesus is taking so long—first of all in me, and then in others I love. Quite honestly, at times it's easier for me to doubt your "whole salvation" commitment to others than to me—which is a pretty arrogant thing to own, even as I say it and pray it. Forgive me, Father.

When I don't live with Paul's certainty about your covenant faithfulness to each of your children, I don't love well.

I become more aware of what bugs me in the lives of others than what encourages me. I get more impatient than accepting, more rigid than relational, and more condescending than compassionate. I start making unnecessary observations, offering unhelpful criticisms, and giving unrequested suggestions—the very things I hate for people to do toward me.

Father, have mercy on me. Free me to accept others the way you have accepted me in Jesus. It's one thing for me to "provoke others to love and good deeds" (see Heb. 10:24) but quite another just to provoke them unto irritation and avoidance. By your grace, help me offer others a nonanxious presence, your welcoming heart, and genuine encouragement. I know you're not calling me to naïveté and passivity, but I also know you're not calling me to act like the fourth member of the Trinity. In Jesus' glorious and grace-full name I pray. Amen.

A Prayer for Focusing
on God's Steadfast, Ceaseless Love

Remember my affliction and my wanderings, the wormwood and the gall! My soul continually remembers it and is bowed down within me. But this I call to mind, and therefore I have hope: The steadfast love of the LORD never ceases; his mercies never come to an end; they are new every morning; great is your faithfulness. "The LORD is my portion," says my soul, "therefore I will hope in him." (Lam. 3:19–24 ESV)

Dear heavenly Father, another day and another delightful deposit of your fresh mercies greets us. You are so grace-full and generous toward us, so we join Jeremiah in calling to mind your great love and your great faithfulness. In fact, we can "call to mind" much more of your love and faithfulness than Jeremiah. Our place in the history of redemption is to be much preferred over his.

Jeremiah lived looking forward to the coming of Jesus and the fulfillment of the promises of the new covenant (Jer. 31:31–34). But we live on this side of those blessed events. How much quicker should we be to praise you, and how much greater should our hope be!

Lord Jesus, you are the reason we aren't consumed with guilt and paralyzed with fear, stuck in our shame and drowning in doubt; for you took the judgment we deserved on the cross and exhausted it. Because of you, God has forgiven all our wickedness and will never remember our sins against us (Jer. 31:34). You became sin for us, and in you we have been declared presently and eternally righteous (2 Cor. 5:21).

Father, it's because of this gospel, this Good News, that we also join Jeremiah in lamenting our wanderings. With humility we still sing, "Prone to wander, Lord, I feel it; prone to leave the God I love." We need the gospel every day and every hour.

Don't let us wander far. When we lose sight of Jesus, make the gall more galling; make the bitterness more bitter; make downcast feel even more downcast. We don't want to ever get used to feeling disconnected from the gospel.

In view of your steadfast love and never-failing compassions, we proclaim, "The LORD is our portion" (see Lam. 3:24). We pray in Jesus' beautiful and bountiful name. Amen.

A Prayer for Trusting, Resting, and Rejoicing in the God of Hope

May the God of hope fill you with all joy and peace as you trust in him, so that you may overflow with hope by the power of the Holy Spirit. (Rom. 15:13)

Dear heavenly Father, meditating on this verse today is like standing under a gentle, steady shower of grace after drought-like conditions; or like waking up on a cool, crisp morning in the mountains of Colorado after a month of high humidity and breath-sucking heat; or like a panoramic train ride through Switzerland in which every scene seems to top the last. Such is the wonder of your Word, the sweetness of the gospel, and the power of hope.

Nothing or no one really has to change for your Spirit to bring us hope in the depths of our hearts, the messiness of our stories, and the angst of our circumstances. Whether it's a Supreme Court ruling or the poor choices of good friends, the canceling of a flight or the loss of a favorite thing, the vacation that didn't happen or the replacement of the air conditioner that had to happen, the cancer that came back or the prodigal that hasn't yet . . . you are still God, you are still in control, and we have more than sufficient reasons to have hope—even overflow with hope.

You gave Jesus to us and for us. Everything that needed to be finished when he was in this world, has been; and everything he's yet to complete will be brought to a glorious, much-more-than-satisfying conclusion. We don't have to like your sense of timing, but we cannot help but love and adore your Son. May your peace rule in our hearts as we wait for the sure and certain fulfillment of our hope. We pray in Jesus' wonderful and merciful name. Amen.

A Prayer for Off-Loading Our Burdens onto Our Gracious Father

Praise be to the Lord, to God our Savior, who daily bears our burdens. Our God is a God who saves. (Ps. 68:19–20)

Dear heavenly Father, what a promise you've made, what a hope we have, and what a God you are. Thank you for being the kind of Father who bears our burdens—as opposed to ignoring, minimizing, or resenting them. To know that you bear our burdens on a daily basis frees us to be honest with you about the things that tend to wear us down and wear us out. Indeed, you are the Father of compassion and the God of all comfort (2 Cor. 1:3–5).

You are the God who saves us—not just from eternal separation from yourself but also in the present realities of life. Father, some of us are overwhelmed with marriage, parenting, and family burdens. Helplessness isn't bad, if it will drive us to you. Help us to want you and your glory more than we want relief and a different story. Protect us from all counsel that might medicate our pain but not identify the real issues.

Father, some of us are fearful, fretful, even rage-full over the political landscape of our country, the legislative shifts in our culture, and the nuclear madness of our world. Lift these burdens from our hearts as you remind us that the throne of heaven is presently occupied (Rev. 4), that Jesus is currently the ruler of the kings of the earth (Rev. 1:5), and that nothing and no one can alter or annul your plans (Isa. 14:27; Eccles. 3:14).

Father, forgive us when we take back the burden of our guilt, even though Jesus has exhausted it; free us when we surrender yet again to the burden of our shame, even though Jesus has broken it.

Rescue us when we feign sovereignty and take on other people's burdens you don't intend for us to carry. Give us grace, wisdom, and power to live and to love to your glory. In Jesus' merciful and mighty name we pray. Amen.

A Prayer for Grace to Forgive Perpetual Offenders

Then Peter came to him and asked, "Lord, how often should I forgive someone who sins against me? Seven times?" "No, not seven times," Jesus replied, "but seventy times seven!" (Matt. 18:21–22 NLT)

Dear Lord Jesus, I've read this story and heard it read, preached it and heard it preached what seems like a gazillion times, but it never grows old and never grows unnecessary. The need for forgiveness and the call to forgive are as daily as breathing, eating, and sleeping.

Jesus, I know I sin against you—in thought, word, and deed—every single day. I also know that through the gospel, I'm completely forgiven, declared righteous, and a beloved child of Abba Father. Hallelujah, many times over!

When I confess my sins, you're neither shocked nor informed, and you know my need of your grace is much greater than I realize. But you also know that my standing in your grace is much more glorious than I could hope or imagine. Nothing compares with the treasures we have received in the gospel.

But Jesus, receiving your grace is often much easier than extending your grace—especially with certain people and in certain story lines. Currently, there are a few "seventy times seven" forgiveness scenarios which are munching on my joy like tiny voracious piranha.

I have been over-the-top generous with forgiveness, but now, Jesus, it's easy to withdraw, be smug, and want them to pay. It'd be easy to gossip and tell others not to trust those who have hurt me. In short, Jesus, I am a mess. I know that saying I forgive isn't the same thing as trusting again, and I know that not forgiving is not an option.

So here's my cry: Come, Holy Spirit, come. Humble and gentle me; settle and focus me. Grant me the want-to, will, and wisdom to forgive as I've been forgiven. Reveal the scandalous wonder of the gospel—to me and through me. I pray in Jesus' holy and loving name. Amen.

A Prayer for the Prodigals in Our Lives

So he got up and went to his father. But while he was still a long way off, his father saw him and was filled with compassion for him; he ran to his son, threw his arms around him and kissed him. . . . The older brother became angry and refused to go in. So his father went out and pleaded with him. . . . "My son," the father said, "you are always with me, and everything I have is yours." (Luke 15:20, 28, 31)

Dear heavenly Father, we praise, bless, and adore you for being the running and pursuing, welcoming and redeeming God that you are. Your mercies are new every morning;

your grace is sufficient for every story; your love is powerful beyond our reckoning.

Just as you have all kinds of prodigals in your family, so do we, and we appeal to you on their behalf today. For those in a "faraway country" of pleasure-seeking, responsibility-evading, pain-medicating madness—do what you must to bring them to their senses. If severe mercy is the only thing that will bring them to saving grace, then Father, be as severe as the wonders of your love necessitate. If things have to get much worse in their lives, then give us the patience, trust, and assurance that you are at work. And should we be tempted to rescue them before your work is done, grant us grace and power to resist doing so.

Father, for our prodigals who haven't gone anywhere but into the blindness of their self-righteousness, the smugness of their self-assurance, and the cocaine of their success and "intactness," run to them, plead with them, and show them how much they need the grace of the gospel. Prodigals on an island of self-sufficiency are often harder to reach than prodigals on a hedonistic holiday.

Father, lest we stay too mentally and emotionally preoccupied with our prodigal friends and family members, renew our experience of your compassion, embrace, and "kisses" for us in the gospel. Our primary calling isn't to fix anybody in life but to know you, glorify you, and enjoy you forever. So may it be. We pray in Jesus' wonderful and merciful name. Amen.

A Prayer for Hearing God's Laugh in a World That Makes You Angry

A little while, and the wicked will be no more; though you look for them, they will not be found. But the meek will inherit the land and enjoy peace and prosperity. The wicked plot against the righteous and gnash their teeth at them; but the Lord laughs at the wicked, for he knows their day is coming. (Ps. 37:10–13)

Dear heavenly Father, I look forward to the day when I will actually hear you laugh—a laughter that already fills the courts of heaven and the chambers of eternity—for that will be the day when every expression of darkness and death, evil and folly, meanness and wickedness will be totally eradicated. It's hard to conceive of our world devoid of every semblance of sin and brokenness and instead filled to overflowing with your goodness, truth, and beauty, but you have promised that day, and Jesus has secured it.

Though not as quickly as we'd like, but more certainly than we can imagine, the day of "all things new" is coming. And as this Scripture highlights, it's not the powerful and proud who will "inherit the earth and enjoy great peace" but "the meek." Therefore, I praise you, Father, for the meekness of Jesus, who like a lamb (the Lamb) was led to the cross—taking our sin (my sin), defeating the devil, and securing the transformation of all things. It is in union with Jesus that we too will inherit the earth, as mind-boggling and heart-humbling a thought as that is; and it's in union with Jesus that we too become humble and meek and thereby useful in your kingdom service.

Father, forgive my fearful fretting, cynical unbelief, and vengeful musings. Vengeance belongs to you, not me. My wickedness deserves your judgment just as much as it requires your grace. Make me a meek man who grieves evil, but one who lives with hope—your son and servant, living in your story to your glory.

So when wicked plots and gnashing teeth seem to be on the increase and righteousness seems to be on the decrease, please, Father, allow us to hear your laughter. May your joy be our strength, your promises be our confidence, and your timing be our schedule. We pray in Jesus' tender and triumphant name. Amen.

A Prayer for Loving People as unto the Lord, Not to Make Them Happy

Serve wholeheartedly, as if you were serving the Lord, not people. (Eph. 6:7) Obviously, I'm not trying to win the approval of people, but of God. If pleasing people were my goal, I would not be Christ's servant. (Gal. 1:10 NLT)

The LORD is for me, so I will have no fear. What can mere people do to me? (Ps. 118:6 NLT)

Dear heavenly Father, of all the traps that are easy to fall into, being shaped by what people think of us is the easiest, daily-est, and deadliest. The acceptance and affirmation of some people can be as addictive as heroin or money; the criticism and anger of others can be as disorienting and paralyzing as the venom of certain snakes; and the withdrawal and indifference of still others can fuel fear and anxieties even more than awaiting the lab results of suspicious cells.

Father, intensify our awareness of your great love for us in Jesus, and free us to love and serve people as unto you—whether our kindness is acknowledged, reciprocated, or ignored. Only your love is better than life. Only through faith union and vital communion with Jesus will we experience the fulfillment of our deepest relational longings—longings that you have given us and intend to fulfill, longings that must be guarded and stewarded with the greatest care.

Help us to break the cycle of living as affirmation junkies and rejection-phobes. Help us to take back the power we have given certain people to either make us or break us. That's not a power they deserve, nor one you intend for any human being to exercise.

Father, we are thankful you don't despise our weaknesses, even when we have to confess the same things to you over and over. We long for the day when we will be made perfect in love. Until that day, keep freeing us from our people idolatries. In Jesus' welcoming and healing name we pray. Amen.

A Prayer for Decluttering and Recentering Our Lives

Don't store up treasures here on earth, where moths eat them and rust destroys them, and where thieves break in and steal. Store your treasures in heaven, where moths and rust cannot destroy, and thieves do not break in and steal. Wherever your treasure is, there the desires of your heart will also be. (Matt. 6:19–21 NLT)

Dear Lord Jesus, a little work in my attic, garage, closet, and drawers this week made these words of yours start blinking at me like a bright neon sign on a dark night—unavoidable. Where did all this stuff come from? Clutter is like zucchini; it just seems to keep spreading and multiplying. How did I accumulate all these things? Once a "treasure," now most of these things are just a bother.

But, Jesus, what concerns me far more than my attic and garage are my mind and heart. The older I get, the less storage space there is, and I don't want to finish my journey into eternity with a distracted mind and a cluttered heart. So, Lord, help me declutter and recenter on you. I want to live more like Mary in a Martha world (Luke 10:38–42). In a world of multiple distractions, I want to finish my days with one great consuming affection, Lord Jesus—making and keeping you my treasure.

I love you because you first loved me, and I'll treasure you to the extent I really believe you treasure us (and me) as your beloved Bride and eternal inheritance. By the Holy Spirit, once again rearrange the price tags in my heart, Jesus. Once again let my uncluttered spirit and recentered heart say, "I consider all things rubbish compared to the surpassing excellency of knowing Jesus" (see Phil. 3:7–10).

Once again let my relationships and schedule, attic and garage demonstrate my delight in you and desire for you. Jesus, I am so glad that you love me the same with or without my clutter, but I know I will love you much better with much less clutter. I pray in your triumphant and tender name. Amen.

A Prayer for Short-Fused Temper Days

Be not quick in your spirit to become angry, for anger lodges in the heart of fools. (Eccles. 7:9 ESV)

Whoever is slow to anger has great understanding, but he who has a hasty temper exalts folly. (Prov. 14:29 ESV)

Dear heavenly Father, thank you for using such attention-getting, heart-convicting images when confronting us with our bad attitudes. I certainly cringe at the thought of being a fool whose heart provides lodging and hospitality for anger, and I take no pleasure in the notion of "exalting folly" by my "hasty temper." Forgive me, Lord, and help me be a better steward of the important and powerful emotion of anger. In what contexts have I had short-fused anger lately?

When I'm in my car and in a hurry—Father, forgive me for committing "heart homicide" toward slow-driving, smartphone-talking, rubbernecking drivers. I get irritated and think and say things that neither honor you nor get me to my destination sooner. I can either leave earlier, or trust that you are sovereign, or both.

When promised delivery times and appointments aren't kept, when flights are delayed and deadlines are missed—it's one thing to be appropriately disappointed, but another to vex, seethe, and cop a bad attitude. Father, by your grace, slay the beast of the idol of control that rears its ugly head in my heart too often.

When people make choices that inconvenience me or complicate my life—oh, Father, just writing these things out convicts me about my self-centeredness. Granted, it's been a way busy, complicated summer, but I've got a way bigger gospel than I've been drawing upon and demonstrating. Forgive me. Thank you for the convicting work of your Spirit and the consoling and transforming power of your grace. I pray in Jesus' kind and loving name. Amen.

A Prayer for Declaring Our Trust in the Lord and Naming the Competition

Some trust in chariots and some in horses, but we trust in the name of the LORD our God. (Ps. 20:7 ESV)

Dear heavenly Father, the battle for our heart's trust is relentless, often vicious, and quite deceptive. As this day begins and continues, we affirm that *only you* are worthy of our worship, love, and trust; and yet we also name the people, places, and things to which we often default in our sin, weakness, and foolishness. In David's day, it was chariots and horses; in our day, the battle for our hearts includes other temptations.

Some trust in their goodness and discipline and niceness, but we trust in the finished work of Jesus and the gift of his perfect righteousness.

Some trust in their spouse's attention and their children's affection, but we trust in the steadfast love and great delight you have for us in Jesus.

Some trust in their stock portfolios, cash margins, and "stuff," but we trust in the unsearchable riches of Christ and the inviolate treasure kept for us in heaven.

Some trust in their physicality and their sensuality, but in sickness and in health, in our youthfulness and in our aging, we trust in the truly beautiful and all-powerful one—Jesus.

Some trust in being smart, wise, and right, but we trust in Jesus, who is our wisdom from God—that is, our righteousness, holiness, and redemption.

Some trust in being included in special groups, circles, and clubs, but we trust in the gift of our union with Christ and the ongoing communion we enjoy with the entire Trinity.

Some trust in their vocational productivity and their standing in the company, but we trust the One who is making all things new and our standing in his grace.

Some trust in their meds and libation and their uppers and downers, but we trust in the One who says, "Come to me, all you who are weary and burdened, and I will give you rest" (Matt. 11:28). Only you, Jesus, can heal and free us.

Father, again we say it: though many people, places, and things incessantly vie for our trust, only you are worthy. In Jesus' beautiful and bountiful name we pray. Amen.

A Prayer for Grace to Enjoy, Not Just Endure, Differences in Others

> May God, who gives this patience and encouragement, help you live in complete harmony with each other, as is fitting for followers of Christ Jesus. Then all of you can join together with one voice, giving praise and glory to God, the Father of our Lord Jesus Christ. Therefore, accept each other just as Christ has accepted you so that God will be given glory. (Rom. 15:5–7 NLT)

Dear heavenly Father, one of the surest indicators of my ongoing need of the gospel is revealed by the way I relate to different personality types when I'm in a hurry or under stress. I've discovered this yet again in this season of having to accomplish many important tasks in a small window of time.

I stand convicted, Lord—convicted that my passion to get a job done quickly often takes precedence over my calling to love people well. Rather than enjoying the diversity of perspectives, insights, and emotional wiring in others, I endure it at best and resent it at worst. Rather than heeding

Paul's words in this Scripture to "accept each other just as Christ has accepted you," I often want (expect) people to see and do things my way—which is "obviously" the best way.

Father, I am so glad you are the God who "gives patience and encouragement," because I need both. I need patience to enjoy and accept the rich diversity of people and perspectives that surround me where I live, work, and play. Forgive me for looking to my Myers-Briggs profile rather than my truer identity in Christ to justify my relational style.

Lord, I need encouragement to know that the older I get, the kinder and more flexible I can become. Suffering from the "hardening of the categories" may be normal, but it isn't necessary. When others tend to grate on my nerves, give me grace in my heart. When I want to roll my eyes in annoyance, help me roll up my sleeves in service.

For your glory, Father, make me more like Jesus. I pray in his wonderful and merciful name. Amen.

2

Praying the Scriptures Verse by Verse

The Glories and Grace of Our Good Shepherd:
Praying through Psalm 23 (NLT)

The LORD is my shepherd; I have all that I need.

Dear Lord Jesus, *you* are my shepherd, my Good Shepherd. You give me everything I need and more than I want. All I need in life is you, plus what you choose to give me.

He lets me rest in green meadows; he leads me beside peaceful streams.

Even the most difficult places in life are like green meadows as long as you are there. And in the desert seasons of my journey and the drought-like conditions of my heart, you quench my thirst with living water and give me a peace that passes all understanding.

148

> He renews my strength. He guides me along right paths, bring-
> ing honor to his name.

By your grace I've learned to boast in my weakness and to
pose and pretend less. For when I come to the end of my
strength, you faithfully meet me there—granting me rest
in my weariness and strength for my tired heart and body. I
am so grateful both that you have marked the path for me
and that you yourself are my Way, Truth, and Life. I want
to honor your name much more than I want to go my way
and get my way.

> Even when I walk through the darkest valley, I will not be afraid,
> for you are close beside me. Your rod and your staff protect and
> comfort me.

Jesus, you never promised me that the journey toward the
new heaven and new earth would be easy, quick, or without
seasons and circumstances that are overwhelming, but you
have promised never to leave or forsake me, even in the darkest
valley. That's all I really need to know—that you are close and
that you love me, and that you won't let anything happen to me
outside of your perfect plan for my life. Even when you have
to discipline me, the goal is my good and always your glory.

> You prepare a feast for me in the presence of my enemies. You
> honor me by anointing my head with oil. My cup overflows
> with blessings.

Jesus, you are taking me to the feast of all feasts, the wedding
feast of the Lamb, but long before that day, you yourself are
my portion, banquet, and feast—Bread from heaven, my
nourishment and satisfaction. Though enemies threaten, you

feed me, anoint my life with your grace and Spirit, and cause my cup to spill over with blessings, for the benefit of others.

> Surely your goodness and unfailing love will pursue me all the days of my life, and I will live in the house of the LORD forever.

Absolutely nothing will keep me out of the new heaven and new earth, and just as certainly, *nothing* can possibly separate me from your goodness and unfailing love—at any time or in any place. Until the day I long for more than any other arrives, I rest in your love and trust in your grace. Jesus, thank you for your promise to never stop pursuing me. I pray in your glorious and powerful name. Amen.

Living by the Rhythms and Pace of Grace: Praying through Titus 2:11–14 (ESV)

> For the grace of God has appeared, bringing salvation for all people,

Dear heavenly Father, your grace "appeared" in my life like the sun burning through the bleakest skyline; like an artesian spring in the middle of the driest desert; like the command Jesus spoke to Lazarus, "Come forth," while I was dead in my sins and trespasses. You brought your saving grace to me, for there's no other way I could have found it. I praise you for the irresistible, indefatigable, inexhaustible grace you have poured out on us generously in Jesus. Grace for *all* people, nonbelievers and believers alike, for none of us is beyond the reach or the need of your grace.

> training us to renounce ungodliness and worldly passions, and to live self-controlled, upright, and godly lives in the present age,

Now that we've been justified by your grace, we're being taught, trained, and transformed by the same grace. You get all the credit. There's no other way we could ever become like Jesus. Father, thank you for working in us both to will and to do the things that honor you. Thank you for calling us to live by the rhythms and pace of grace—saying yes to more of Jesus and no to the things that dishonor you and rob us.

> waiting for our blessed hope, the appearing of the glory of our great God and Savior Jesus Christ, who gave himself for us to redeem us from all lawlessness and to purify for himself a people for his own possession who are zealous for good works.

What a blessed hope you have given us—Father, thank you for your commitment to complete the good grace work you began in us. When Jesus returns, we will see him as he is, and we will be made completely like him! Until then, keep burning the dross from our lives; keep rescuing us from under-believing the gospel; keep intensifying our love for holiness, beauty, and good works. We pray in Jesus' exalted and loving name. Amen.

The Longing for a Gospel-Shaped, Grace-Filled Heart: Praying through Matthew 5:3–10

> Blessed are the poor in spirit, for theirs is the kingdom of heaven.

Lord Jesus, now that I'm no longer condemned for my sins, convict me quickly and deeply. Keep me always aware of my need for more grace and more of the Spirit's work in my life. I want to be a chief repenter in my relationships.

> Blessed are those who mourn, for they will be comforted.

151

Free me to grieve about the ways I love poorly—not making lame excuses or insincere promises. Grant me godly sorrow and the comfort you alone can give.

Blessed are the meek, for they will inherit the earth.

I love humility in others; grow a more humble heart in me, Jesus, for surely, I have plenty about which to be humble. By grace, make me more gentle and less defensive.

Blessed are those who hunger and thirst for righteousness, for they will be filled.

Now that you are my legal righteousness, Jesus, intensify my hunger for becoming a more righteous man and someone who works tirelessly and hopefully for justice in my community.

Blessed are the merciful, for they will be shown mercy.

As I have received so much mercy in the gospel and daily mercies from my Father, may I be far more merciful in my relationships and in situations that tend to aggravate me. I want to lead with kindness, not rightness.

Blessed are the pure in heart, for they will see God.

Jesus, I long for the day when I will see you as you are and will be made like you. Until then, grant me a purer heart, a single heart, a whole heart with which to love, worship, and serve you.

Blessed are the peacemakers, for they will be called children of God.

You are my peace, Jesus. You have reconciled me to God by your life, death, and resurrection, once and for all. Hallelujah!

By the Spirit, use me as a peacemaker in my relationships and community. Forgive me when I care more about winning than loving.

> Blessed are those who are persecuted because of righteousness, for theirs is the kingdom of heaven.

If I am to be persecuted for anything, may it be for living out the implications of the gospel in my community. May the gospel be the only offensive thing about me, Jesus. In your glorious and grace-full name I pray. Amen.

Returning to Gospel Sanity and a Heart of Worship: Praying through Psalm 73:21–26 (NLT)

> I realized that my heart was bitter, and I was all torn up inside. I was so foolish and ignorant—I must have seemed like a senseless animal to you.

Dear heavenly Father, I can handle getting lost on a trip a lot better than getting disconnected from a vital, robust relationship with you. Because when my fellowship and communion with you get broken, I can start acting, like Asaph, like a "senseless animal." I get grumpy and critical, whine more than I worship, complain quicker and longer. I start acting like a spiritual orphan—like I don't have you as my loving, sovereign, grace-full Father.

> Yet I still belong to you; you hold my right hand. You guide me with your counsel, leading me to a glorious destiny.

Then, as the Holy Spirit applies the gospel to my heart yet again, I come back to my senses. More importantly, I come back to you. Abba Father, I belong to you, and that's all that really matters. You hold my right hand with a grip of grace, even when I try to pull away. You're actively guiding me—working in all things for my good and your glory, even when I don't see it or feel it. And you will bring your work in me to completion and bring me safely into the new heaven and new earth. What a Father, what a gospel, what peace!

> Whom have I in heaven but you? I desire you more than anything on earth. My health may fail, and my spirit may grow weak, but God remains the strength of my heart; he is mine forever.

In my most gospel-sane moments, I gladly affirm—even shout—Father, you are *all* I want and *more* than I need. I desire you more than getting my way and getting more stuff, more than being in control—even controlling you. You don't guarantee me perfect health or easy circumstances in life, but you have given me yourself, the righteousness of Jesus, and a perfect future. I am yours and you are mine, forever. Hallelujah! I pray in Jesus' wonderful and merciful name. Amen.

When You Begin to Wonder
If God Will Ever "Show Up" Again:
Praying through Psalm 42:1–5 (ESV)

> As a deer pants for flowing streams, so pants my soul for you, O God. My soul thirsts for God, for the living God. When shall I come and appear before God?

Dear heavenly Father, when weariness begins to outlast grace, heaviness feels more daily than hope, and things we thought would change for the better continue a downward spiral, where can we go but to you? Father, we crave your heart-renewing, perspective-giving, thirst-satisfying presence. More than anything else, we need an artesian spring of your living water to well up in the desert of our discouragement.

> My tears have been my food day and night, while they say to me all the day long, "Where is your God?"

Whether it's from the devil, the culture, or our own unbelief, we're tired of the chorus that keeps calling your faithfulness, goodness, and might into question. Father, that you love us in Jesus and that you are in control of all things is our theology and profession; make it our doxology and possession—even if some things don't change till heaven.

> These things I remember, as I pour out my soul: how I would go with the throng and lead them in procession to the house of God with glad shouts and songs of praise, a multitude keeping festival.

Memories of days when we felt your thick enlivening presence in our midst and your liberating heart and hand upon us—those memories sometime mock us but more often woo us. Father, we *long* to be restored to the joy of our salvation, to our first-love relationship with Jesus. We want this more than we want circumstances to change, life to be easy, and all of our burdens lifted.

> Why are you cast down, O my soul, and why are you in turmoil within me? Hope in God; for I shall again praise him, my salvation.

Father, you know all the details of our broken stories and aching hearts; what *we* know is that you are good, that you can be trusted, and that hope is the order of this day. Because the gospel is true, hope is *always* the order of any day. We pray in Jesus' strong and loving name. Amen.

Revealing the Life of Jesus through Our Tiredness and Weakness: Praying through 2 Corinthians 4:7–10

But we have this treasure in jars of clay to show that this all-surpassing power is from God and not from us.

Dear Lord Jesus, to have you plus nothing makes me as rich as anybody in the history of the universe. To have you plus everything wouldn't make me any richer than he who has you alone. You are the treasure all other currencies mimic and counterfeit. *Nothing* compares to the excellency of being loved by you and knowing you.

You inhabit my weakness like an original Rembrandt painting in a picture frame of straw, or like the Hope Diamond mounted in a necklace of tinfoil and Scotch tape. You get all the attention and honor, and I get the supreme privilege of simply being used of you. Just as it should be, and just as I want it to be.

We are hard pressed on every side, but not crushed; perplexed, but not in despair; persecuted, but not abandoned; struck down, but not destroyed.

Unlike Paul, I haven't been in a season of persecution, but I totally relate to his images of being hard pressed and perplexed, and I'll throw in frazzled, head-spinningly busy, and

primed for Sabbath rest, renewal, and refreshment. The stories, demands, and emotional expenditures of these past few
weeks have taxed my limits and driven me to you—which is
a good thing. In all of it, I've been keenly aware of your presence, shocked at the strength you've given me, and thankful
for what I see you doing.

> We always carry around in our body the death of Jesus, so that
> the life of Jesus may also be revealed in our body.

Jesus, I am fine—actually *happy* to do life accepting my
limits and boasting in my weaknesses, as long as your life is
revealed in me and through me. I don't feel the need to be
as competent as many of my gifted friends, but I *do* want to
finish my life as a conduit of your beauty and love, mercy and
grace. I pray in your tender and triumphant name. Amen.

Longing for a Fresh Crop of the Spirit's Fruit in Our Lives: Praying through Galatians 5:22–23 (NLT)

> But the Holy Spirit produces this kind of fruit in our lives: love,
> joy, peace, patience, kindness, goodness, faithfulness, gentle-
> ness, and self-control.

Dear heavenly Father, to start with, *thank you* for sealing me
with your Spirit (2 Cor. 1:22), indwelling me by your Spirit
(Rom. 8:9), and transforming me through the Spirit's work
(2 Cor. 3:18). It's my only hope and my overwhelming joy.
Yes indeed, I want my life to be marked more fully by this
kind of fruit—the Spirit's fruit.

Love—Father, keep me alive to how much Jesus loves me, for Jesus' love is compelling and transforming, and it sabotages my every excuse for loving poorly.

Joy—Transcending my circumstances, both hard ones and delightful ones, give me a core of joy, Father—your joy.

Peace—Father, may your peace trump my worries and fears, my unbelief and foolish penchant for trying to control things and people. You are God and I am not.

Patience—Father, my hurried spirit, inflexibility, and lack of spontaneity often rob me (and others) of being present and enjoying the moment. Forgive and free me.

Kindness—Help me to major in kindness over rightness, Father. There is always enough of your grace for being kind. I have no excuses for curtness or rudeness.

Goodness—Father, I know my good works earn me "squat," but your goodness in me is a mercy magnet for people needing hope and help. Grant me more gospel goodness.

Faithfulness—Forgive me when I make promises lightly or fail to follow through on little stuff and big stuff. Great is your faithfulness—that's not just a great hymn; it's who you are. Make me more like you.

Gentleness—Gentle my rough edges, harsh words, and quick reactions, Father. Cultivate a nonanxious spirit within me that welcomes the broken.

Self-control—Whether it's with my eating or speaking, my listening or my spending, my exercise or spiritual discipline, Father, forgive me for confusing laziness with grace. Empower me for the freedom of self-control and taking responsibility for myself.

There is no law against these things!

Father, thank you that it's impossible to be too zealous for the Spirit's fruit; we cannot go overboard with wanting to be like Jesus. You began this work in our lives, and you will bring it to completion. Show us what living by the Spirit looks like—how to surrender, how to trust, how to hope. We pray in Jesus' loving and powerful name. Amen.

The Who, What, and How of Jesus' Prayer: Praying through Matthew 6:9–13

This, then, is how you should pray: "Our Father in heaven, hallowed be your name,

Dear Lord Jesus, thank you for giving us this remarkable prayer, but even more so, thank you for making it possible for us to know God as Abba Father. We dare call God "our Father" only because of your finished work on our behalf. You were forsaken by God on the cross so that we could be adopted by him in life. We praise, bless, and adore you for being so great a Savior and giving us so awesome a salvation.

your kingdom come, your will be done, on earth as it is in heaven.

Oh, how we long for the day when the perfect, full, and glorious reign of God will come on earth—when the "old order" will be completely gone and all things will be wondrously and eternally new. Life in the new heaven and new earth will be far beyond anything we could ever hope or imagine, thanks to you, Jesus. As grace does its work in our hearts, increase our joy in obeying you and doing the will of God to the glory of God, as we long for that day.

Give us today our daily bread.

Until the kingdom fully comes, we look to you to meet *all* of our daily needs (spiritual, physical, and emotional), for you are glorified in our dependence and joyful in your generosity. Give us what we need and an abundance to share with our neighbors.

And forgive us our debts, as we also have forgiven our debtors.

Jesus, we know we don't earn more forgiveness by being forgiving toward others, but how can we claim your forgiveness if we don't work hard at forgiving others? Help us in our struggle to forgive as we've been forgiven.

And lead us not into temptation, but deliver us from the evil one."

Jesus, make us ever wise to the schemes of our enemy, the devil. He's a defeated foe but far from being eradicated. Protect us from him, but also rescue us from our perfectly forgiven but yet-to-be-perfected hearts. There is no sin to which we are immune, and yet (hallelujah!) no sin beyond your power to redeem. We pray in your magnificent name and for the glory of our God. Amen.

How Our Relationship with Jesus Is to Impact All of Our Relationships: Praying through Philippians 2:1–4

Therefore if you have any encouragement from being united with Christ,

Dear Lord Jesus, do I have any encouragement from being in union with you? What a blessed rhetorical question! Let's see . . . because I'm united to you, *all* of my sins are forgiven, your righteousness has been declared to be *mine*, I'll *never* be condemned for my sin again, and God delights in me *as much* as he delights in you. That's a start!

if any comfort from his love,

Do I receive any comfort from your love? More than I can measure. Only your love is better than life and will never let go of me. Only your love satisfies the longings of my soul, heals the brokenness of my story, and breaks the chains of my foolishness.

if any common sharing in the Spirit, if any tenderness and compassion,

Does the Holy Spirit mediate your tenderness and compassion to me? Every hour of every day—even when I ignore it, deny it, or fail to take advantage of such graces. It's your tenderness and kindness that lead me to repentance, and it's your compassion that frees me to own my weakness before you, time and again.

then make my joy complete by being like-minded, having the same love, being one in spirit and of one mind.

Here's where the power of your resurrection must come into play, Jesus. Loving others with the love you lavish on me is easy toward some, difficult toward others, and seemingly impossible with some people, whose names I don't even like to bring to mind. Help me, Jesus. You never said loving well is less than demanding and messy.

Do nothing out of selfish ambition or vain conceit.

161

Do *nothing* from the motivations of selfishness and vanity? Really? Jesus, one day I'll do this perfectly, but right now I'll just concentrate on this present day. Grant me this kind of other-centered grace for today, Jesus. Then we'll deal with tomorrow in the morning.

> Rather, in humility value others above yourselves, not looking to your own interests but each of you to the interests of the others.

Jesus, only because you humbled yourself in death can I even think about humbling myself toward others in life. Only because you put our interests before your glory dare I think about dying to my self-preoccupation and serving others today. Only because the gospel is true do I have any hope that I can actually live and love this way at all. I pray in your glorious and grace-full name. Amen.

When Our Sufferings Feel Like Too Much: Praying through Psalm 13 (ESV)

> How long, O LORD? Will you forget me forever? How long will you hide your face from me?

Dear heavenly Father, I bless you that these difficult words were first sung by your people in worship at the temple, for they show us that some seasons and sufferings in life cause us to wonder about your goodness and question your faithfulness. Yet you are neither offended nor affronted when we feel this way. You welcome us in our woes, and if we don't bring our cries and confusion to you, where can we go?

Indeed, Father, there are some times when it feels like you have forgotten us or are hiding from us. For some of us, that moment is now and that season has been going on for quite a while. Help!

> How long must I take counsel in my soul and have sorrow in my heart all the day? How long shall my enemy be exalted over me?

The worst thing about not sensing your heart and hand, Father, is that we're left to the shallow waters of our own counsel and the voices of mockers and haters. "I thought you said Jesus was enough. Where's your mighty and merciful God now? Didn't you tell me God wouldn't give you too much?" Father, we don't want the voices of darkness to prevail. We don't want our suffering to sabotage our trust in your sovereignty. Come, Lord.

> Consider and answer me, O Lord my God; light up my eyes, lest I sleep the sleep of death, lest my enemy say, "I have prevailed over him," lest my foes rejoice because I am shaken.

Meet us in this hard, difficult place. It's not our pride but your praise that we care about the most. As much as our bodies and hearts may hurt, the gloating of your enemies hurts even more. For the sake of your name, bring the power of your hand.

> But I have trusted in your steadfast love; my heart shall rejoice in your salvation. I will sing to the Lord, because he has dealt bountifully with me.

Father, this we know for sure: your steadfast love for us in the gospel is unquestionable and inexhaustible. Though our rejoicing and singing may presently be reduced to a still, small voice, we bless you for dealing bountifully with us through the finished work of Jesus. This pain, heartache, and season soon will pass. May soon be *sooner*. Until then, we unabashedly and unhesitatingly proclaim that we are your beloved children and you are our grace-full God. We pray in Jesus' wonderful and merciful name. Amen.

Shutting Down Our Whines with Worship: Praying through Romans 8:31–37 (NLT)

What shall we say about such wonderful things as these? If God is for us, who can ever be against us?

Dear heavenly Father, when I consider your great love for us in Jesus, how is it possible for me to indulge in whining, justify my complaining, or linger in griping? When I do the mercy math, all the wonderful things you are to us and have done for us *far* outweigh all the provocations, irritations, and exasperations of life.

Since he did not spare even his own Son but gave him up for us all, won't he also give us everything else?

You gave Jesus *to us* and *for us*; of course we can trust you for everything else we need and for bunches more you simply delight to give us.

Who dares accuse us whom God has chosen for his own? No one—for God himself has given us right standing with himself. Who then will condemn us? No one—for Christ Jesus died for us and was raised to life for us, and he is sitting in the place of honor at God's right hand, pleading for us.

You made us, chose us, bought us, reconciled us, and delight in us. Who cares what anybody else thinks, says, or feels about us? Forgive us for giving any other voice more power over our hearts than yours—whether it's the accusations of the devil or the meanness of people, the contempt of our shame or the flattery of the world.

> Can anything ever separate us from Christ's love? Does it mean he no longer loves us if we have trouble or calamity, or are persecuted, or hungry, or destitute, or in danger, or threatened with death? (As the Scriptures say, "For your sake we are killed every day; we are being slaughtered like sheep.") No, despite all these things, overwhelming victory is ours through Christ, who loved us.

Through the hardest parts of life and the most joyful ones; in the crazy-making seasons and the oasis-like breathers; in the stories that vex us and the relationships that test us—you love us, will never leave us, and will complete us. Father, we praise, bless, and adore you. In Jesus' merciful and mighty name we pray. Amen.

3

Prayers for Preaching the Gospel to Our Hearts

Jack Miller, my spiritual father of twenty-one years, modeled and taught me the discipline of "preaching the gospel to yourself." We're always talking to ourselves, so why not fill the conversation with the life-giving, heart-transforming truth of the gospel? The following prayers are examples of how we can preach the gospel to ourselves by praying the Scriptures into our hearts. This isn't "mind over matter" or merely the power of positive thinking; it's the gospel for the whole of life.

We Are Image Bearers of God— Wonderfully Made

I am fearfully and wonderfully made. (Ps. 139:14)

Father, before I was broken, I was beautiful—made by your hands and for your glory. Thank you for creating me in your image and for now renewing me to become like Jesus. Help me to reject all the old tapes, messages, and voices that convinced me I was worthless and useless. The gospel has always been your Plan A for my life. By your grace, continue to heal, change, and free me.

We Are Completely and Exhaustively Forgiven

In him we have redemption through his blood, the forgiveness of sins, in accordance with the riches of God's grace. (Eph. 1:7)

Heavenly Father, thank you for forgiving all of my sins, *all* of them. Sins I've committed in my thinking, with my words, and by my choices. Sins in the past, sins of today, and the sins I have yet to commit. Such forgiveness is almost too good to be true; and it would be, if you hadn't sent Jesus to be our perfect Savior. The riches of your grace have proven to be more than sufficient for the bankruptcy of my sin. I praise and bless you.

For his unfailing love toward those who fear him is as great as the height of the heavens above the earth. He has removed our sins as far from us as the east is from the west. (Ps. 103:11–12 NLT)

Holy and gracious God, though my grasp of your grace often fails me, your grasp of me is as unfailing as your love is. Thank you for taking my sins immeasurably far away from me. Oh, how I love the geography of your grace—as far as the east is from the west. Through the gospel, I'm no longer afraid of you as my Judge, but take me deeper and deeper into an affectionate reverence for you. Your love is so compelling and transforming.

> I will remember their sins and their lawless deeds no more. (Heb. 10:17 ESV)

Almighty and loving Father, I know you don't really have amnesia about my sins, but you have promised me something far better. You will never, ever remember my sins against me, because you have remembered them against Jesus on the cross. He took the judgment I deserve that you might give me the grace I could never earn. Hallelujah, what a Savior! Hallelujah, what a salvation!

We Are Washed Clean and Guilt Free

> Though your sins are like scarlet, they shall be as white as snow; though they are red as crimson, they shall be like wool. (Isa. 1:18)

Gracious God, as hard as it is to imagine, and despite everything my discouraged heart tells me, you have washed me clean through the blood of Jesus. In your sight, I cannot be more guiltless, heart-clean, and pure. Thank you, thank you, thank you. I believe this is true; help my unbelief. The riches of your grace continue to astound me.

> So now there is no condemnation for those who belong to Christ Jesus. (Rom. 8:1 NLT)

Lord Jesus, through the gospel, my permanent address is now "in Christ" and my eternal song is "no condemnation." I praise, bless, and adore you for this astonishing and liberating news. I will never be held guilty for my sins again, for you took my guilt on the cross. There is now NO condemnation hanging over me—not a scintilla, even for a nanosecond—none, nil, zip, zilch. Make this Good News more real to me than ever.

We Have Been Declared Legally and Completely Righteous in Christ

He [God] made Him [Jesus] who knew no sin to be sin on our behalf, so that we might become the righteousness of God in Him. (2 Cor. 5:21 NASB)

Most glorious and grace-full Jesus, what wondrous love is this, indeed! As my substitute in life, you lived a perfect life of obedience, thus fulfilling every demand of the law for me. And as my substitute in death on the cross, you completely exhausted God's judgment against my sin. I am totally forgiven, perfectly righteous, and eternally free in you. Hallelujah, many times over! Take me deeper and deeper into the reality of this Good News.

You were washed, you were sanctified, you were justified in the name of the Lord Jesus Christ and by the Spirit of our God. (1 Cor. 6:11 ESV)

*Father, Son, and Holy Spirit—glorious Trinity—*this one verse reminded me how the whole Godhead has secured my irrevocable, magnificent salvation. Wow . . . how astonishing, comforting, and humbling. Father, you washed and justified me through the finished work of Jesus, and by the Holy Spirit you set me apart for yourself and have sanctified me. I am undone with joy, filled with gratitude, and set free to love and serve you. Eternal thanks and praise to you!

God Loves Us Just as Much as He Loves Jesus

I have loved you, my people, with an everlasting love. With unfailing love I have drawn you to myself. (Jer. 31:3 NLT)

Most gracious and almighty God, supersize the chambers of my heart that I might take in more of the wonder of this Good News. You have drawn me to yourself with an unfailing, irresistible, powerful love—not because of anything in me but because of everything in you. And now, because of what you have done for me in Jesus, once and for all, you love me with an unwavering, everlasting love. I cannot add to your love for me, and I cannot take away from it, because it's not about me, it's all about Jesus. I'm undone with peace.

I am in them and you are in me. May they experience such perfect unity that the world will know that you sent me and that you love them as much as you love me. (John 17:23 NLT)

Dear Lord Jesus, this one verse exposes how little I "get" the gospel and what a neophyte I am in grasping the wonders of God's grace. Let me get this right: you are telling me that God the Father loves me as much as he loves you. This is astonishing! How can it be? I know the right answer, but wrap the right answer tight around my heart and drive it deep into my spirit. My heavenly Father loves me just as much as he loves you because of everything *you* have done for me. You earned my salvation for me, Jesus—completely and forever. When you spoke those words from the cross, "It is finished!" you were speaking on my behalf, just as much as for anyone else. This isn't just a "game changer," Jesus; it's an "everything changer." Arise my soul, arise, and shake off your guilt, shame, and unbelief. Wow!

> See what great love the Father has lavished on us, that we should be called children of God! And that is what we are! (1 John 3:1)

Heavenly Father, this is one of my favorite commands in the Bible to obey. Absolutely, I want to see *everything* you will show me about the great love that comes with being your adopted children. So by the Holy Spirit, open my heart's eyes to behold the height, depth, width, and breadth of your affection for me in Jesus. And oh, how I love the word *lavish* when it's attached to your love. You haven't dribbled, trickled, or sprinkled your love on us; you have *lavished* it! To be your child is like standing under the life-giving Niagara Falls of your grace. Thank you, now and forever.

We Are Delighted In and Enjoyed by God, and There's Nothing We Can Do about It

> The LORD your God is in your midst, a mighty one who will save; he will rejoice over you with gladness; he will quiet you by his love; he will exult over you with loud singing. (Zeph. 3:17 ESV)

Magnificent and merciful Lord, this portion of your Word contradicts so many wrong notions I've had about you, and it invites my heart to go to places your Spirit alone can take me. Oh my goodness! Such doxological wonder and heart overload, because the gospel is true—right now, in this very moment, you greatly delight in me. You're not irritated or disappointed with me. You are committed to quiet me with your love, not shame me with rebukes. You "exult" (what a powerful word) over me, and not just with singing but with *loud* singing. Father, enable me to hear you serenading me in the gospel, in this very moment and forever. I praise, bless, and worship you for so great a salvation, and so great a Savior as Jesus.

> So Christ has truly set us free. Now make sure that you stay free, and don't get tied up again in slavery to the law. (Gal. 5:1 NLT)

Lord Jesus, there is no freedom like the freedom we have in you. To be free from the law's demands is astonishing, exhilarating, and (hallelujah) true! And yet my default mode always seems to be towards performance-based living. By the power of the gospel, keep liberating me from all forms of legalism, pragmatism, moralism, and all other "isms" that contradict free grace. I am no longer a slave to the law but a beloved child of God, all because of what you have done for me.

> There is no fear in love. But perfect love drives out fear, because fear has to do with punishment. The one who fears is not made perfect in love. (1 John 4:18)

Abba Father, many times my heart has to catch up with my head, especially in matters of grace. Theologically, I know that when Jesus died on the cross, he took all the punishment I deserve. Your wrath was poured out on Jesus completely, and now you pour out your love on me fully. I know this is what the Bible teaches, but make it palpably real to my heart, Father. By the truth of the Holy Spirit, drive out these residual fears in my heart that haunt me with threats of condemnation and judgment. May your perfect love drive out everything that contradicts your declaration that I am fully and eternally accepted in Christ. Shut the mouth of the devil with Jesus' bold affirmation, "It is finished!"

We Have Been Sealed and Are Indwelt by God's Spirit

In him you also, when you heard the word of truth, the gospel of your salvation, and believed in him, were sealed with the promised Holy Spirit, who is the guarantee of our inheritance until we acquire possession of it, to the praise of his glory. (Eph. 1:13–14 ESV)

Gracious Father, thank you for enabling me to hear and believe the gospel. My salvation is all of grace. You have sealed me with the promised Holy Spirit—who is an inviolate sign that I belong to you, now and forever. You began my salvation, and you will bring it to conclusion one day. By the Holy Spirit, you assure me that I belong to you and guarantee my final inheritance. Nothing can separate me from your love or move you to disinherit me. Signed, sealed, and delivered, I'm yours!

> Don't you realize that your body is the temple of the Holy Spirit, who lives in you and was given to you by God? (1 Cor. 6:19 NLT)

Most loving and gracious God, I know this verse is offered as a rhetorical question, but sometimes I *don't* realize that you have given me the permanent indwelling of the Holy Spirit. And when I forget, I start acting like a spiritual orphan, and I fall back into fear and some form of self-salvation or performance-ism. Thank you for giving me your Spirit, Father. You sent him into my heart to constantly remind me that I am your beloved child. I'm not my own; I'm yours. Hallelujah! The Spirit is also faithfully at work in my life to make me like Jesus, for there's no other way that could ever happen. Thank you, Father; thank you.

We Have Been Adopted as Beloved Children of God

> So you have not received a spirit that makes you fearful slaves. Instead, you received God's Spirit when he adopted you as his own children. Now we call him, "Abba, Father." (Rom. 8:15 NLT)

Abba Father—how I love to call you by that name. When you drew me to Christ, you forgave all my sins; you declared me to be righteous in Christ; and then you adopted me as your very own and beloved child. Amazing, astonishing! I still have a hard time taking in all this goodness, Father. That's why you have given me your Holy Spirit. He's the only one who can powerfully combat the spirit of fear that is ever lurking, so wanting to lure me back into the dungeon of guilt and shame.

But it's true, it's true, it's true: I'm no longer a slave. Jesus is my righteousness, the Spirit is my guarantee, and you are my Father. You cannot love me more, and you'll never love me less.

We Are Confident of God's Acceptance, Not Fearful of His Rejection

Therefore, since we have such a hope, we are very bold. (2 Cor. 3:12)

Father, it feels so good to be set free from the old "He loves me; he loves me not" spirituality. Because the gospel is true, I can be bold, assured, and at home in your presence. Hallelujah, there's no more need to pose or pretend with you, Lord. I've traded in my "fig leaves" for the righteousness of Jesus.

By your grace, I discovered my condition was far worse than I ever imagined, but I've also discovered you love me far more than I could have hoped or dreamed. I'm no longer afraid to die and face judgment, and I'm learning to be less fearful to face the challenges of life and opinions of men. Grant me even greater freedom, Father.

So let us come boldly to the throne of our gracious God. There we will receive his mercy, and we will find grace to help us when we need it most. (Heb. 4:16 NLT)

Dear Lord Jesus, it's only because you went gladly to the cross of judgment that I now come boldly to your throne of grace. I don't come "hat in hand" but as someone who is safely in *your* hand. For such freedom, welcome, and love, I worship and adore you, and for the promise of fresh mercy and sufficient grace, I now trust you. Hear my plea and supply what you will. You are a most wonderful and merciful Savior!

We Are Free from Performance-Based Living

But we have this treasure in jars of clay to show that this all-surpassing power is from God and not from us. (2 Cor. 4:7)

Gracious and loving Father, it feels so good to be done with "doing more and trying harder." It's so liberating to know that far from denying and despising my limitations, the gospel actually calls me to accept them. Take this "jar of clay" and release the aroma of grace through me today—in all of my relationships and everywhere you send me. I'm done with trusting in my "grit"; I will rely on your grace for the power I need to live and love to your glory.

Each time he said, "My grace is all you need. My power works best in weakness." So now I am glad to boast about my weaknesses, so that the power of Christ can work through me. (2 Cor. 12:9 NLT)

Lord Jesus, if your power works best in my weakness, then I gladly humble myself before you today, with palms up in praise and surrender. You are my righteousness and sufficiency; my help and my hope; my life and my freedom. Work in me and through me to your glory today. Free me from any need to be noticed and appreciated. I love being loved by you and living as a conduit of your life-giving grace.

We Are Never Alone
and Will Never Be Abandoned

Do not be afraid or discouraged, for the Lord will personally go
ahead of you. He will be with you; he will neither fail you nor
abandon you. (Deut. 31:8 NLT)

Father, thank you, thank you, thank you for the promise of
your perpetual presence. When I'm afraid to be alone, you
won't let me be. When I want to be alone, you won't let
me be. When I need you to come through for me, you will.
When it feels like you're not coming through for me, you
are. When I'm discouraged, you don't despise, chide me,
or revile me; you enter, engage, and encourage me. When
I'm afraid, you don't say, "Buck up, be strong," you say, "I
understand, I'm here." I praise and adore you.

Our Sovereign Father Is Working
in All Things for Our Good

And we know that in all things God works for the good of those
who love him, who have been called according to his purpose.
(Rom. 8:28)

Father, you are God and I am not. Hallelujah! You've num-
bered my hairs and my days; you appoint my joys and my
pain; you give and you take away—blessed be your name,
because the main thing I'm glad you've given is Jesus,
and the main thing I'm glad you've taken away is my sin.
Your sovereignty is my sanity, and your reign is my joy. Of
course you're working in all things for my good and your

glory—even when I cringe, doubt, and struggle with your sense of timing. The gospel convinces me of this. One day it will all make sense. But for now you bottle my tears, and one day you will wipe them all away. I am blessed beyond all sensibility. Hallelujah!

We Are New in Christ
and Part of the New Creation Order

> Therefore, if anyone is in Christ, the new creation has come: The old has gone, the new is here! (2 Cor. 5:17)

Dear Jesus, my favorite and most eternal address is "in Christ." In you, I have more than I need and realize and everything I want and could ever hope for. When God rescued me from the dominion of darkness and hid my life in you, I became a part of the new creation era. Every promise in the Old Testament finds its emphatic "Yes!" in you. Every vision of the Messianic age will be fully realized because you completely fulfilled the work God gave you to do. You are the Lamb of God who took away my sin; the Lord of Lords, who is making all things new; and the Lamp of the New City, whose glory will radiate the new heaven and new earth. Hallelujah, what a Savior you are! Hallelujah, what a salvation we have in you!

We Are Co-Heirs with Christ
of the New Heaven and New Earth

> Now if we are children, then we are heirs—heirs of God and co-heirs with Christ. (Rom. 8:17)

Heavenly Father, just being your beloved child is enough, but according to your Word, you have also given me an inheritance beyond anything I could hope or imagine. By the gospel, you have legally made us co-heirs with Jesus of the new heaven and new earth. Jesus wasn't exaggerating when he said we will inherit the earth (Matt. 5:5). Everything that's coming to him is coming to us. How astonishing, humbling, and liberating. Father, this overloads the "circuit board" of my heart. Your kindness and generosity are beyond measure. Forgive me for whining about what I don't have, reaching for what I don't need, and under-believing what is already mine.

We Are Chosen and Set Apart to Live in God's Story to His Glory

But you are a chosen race, a royal priesthood, a holy nation, a people for his own possession, that you may proclaim the excellences of him who called you out of darkness into his marvelous light. (1 Pet. 2:9 ESV)

Father, by your grace you have freed me from a self-centered life of giving you bit parts in my story, and you have written me into your big story of every-nation redemption and cosmic renewal. I'm not choice, I'm chosen; I'm not royal, but I've been reborn into the eternally royal family; I'm not a bit holy in myself, but I am perfectly holy in Christ; I'm no longer my own (hallelujah!), but I am your own possession (double hallelujah!). And for the rest of my life and throughout eternity, I have been given the privilege of declaring the excellences of your grace and the wonders of your love. I never want to go back to my silly little story of the quest for personal peace and affluence.

> For we are co-workers in God's service; you are God's field, God's building. (1 Cor. 3:9)

Yes! The pressure is off. Father, thank you for showing me that the gospel isn't about what I'm to do for you but is all about what you've done for me in Jesus and what you're doing through me for your glory. We are your co-workers, in your service, in your field, and in your building. We all matter, but none of us is the point. We all have a part to play in your story, but your story will progress with us or without us. This makes me want to be about the delights, design, and demands of your kingdom more than ever. It's not about me; hallelujah, it's not about me! The pressure is off and the praise is on!

We Are Ambassadors of Christ, through Whom God Is Redeeming His Family

> So we are Christ's ambassadors; God is making his appeal through us. We speak for Christ when we plead, "Come back to God!" (2 Cor. 5:20 NLT)

Whew! Nobody's salvation is "on my head." Jesus, there was a time when I used to carry an unbearable burden—the salvation of my family and friends. But I'm an ambassador, not a savior; a messenger, not the Messiah; a witness to grace, not a raiser of the dead—that would be you. Thank you for the privilege of being a means by which you are redeeming your Bride from every nation. Free me to love well, share the gospel freely, and trust you eminently. All of history is bound up with your commitment to populate the new heaven and new earth with your people. Use me, any way you please and choose, in that history-defining story. I'm an ambassador; you're the King.

We Have a Secure and Glorious Future

"For I know the plans I have for you," says the LORD. "They are plans for good and not for disaster, to give you a future and a hope." (Jer. 29:11 NLT)

Dear Father, I know this verse isn't a private verse for me to claim; it's your megapromise that claims me, all of your people, and the entire cosmos. Hallelujah, many times over! Because of Jesus' finished work, I'm a part of your story of unimaginable redemption and cosmic restoration. I don't have to be afraid of *anything*—dying or living. The gospel of your grace confirms you are unequivocally and incomparably good. The truth of your Word affirms that our future is crammed full and bursting at the seams with hope. No eye has seen, ear heard, or mind imagined what you have prepared for those you love, and I love you only because you first loved me and gave Jesus on my behalf. Enough said, except, "Glory!"

And I am certain that God, who began the good work within you, will continue his work until it is finally finished on the day when Christ Jesus returns. (Phil. 1:6 NLT)

Father, my salvation is a work I didn't begin and you alone can finish. I could never perform my way out of my sin or earn my way into your love. From beginning to end, my salvation is all of grace—the whole redemptive enchilada. I contributed nothing but my sin, and you gave everything in your Son. Oh, the peace, joy, and freedom that comes with really believing the gospel is as complete and good as you declare it to be. And oh, the wonder of realizing that one day I will be as lovely as and as loving as Jesus, for you *will* complete this good work of grace in my life. For so great a salvation, I worship you; for so great a Savior, I adore you.

4

Prayers for Expressing Our Feelings, Stories, and Struggles to God

One of the ongoing blessings I receive from my book *Everyday Prayers* and from my daily prayer blogs is to hear this recurring sentiment: "Thank you for helping me voice what I was feeling but didn't know how to express to God." I cannot overstate how much that means to me. God has given me a love for himself, his gospel, and words, and it's simply my delight to combine all three in service of his people.

This next section of prayers is specifically designed to help those who struggle with particular situations and story lines find their voice before God. These topics were given to me by some of my trusted counselor friends, who longed to have prayers written for some of their clients. Though this grouping isn't exhaustive, I hope it will serve as a paradigm for many other issues we and our friends face. God is honored when we pour out our hearts to him honestly, without filters or faking anything, and with the resources of his grace in view—even when it's a distant view.

Prayers of the Anxious and Depressed

Bend down, O Lord, and hear my prayer; answer me, for I need your help. (Ps. 86:1 NLT)

Father, the weight of the darkness makes it difficult for me to wait for your deliverance. Hold me tightly, for I feel my grasp of you growing weaker and weaker. Will this sorrow ever lift? Will my fears always outnumber my hopes? Will my heart ever sing again?

I would completely despair if you hadn't written the gospel upon my heart. If the word of your grace wasn't penned with indelible ink, the accuser and condemner would have long since erased all memory of your goodness from my soul. Though my conscience and emotions mock me, I rest in your promise that I am yours, that you love me, and that you will never leave me. In Jesus' name I pray. Amen.

Why, my soul, are you downcast? Why so disturbed within me? (Ps. 43:5)

Father, I feel like a leper in a world of healthy people. I am alone, and I choose aloneness over the threat of judgment and more shame. Please keep people like Job's friends far from me. I'm not a project to be fixed, a riddle to be solved, or a waif to be pitied. Who can possibly understand what it feels like to be me? Who will meet me in this pain? Only you, my God, only you can.

I'm sorry that I cannot run to you, Father. I have no strength and little will. The best I can do is to collapse on Jesus. So I fall on the One who took my place and bore my shame. Meet me here, Father, and pour your mercy upon me. For Jesus' sake, I make my plea. Amen.

How long, O LORD? Will you forget me forever? How long will you hide your face from me? (Ps. 13:1 ESV)

Father, I want to be near you, but at the same time, I want to keep my distance. I understand why Adam hid from you, but I also am angry and confused that you seem far away. Lord, I'm a mess, in desperate need of your mercy. I know what I believe, but feelings of dread and voices of darkness have worn me out. I'm heartsick, body-weary, and weak-willed.

Yet I will look to you, Father, and for you. In the past, you have dealt with me graciously—I cannot deny that. In my most sane moments, I know you are good. I'm afraid to hope, but I'm more afraid not to hope. Come, Lord, come. Let me see Jesus again—through my tears. I remember and long to be restored to the days of grace and peace. Father me, Father. In Jesus' name I pray. Amen.

Prayers of a Victim of Abuse

The LORD is close to the brokenhearted; he rescues those whose spirits are crushed. (Ps. 34:18 NLT)

Father, I'm thankful your shoulders are broad and your heart is big, because I finally have the courage to come to you with my pain, my story—my confusion. Where were you when I was abused? Where were you when my innocence was assaulted and my heart was pillaged, when my body was violated and my world was vandalized? Where were you, Lord? Were you too busy? Were you away in some other part of the world? Were you watching? Thank you for not being affronted and for not shaming me for asking.

Father, I don't think I'm looking for answers as much as I'm craving your undivided attention, your listening, and your presence. For years, I've struggled to name the pain and own the shame, to not lose my heart and to find my voice. I've felt deeply disconnected, wanting intimacy but fearing it, even avoiding it. I often wondered what was wrong with me—fearing the worst, minimizing the obvious.

Blessed be the day I was finally able to own my abuse. Cursed be the day it happened. Hallelujah for the day I'll be completely healthy and whole. Until then, Father, I have a lot of healing left in front of me. Give me courage and grace. Keep me far from those who would heal my wounds lightly. Lead me at the pace of grace. May a story I wish I could blot from my history become a means of mercy and hope for others. Continue to comfort me that I might comfort others, Father. In Jesus' name I pray. Amen.

My flesh and my heart may fail, but God is the strength of my heart and my portion forever. (Ps. 73:26 ESV)

Gracious Father, my flesh and my heart still reel from the damage of my abuse. How long, O Lord? When will these episodes of heart pain and soul shame go away? When will my triggers become less and less hair triggers? Will my haunting ambivalence ever give way to a nonanxious presence? Will I ever feel normal, whatever normal is?

I want to trust again, Father. I want safe touch, without fear. I want a playful heart. Help me, Abba; give me strength and will to stay present in this journey. You are the strength of my heart and my portion. I have no other hope, refuge, or safe place in life.

With the same mercy you first welcomed me, show mercy to me again and again. By the same grace you saved me and made me yours, heal me and free me. With the same Spirit you raised Jesus from the dead, breathe more life into the dry bones of my soul. When I want to run away, grab me. When I want to look away, look into my eyes with your gaze of grace. When I want to numb out, don't let me. In Jesus' wonderful and merciful name I pray. Amen.

Jesus wept. (John 11:35)

Dear Lord Jesus, no one has been more necessary, precious, and faithful to me in my healing journey than you. I heard the old gospel song long before I believed it: "No one understands like Jesus." It's true—truer than I ever imagined or hoped. You felt the shame and disgrace, the agony and ignominy of sexual abuse long before I did. Stripped naked and abused, mocked and jeered, publicly exposed and openly humiliated, all for us—you endured all of this for us.

You created the world and sustain all things by the power of your Word, yet you became helpless and powerless for us. I'm glad you're all-powerful, but I needed to discover you as all-merciful. I praise, bless, and adore you, Jesus, for the depths of your suffering and the wonders of your love. I wish I'd understood this part of your story—this dimension of the gospel—much sooner. Maybe I would have posed and pretended less.

It's not that your compassion makes my sexual abuse more acceptable or its impact less critical, but I do feel less conflicted and less alone. The tears you wept outside Lazarus's tomb, you weep in full view of my abuse. One day you will wipe away all my tears and fully redeem the pain behind those tears. Until then, I will trust you with my heart, hurts, and hopes. In your compassionate name I pray. Amen.

Prayers of a Spouse Betrayed by Sexual Sin

It is not an enemy who taunts me—I could bear that. It is not my foes who so arrogantly insult me—I could have hidden from them. Instead, it is you—my equal, my companion and close friend. What good fellowship we once enjoyed as we walked together to the house of God. (Ps. 55:12–14 NLT)

Father, I'm not sure if I'm more mad or sad right now, but I am deeply hurt and really angry. I come to you now because I fear what I might otherwise choose to do. In my hurt, I want to repay tenfold. In my shame, one minute I want to hide and the next I want to humiliate my spouse. I feel so stupid. Why didn't I see this coming? Is it me? Is this my fault?

Lord, where do I go from here; what do I do next? Even as I want to hear from you, I'm afraid of what you will say. I'm embarrassed and don't want anybody to know; I'm enraged and want everybody to know. Help me, Father. Lead me to the sanest and wisest people in my circle of friends. It's going to be hard, but not as hard as if I try to do this all by myself.

I can't even think about forgiving my spouse yet, but I can't afford to ignore my own weakness, brokenness, and sin. Father, grant me grace for this moment and for what's ahead. Though I say it feebly, I am sincere when I say I want your glory more than I want revenge. In Jesus' name I pray. Amen.

Then Jesus said, "Come to me, all of you who are weary and carry heavy burdens, and I will give you rest." (Matt. 11:28 NLT)

Jesus, I am so tired of the broken promises, failed commitments, and abused trust. I don't want to risk hoping again—not anytime soon, anyway. It just hurts too much. I hate pornography, I hate pornographers, I hate my spouse's porn problem, and I hate hating so much. I am weary beyond my ability to put up with any more of it. I cannot carry the heavy burdens of this broken record that just keeps on playing. That's why I'm coming to you, Jesus. I need you, Jesus, to be Jesus to me, more than ever.

I don't want to crumble under the weight of my own bitterness and resentment, and I know, at least in my head, that my sin is just as worthy of judgment as anyone else's, including that of my spouse. So help me, Lord Jesus. I cannot read the Gospels without seeing how welcoming, patient, and compassionate you were with those trapped in sexual sin and brokenness, and I cannot believe the gospel without extending the grace I freely receive to others.

I'm glad you're praying for my spouse, because I'm having a hard time doing so. Please bring to me, and us, the community we need in these next hours, days, and weeks.

Thank you for your promise of rest, Jesus, for I'm desperate for rest—now and moving forward. Gratefully I pray in your loving name. Amen.

> Dear brothers and sisters, if another believer is overcome by some sin, you who are godly should gently and humbly help that person back onto the right path. (Gal. 6:1 NLT)

God of restoration and all hope, I bring my husband before you today, acknowledging that I'm just as much in need of your mercy and grace as he is. Though I want to throw stones, it's important for me to throw myself at your feet. Sexual sin has damaged our relationship. That which was meant for beauty and intimacy has become a source of darkness and disconnect. But as much as I feel like my husband is my adversary right now, I know our greater adversary is the devil himself. Don't let me forget this. Truly, evil hates beauty.

Father, keep my husband from self-contempt and even greater shame. I know he's sorry, but only you know his heart. Grant him deep repentance, healing community, and above all, a fresh encounter with your love and grace. I cannot be his Savior.

As for my heart, you know what I need, Father. I need sisters who have walked this path before, counsel that will fix my eyes on Jesus, and hope. I know things impossible with me are possible with you. I've believed that for other friends; now help me believe it for myself. With raw pain and fresh tears, I honestly want you to write a story of redemption and restoration in our marriage. In Jesus' name I pray and trust. Amen.

Prayers of Those Gripped by Shame and Guilt

Instead of your shame there shall be a double portion; instead of dishonor they shall rejoice in their lot; therefore in their land they shall possess a double portion; they shall have everlasting joy. (Isa. 61:7 ESV)

Dear heavenly Father, though I feel so unworthy to call you that name, I come to you today saddled with guilt and paralyzed with shame. Why do I keep doing the same things? Why must I offer the same confession? Surely, you must be fed up with me—regretting you saved me and made me your child. Those thoughts pummel my conscience and haunt my dreams. The accuser of the brethren has found an easy prey in me of late. Regretfully, I've listened to his condemning chorus.

I so want to make excuses for myself, or impose some kind of self-imposed penance to earn my way back into your favor—foolish man that I am. But groveling will never do what your grace alone can accomplish. It's your kindness that leads me to repentance and your Word that propels me to Jesus, again and again.

According to your Word, you have promised your rebellious children a double portion of grace, instead of shame; a secure place in the land, not banishment to the wilderness; and everlasting joy, not perpetual sorrow. How can this be, Father? How can this be?

Though I have no power to change myself, you have made a covenant to change me. What amazing love you have lavished on us in Jesus. Father, I do repent, and though the day of no more sin is in front of me, the day of no more condemnation is here. In Jesus' holy and loving name, I pray. Amen.

191

Looking to Jesus, the founder and perfecter of our faith, who
for the joy that was set before him endured the cross, despising the shame, and is seated at the right hand of the throne of
God. (Heb. 12:2 ESV)

Dear Lord Jesus, I would surely despair, but for the truth
of this Scripture and the scope of its hope. Once again,
I've been hijacked and held hostage by shame. Wounds
from the past, failures in the present, and uncertainties in
the future—all three have joined forces to sabotage my joy
and peace. I feel insecure, fragile, and unusually fearful.
As much as I hate navel-gazing in others, it has been hard
to resist the downward pull into self-preoccupation and
self-contempt.

Fortunately, I hate shame more than I'm disgusted with
myself. I have you to thank for that, Jesus, for you despised
the shame of the cross by taking its judgment and giving
us your righteousness. You loathed shame by your love for
us—you battered it by the brokenness on the cross.

Once and for all, you have destroyed the legal claims of our
guilt and have crippled the lingering power of shame. The joy
coming to you after the cross was far more compelling than
the shame you took upon the cross. Jesus, you have shamed
shame for us. Hallelujah, hallelujah, hallelujah!

Jesus, you are the founder and perfecter of my faith. I cannot change my past, present, or future. That's your domain
and delight. In the coming hours and days, help me lock my
gaze on you. I'm tired of looking at me. I want to see more
of your beauty and more of who I am in you. Thank you,
Jesus; thank you. Amen.

I sought the Lord, and he answered me and delivered me from all my fears. Those who look to him are radiant, and their faces shall never be ashamed. (Ps. 34:4–5 ESV)

Dear Lord Jesus, in my bouts with shame, usually the last thing I want to do is seek you, for I fear being seen—I dread being found out, frowned upon, and forsaken. Such is the depth of my unbelief and a sign of how little I "get" the gospel. For you have always welcomed me in my brokenness and weakness. The gospel has put an end to posing and pretending. I praise, bless, and adore you, Jesus, for your kindness, compassion, and gentleness.

When I confess my sins to you, you're never informed, shocked, or surprised. For you know everything I know and much more. I'm probably aware of only 4 percent of my sin, but you know the other 96 percent as well, Jesus, and have forgiven all of it. I no longer wear the burden of my guilt but am clothed in the robe of your righteousness. I believe this, Jesus, but keep freeing me from the tenacious hold, crippling power, and condemning lies of unbelief.

Oh, for the day when I will never again doubt your love or get disconnected from the power of the gospel; when I'll never again get sucker-punched by shame or be blindsided by fear. That day cannot get here too soon, Jesus. Expectantly and gratefully I pray, in your compassionate name. Amen.

Prayers of the Addicted

And I am convinced that nothing can ever separate us from God's love. Neither death nor life, neither angels nor demons, neither our fears for today nor our worries about tomorrow—not even the powers of hell can separate us from God's love. No power in the sky above or in the earth below—indeed, nothing in all creation will ever be able to separate us from the love of God that is revealed in Christ Jesus our Lord. (Rom. 8:38–39 NLT)

Blessed Father, I hate the very thing I've learned to accept— my addiction. Only your grace was sufficient to show me how out of control, needy, and dangerous I was. Only your grace provided the right circumstances, time, and people to bring me to the end of myself, that I might come to you. Only your grace was powerful enough to rescue me from my guilt and begin healing my shame. Only your grace has given me reason to hope and resources for growth. Only your grace, Father; only your grace. I trust you for ongoing grace to accept the things I cannot change, courage to change the things that I can, and wisdom to know the difference. Nothing and no one can ever separate me from your love, and nowhere and at no time will I ever be cut off from your love. Thank you, thank you, thank you, in Jesus' name. Amen.

So if the Son sets you free, you will be free indeed. (John 8:36 ESV)

Lord Jesus, my addiction doesn't define me; you and your immeasurable, irrevocable, inexhaustible love for me do. And even as I long for the day when I will no longer even be tempted to act out foolishly and destructively, so I trust you for sufficient grace until that day. One day at a time, Lord; indeed, one day at a time. When my brokenness is raging, let me see more of your beauty, Jesus. When I'm most tempted to medicate my pain, meet me in my weakness with your mercy and grace. When I want to run from you, don't let me.

When the voice of the condemner and accuser shouts at me, may your singing over me in the gospel get ten times louder. When I fail, let me fall on you again and again and again. My name isn't addict; it's beloved. I am yours, Jesus—not defined by the pain I carry or the substance I abuse, the people I've hurt or the promises I've broken. I will be whole one day; I want to get healthier this day and tomorrow.

Holy Spirit, you are my higher, present, and sufficient power. Addiction is powerful, very powerful, but you are the power of resurrection and hope. Thank you for making the gospel real to me when my addiction seems even more real. Thank you for revealing your power through my community and sponsor. I dare not walk this journey alone. Thank you for being more powerful to redeem than my addiction is to destroy. Continue to witness to my heart about my sonship. I am no longer a slave to my addiction; I'm a beloved child of God. Continue to strengthen me when I am weak, which means I need your strength daily. Continue to rescue me from the lies that I will never change, can never be trusted, and will never be free. Bring the serenity of God's grace to bear upon my thoughts, emotions, and choices. In Jesus' name I pray. Amen.

Prayers of Those Hiding and Covering Sin

When I refused to confess my sin, my body wasted away, and I groaned all day long. (Ps. 32:3 NLT)

Dear God, I'm tired of running from you, and yet I'm also afraid of being found by you. I hear that you are a loving and compassionate God, but how can that be? Do you really know what I have done? I am ashamed; I want to be different, and yet I have no power to change. Is Jesus for real? Can he save me . . . will he? Have mercy, on me, God; have mercy. Amen.

But the Lord God called to the man, "Where are you?" (Gen. 3:9)

Father, I know exactly what I'm doing—the impossible. I'm trying to hide from you, the One who sees everything. But my pain has been greater than your praise, and getting some form of relief has taken over my life. I'm not proud of it, but I'm not sure I'm ready to deal with the issues yet either. I've tried so hard to keep things together, but I can't do this dance much longer. I know I'm a prodigal. I know you're good. I want to come home. Help me, please. Amen.

What benefit did you reap at that time from the things you are now ashamed of? Those things result in death! (Rom. 6:21)

Have mercy, on me, dear God; have mercy. I give up. I surrender. I am so ashamed of myself. I feel like such a fool. How could you possibly welcome me or want me? I used to walk closely with you. I remember when your love first captured my heart. I was so free, so happy, so content. Why didn't I see this coming? I know better. I want to beat myself up, but that wouldn't accomplish anything. I'm tired of my sin. I'm tired of talking to myself. I'm done with wondering what people will think of me. All I know to do is to throw myself at your feet and cry for mercy, Father. Please forgive me, for Jesus' sake. I won't make any promises. I'll just trust yours. Humbly I pray. Amen.

The fleeting pleasures of sin. (Heb. 11:25)

God, I'm not sure if this is a prayer or if I'm just talking to myself, but here goes. The main joy and pleasure I've experienced in life have come from things I've always been told are sinful. I love sex. I love alcohol. And I love the things money can buy me. But it's never enough. I'm sitting here all alone, maybe in a brief moment of sanity, wondering if there's a different way. I've heard about Jesus. I've heard about your grace. But it seems surreal, too good to be a true story. But at this point, I'm open to almost anything. Jesus, if you are real, if you do receive people like me, if you can change me—please do so. Reveal yourself to me, I pray. Amen.

Prayers of Those Who Feel Forsaken and Abandoned by God

Afterward Job opened his mouth and cursed the day of his birth. (Job 3:1 NASB)

Father, I know the verses, I know what the Bible teaches, I know what I'm supposed to say, but right now I'm just worn out, empty, and confused. I'm not sure if I'm more mad or sad. I don't understand why you cannot share some of my troubles and heartaches with others. I know better, but it feels like you're picking on me. It's hard not to conclude this is payback time in my life—like you're getting even for the years I ignored you and openly rebelled.

But I know better, Lord. In my heart of hearts, I know Jesus paid the price for all my sins. I know you're not mad at me, though it feels that way. I know I'm forgiven and I'll go to heaven when I die. But how long is it going to hurt this bad, Father? When will relief come? When will life get easier? I don't want to wait till heaven. For your glory, lift this load, please, Lord. I don't want to dishonor you with my thoughts or words. Meet me, Father. Amen.

> This is what the LORD says: "A cry is heard in Ramah—deep anguish and bitter weeping. Rachel weeps for her children, refusing to be comforted—for her children are gone." (Jer. 31:15 NLT)

Dear Jesus, if I thought begging would help, I'd crawl on my knees. I'd do anything. You said to let the little children come to you, and that's what I'm doing, but seemingly to no avail. Please, Lord, please heal my child. Give me her pain. I'd gladly take it. She looks at me with questions in her eyes for which I don't have an answer, Jesus. Please help us.

As I hold her, hold us, Lord. Where can we go but to you? Who do we have but you, Jesus? You know what abandonment feels like; that's why I come to you boldly with the searing pain of my heart. Have mercy on us, Lord. Heal my baby. If you never do one more thing for me, please show my daughter your kindness and power. Amen.

> You deceived me, LORD, and I was deceived; you overpowered me and prevailed. I am ridiculed all day long; everyone mocks me. (Jer. 20:7)

Lord, I need the freedom you promise us, because I'm going to test the broadness of your shoulders and the bigness of your heart. I'm fed up, toast, done. I've had it with your people. If feels safer outside the church than inside it. I get better treatment from pagans than from your people. At least my non-Christian friends sit with me and listen. Believers just want to fix me—want me to "get over it." So much for vulnerability and transparency.

And yet, God, as angry as I am, I refuse to be a prisoner to my cynicism. If that happens, they win and I lose. I knew the church was messed up when I joined it, because I knew my own stuff. So help me sort through these feelings, God. At least your Word pulls no punches. I really don't see many admirable people in the Bible. We're all in need of what you alone can give—mercy and grace. Meet me here, Lord; just don't leave me here. I don't want to be old, mad, and alone. Thank you. Amen.

A Prayer of Someone Suffering with Mental Illness

Dear Father, the world I inhabit is filled with contrasting, often clashing feelings. Some days—or hours—I love you and sense your presence; other moments you threaten my existence and I do not trust you. Hold me tightly in those hours. When I push you away, move closer still. Though my thoughts and words often deny your goodness, and even your existence, in my heart of hearts I know I am yours. I adore you even when I feel hatred for you.

In the darkest hours, stay patient; stay present. When the voices in my head are louder than your singing voice, sing louder, Father; sing even when I choose not to listen. When I feel like no one cares, no one understands, no one can be trusted—into those vulnerable, lonely spaces, breathe grace and bring hope. I have no joy in hurting people who are trying to help me. Let them know that. Help me show that.

Father, I long for the day when Jesus will make me whole. I am so glad he loves me as much in this day as he will in that day. Make that Good News so real in the deepest places of my broken being. I love you, Father, and pray in Jesus' name. Amen.

A Prayer of Someone
Whose Spouse Suffers with Mental Illness

Dear Jesus, no one understands the world of brokenness better than you. No one has more kindness, patience, and forbearance. No one is a greater or more gracious Savior. No one is more committed to showing mercy, giving peace, and healing pain. I need all of the above, Jesus, all of the above.

My spouse is a gift to me, Jesus, even though at times I am spent, overwhelmed, and angry, and I simply don't know what to do and how to love. I thank you for the opportunity to need you, know you, and walk with you in ways I never would have planned. I truly want to love my broken spouse as you love me, Jesus—with my own brokenness, messiness, and neediness. I meant those words we spoke, "for better or for worse, in sickness and in health," for this is the way you love us.

I praise you for the days of normalcy, sweetness, and beauty. Though I wish those days were longer and more numerous, nonetheless, I thank you, Jesus, for every foretaste of the unbroken kindness and wholeness that awaits us at your return. My beloved spouse will be as lovely and as loving as you, Jesus, and so will I. Hasten that day, Jesus.

I want to trust you even more in the days of darkness, confusion, and exhaustion. Jesus, thank you that I don't have to pretend or deny how hard it is at times to love my spouse well. Some days I simply run out of patience and indulge feelings of resentment. I start thinking that I deserve better, easier, and kinder. Into those moments infuse fresh grace, heavenly perspective, and the power of the gospel. I humbly and gratefully pray, in your loving name. Amen.

A Prayer of Someone Fearing They've Been Disqualified from God's Service

Dear Father, I miss serving you, with an ache that keeps me up at night. I've owned the foolishness of my choices and the consequences of my sin. I understand why our leaders disciplined me. I too share their commitment to guard the peace and purity of our community. But please assure me this doesn't mean I'll never experience the joy of sharing your Word again. You've restored me to yourself and to my family of believers; please restore me to your service, Father. Silence the condemning voice of the accuser; grant our leaders wisdom as we walk this journey together; and give me a humble and patient heart to wait upon you, Lord.

Dear Jesus, though our leaders are ready for me to serve again, my confidence is crippled, shame lurks near the door of my heart, and I still battle the voices of condemnation. I know you have forgiven me, but I've yet to regain a sense of your delight. Please lift this burden and free my heart. The

Scriptures assure me that your strength is made perfect in weakness, but my heart tells me my weakness has disqualified me from your service. Jesus, your Word is greater and more trustworthy than my heart. Help me as I make myself available again to our church family. Thank you for your kindness to me in this season of restoration. I do love you, and I've so missed using my gifts for your glory. Humbly and expectantly I pray. Amen.

5

Prayers for Listening to the Heart of God

This next section of prayers invites us to assume the posture of listener rather than intercessor. Too often we do all the talking in prayer. But prayer is meant to be dialogue shaped by the gospel and fueled by the Holy Spirit. God initiates and we respond, which is the rhythm of worship.

Indeed, there are seasons of life or moments in a day in which our greatest need is simply to allow the great truths of the Scriptures to wash over us, bringing perspective and peace, renewal and hope. I've chosen certain Scriptures as the basis for these listening prayers, from which I have written a brief meditation, expressed in the form of God speaking directly to us. But listen up and pay careful attention to what I'm about to say: I don't offer these meditations as words God gave me directly; rather, they are thoughts expressing the wonderful implications of these Scriptures and the gospel, confirmed by the unified voice of the Bible.

This section of prayers is written in the spirit and style of some of our favorite hymns, in which the hymn writer uses portions of the Bible as the basis of his text and then applies them in the first person voice of God. "How Firm a Foundation" (written by John Rippon in 1787), is a perfect example. Every line in this hymn is "biblical," but no word-for-word quotation from a text of Scripture is used. The first two verses introduce the other verses, in which Rev. Rippon grounds the hymn in the trustworthiness and comprehensive applicability of God's Word: "How firm a foundation, ye saints of the Lord, is laid for your faith in His excellent Word!" Then he writes the remaining verses drawing from Old and New Testament texts: "Fear not, I am with thee, O be not dismayed; For I am thy God and will still give thee aid. . . . The soul that on Jesus has leaned for repose, I will not, I will not desert to its foes; That soul, though all hell should endeavor to shake, I'll never, no never, no never forsake."

My response to this hymn is "Hallelujah!" Accordingly, I encourage you to engage with and "soak" in the following devotional thoughts and prayers. Read through them *slowly*, lingering as you go. Pay the greatest attention to the Scripture introducing the meditation, for that is where the liberating power resides. I would also suggest having a pen and a prayer journal close by for writing a prayer in response to what the Lord stirs up in your heart. This should be a prayer journal for your eyes only, so you'll enjoy the freedom to express the fullest range of your thoughts and emotions to God.

I belong to my beloved, and his desire is for me. (Song of Sol. 7:10)

Indeed, you belong to me, my child, and I love you more than you ever hoped and desire you more than you can possibly imagine. No matter your failures or feelings, no matter the defaming names you wear or the shameful things you have done, in full view of your struggles and knowing all your burdens, I have redeemed you and you are mine.

Though you doubt many things, you don't have to doubt what I think of you. I love you as much as I love my Son, Jesus—for I've hidden your life in his, and made his righteousness yours. I cannot love you more, and I will never love you less. Rest, my child, and be at peace. Know that the grasp of my grace is tighter than your grip on me.

When in doubt, I will meet you right there. When in joy, know that I intend even greater joy for you. When in weakness, my strength is made perfect in that very place.

The Lord your God is in your midst, a mighty one who will save; he will rejoice over you with gladness; he will quiet you by his love; he will exult over you with loud singing. (Zeph. 3:17 ESV)

Of course you find it hard to believe that I could possibly love you like this. When you look at the good works, wise choices, and great sacrifice of others, you feel unworthy and undeserving. But I don't want you to look at people in comparison but to my Son in adoration. Jesus is the Author and Perfecter of your faith. He is your righteousness, holiness, and redemption. I am mighty to save you, because he was fully obedient for you.

Right now, in this very moment, I am rejoicing over you with gladness—great gladness and delight—for you not as you should be, not as you will be, but as you actually are. I will quiet all the restless places in your life with my love—your wounds and fears, your worries and tears. I am singing over you loudly and joyfully in the gospel. Listen carefully, and may the sound of my voice mute the noise of your doubt, the roars of the dark lion, and the clamor of the world.

I have loved you, my people, with an everlasting love. With unfailing love I have drawn you to myself. (Jer. 31:3 NLT)

I loved you before the world began—before you showed any promise or made a single promise, I loved you. I never looked to what you would do for me, but only to what I would do for you. I sent Jesus into the world to you and for you. His life of perfect obedience and his death of perfect surrender, I now consider yours. You are legally mine but also delightfully and passionately mine.

That is why my love for you is unwavering and unfailing. You cannot add to it or take away from it. I will cease to be God before my affection for you will wane or fail, be exhausted or be withdrawn. Even when I discipline you and bring the pain of correction into your life, it's from a heart of compassion and kindness. I will humble you, but I will never humiliate you; I will shape you, but I will never shame you, for I have drawn you to myself, and you are mine.

Who then is the one who condemns? No one. Christ Jesus who died—more than that, who was raised to life—is at the right hand of God and is also interceding for us. (Rom. 8:34)

Why do you condemn yourself, my child? Why do you listen to the voice of the accuser, slanderer, and liar? There is now, and never will be, any condemnation left for your sin. Rejoice and be glad, for Jesus has exhausted my judgment against you. I will never remember your sins against you, for I have remembered them against him. I will never deal with you according to your iniquities, because I dealt with Jesus according to your iniquities.

You will never be more criticized than you were by Jesus' cross, yet at the same time, you will never be more celebrated and loved. Because of your sin, Jesus had to die for you, but because of his love, he was glad to die for you—the just for the unjust, the lovely for the loveless, the righteous one for the rebel you. We cherish you this much.

I know you believe this Good News, but I intend for you to glory in it all the more—to boast in it, rest in it, be transformed by it, my beloved children. He who died for you, now ever lives to pray for you. He who came as your Savior is coming back as your Bridegroom. Be done with the lies.

But the LORD God called to the man, "Where are you?" (Gen. 3:9)

As surely as I asked your first parents this question, so I ask you as well. Where are you, my beloved? I ask for your benefit, not mine. I know where you are—for you cannot hide from me, and you certainly cannot outrun me, and there's no need to do so.

Why all your posing and pretending? Why all your busyness and drivenness? Why do you try so hard not to need my mercy and grace? Do you honestly think your weakness and brokenness will surprise or shock me? Have you ever known me to be harsh or shaming, unforgiving or unkind?

I don't need your tears of regret or your promises of reform. They are no more effective than fig leaves. Just collapse upon Jesus afresh, for he is your covering and peace, your righteousness and hope, your freedom and joy. I'm not looking for you to do anything for me. I'm just looking for you. I want you. I love you. I see you.

The Spirit himself bears witness with our spirit that we are children of God. (Rom. 8:16 ESV)

Oh, my daughters and sons, I so want you to realize you're no longer slaves or orphans but my totally known and greatly beloved children. By the same Spirit I spoke the world into existence, and with the same Spirit I anointed my prophets and kings, I have sealed you and now indwell you.

Listen to my Spirit. He is gently and persistently serenading you—singing the Good News of your adoption, declaring the freedom of your redemption, regaling the greatness of my affection. I am the Father you always wanted. No other father could be to you what I am. I have redeemed your past, I am engaged in your present, and I have secured your future. Be still and know that I am God. Be still and know that I am good. Be glad and call me Abba Father.

When you go through deep waters, I will be with you. When you go through rivers of difficulty, you will not drown. When you walk through the fire of oppression, you will not be burned up; the flames will not consume you. (Isa. 43:2 NLT)

My child, I never promised you a pain-free life or an easy journey into the new heaven and new earth. But I did promise you that I would never leave you or forsake you, even though you feel alone and overwhelmed at times. You live in a broken world, but you have a sovereign Father.

When—not if—you go through rivers of difficulty, the fire of calamity, and the hardship of providence, I am right there with you. As surely as I number your hairs and your days, I bottle the very tears I will wipe away one day. I will limit your suffering and pain, but I will never limit my mercy and grace for you.

Do not fear, but do not pretend either. Some things will only make sense when you are home. But never forget, I'm not only with you, I am for you. Nothing can separate you from my love. Bring me your confusion and doubts, your sadness and fury. You'll never affront me; I'll only love you.

I remember the devotion of your youth, how as a bride you loved me and followed me through the wilderness. (Jer. 2:2)

I am jealous for your heart, my beloved. I redeemed you because I love you and want you for myself. I remember the joy you felt when I first called you by name and poured my grace upon you. Your first love was an aroma of praise, a delight to my heart. Do you remember those days—their sweetness, freedom, and peace?

Yet the battle for your heart continues. Guard your heart, my beloved, and be careful not to give your affection to other suitors. Your great enemy has lost you for eternity, yet he remains committed to wooing you away from me. Know his schemes, and be wise. He comes to steal, kill, and destroy. I have come to give you life in abundance and myself without reservation.

Come to me, all who labor and are heavy laden, and I will give you rest. (Matt. 11:28 ESV)

I know your weariness, heartaches, and burdens. And I know you are tempted to either deny and pretend or withdraw and despair. I don't need you to be sufficient, and I don't want you to linger in anguish. I want you to come to me; come to me right now. You don't have to go far, for I am right here with you. I will give you rest.

Rest from thinking that I'm disappointed in you.

Rest from the desolation of isolation.

Rest from thinking you should be better by now.

Rest from taking on more than I've given you.

Rest from the lies and condemning voice of the accuser.

Rest from the idolatry of your capability.

Rest from the false guilt of your failure.

Rest from the real shame of your past.

Rest from the uncertainties of your future.

Rest to be a Mary in a Martha world.

Just collapse on me right where you are, for where you are, I AM.

As a bridegroom rejoices over his bride, so will your God rejoice over you. (Isa. 62:5)

Beloved, I delight to rescue you from all the wrong notions you've had of me for years, for they have robbed you of much peace, joy, and freedom. But more important than what you think of me is what I think of you. What do I think of you? I love you with great passion and delight, as your Bridegroom, for I have betrothed you to myself. I am the Spouse you always wanted, and you are the Bride for whom I gladly died and will joyfully return.

Don't be afraid, for you'll never shock me with your weakness or surprise me with your failings. I know all and have forgiven all. I've replaced your garments of guiltiness with the wedding dress of my righteousness. No one can blame you, for I have claimed you as my own. On the day of our wedding, my delight in you will be great, but no greater than it is today, even in this moment. Rest in my love; linger there, be healed, be free.

Fear not; you will no longer live in shame. Don't be afraid; there is no more disgrace for you. (Isa. 54:4 NLT)

No more, my child, no more is shame your prison, home, or name. You have no reason to hide, no need to fear, no cause to blame yourself or anyone. The weight of your guilt is lifted; the power of your shame is broken; the doubts in your heart are groundless.

When I see you, I see the perfection of my Son—for I have hidden your life in his. My grace has more than replaced your disgrace, for Jesus fulfilled the law for you and exhausted its judgment against you. I have raised you to newness of life and have given you a new heart and new name, a perfect record and a sure future.

Though the devil accuse you, people deride you, and your own thoughts indict you, I declare you to be righteous in my sight—known and desired, welcome and enjoyed. Believe it, and believe it even more.

Fear not, little flock, for it is your Father's good pleasure to give
you the kingdom. (Luke 12:32 ESV)

My beloved daughters and sons, don't retreat, don't pull
back, and don't turn in on yourselves. I want you to live not
as ingrown cloisters of fear but as outgoing communities
of faith—women and men set free to love as you are loved
and serve with the servant love of Jesus. As surely as I gave
the true King for your salvation, so I give you my kingdom
with pleasure. I rescued you from your little fiefdom of self
to serve in my transforming kingdom of grace. Why settle
for less? Don't be afraid. Things are not as they appear.

It has always been my plan to fill the earth with the goodness, truth, and beauty of Eden, and I haven't changed my
mind. That's not a job for you to do but a story for you
to live—my story of redemption and restoration. Be good
neighbors and love well; do excellent work and be generous;
advocate for justice and extend my mercy; preach the gospel
and create beauty. Listen to me: your labors of love will never
be in vain, for I will bring my good work to completion—in
you and through you. My kingdom has come, and my kingdom is coming in fullness.

Dear children, keep yourselves from idols. (1 John 5:21)

Dear children—for you are very dear to me—give me your
hearts. I have your hearts for eternity, but I want your affection today. I have bought and washed your hearts; I will
beautify and one day perfect your hearts. But just as Eve was
tempted and seduced, so do you face other lovers and empty

idols clamoring for your devotion. Don't be naïve. You will be prone to wander until the day you are filled with my wonder.

How do you keep yourselves from idols? Gaze upon my beauty in the Scriptures, dear children; marinate in my love for you in Jesus—the only love that is better than life, the only love that is enough, the only love that will never let go of you.

Bring me your brokenness and weakness, your disappointments and pain, your failures and sin. Though your idols promise relief, I'm the only one who will welcome and accept you, heal and free you, stay present and never give up on you. I understand your pain and longings, and I can handle your anger—even your anger with me. I give you daily mercies, because you need my mercy daily.

Blessed be the God and Father of our Lord Jesus Christ, the Father of mercies and God of all comfort, who comforts us in all our affliction, so that we may be able to comfort those who are in any affliction, with the comfort with which we ourselves are comforted by God. (2 Cor. 1:3–4 ESV)

Do not hoard your sorrows, my daughters; do not waste your suffering, my sons. These are grace gifts to you—a means by which I intend to gentle you, not harden you; increase your compassion, not intensify your sadness; free you to enter the pain of your friends, not cause you to withdraw into your chamber of self-pity.

I am your Father of mercy, yet sometimes my mercy is severe. Of course I will give you more than you can handle. It's one of the main ways I rescue you from yourself and draw you closer to me. I made you for a life of rich fellowship with me and for loving and serving your neighbors. I want you to rely not upon yourself but upon me, the God who raises the dead.

I am your God of all comfort. Whatever your affliction, I promise you sufficient grace—grace that will be enough for you and for your friends and neighbors. One day I will wipe all of your tears away, redeeming the pain behind those tears. In light of that day, love to my glory in this day. I don't need you to be competent in the presence of your neighbor's suffering, just present and kind. This morning, and the next, and the next, I pledge you my steadfast love and new mercies.

6

Prayers of Lament

A lament is an impassioned cry, born out of a story or experience that seems to contradict God's revealed character, ways, or promises. Not to be confused with a dirge, a biblical lament most often follows the pattern of addressing God, stating the complaint, offering requests, and concluding expressions of trust or praise. How important were laments in the worship culture of Israel? Laments—either corporate or individual—make up over a third of the book of Psalms, at least sixty-five of the entire collection of one hundred fifty psalms.

The typical flow to a biblical lament, in most cases, follows this rhythm:

Address: God is named
Complaint: the issue is stated
Trust: an affirmation is expressed

Request: a cry for provision or deliverance is offered

Praise: God is blessed

This genre of prayer underscores the fact that the gospel puts an end to all posing and pretending. God wants us to bring our pain and confusion, anger and consternation to him. His shoulders are broad enough and his heart big enough to take whatever we need to express to him.

Lamenting Evil in the World

Holy and righteous God,

Don't you see? Don't you care, Lord? Fools revile you, daring you to take action. Evil men flaunt their excesses, without conscience or concern. It grieves us; it angers us. Women, children, and the elderly are shown no mercy. When will it end, Lord? When will the day of justice come?

We don't question your power; just your timetable. We don't question your plan; just its execution. Our hope is in you, Lord. There is no other God.

So until the day you put all things right, Lord, pour out your Spirit upon your people. Grant leaders wisdom, children comfort, and your church courage. Whether by our living or by our dying, we want to honor you.

When we're tempted to repay evil for evil, harm for harm, or hatred for hatred, grant us grace and restraint, O Lord. When fears loom and doubts increase, show us Jesus' empty tomb and your occupied throne. You alone, O God, are worthy. We praise, bless, and adore you, in Jesus' name. Amen.

Lamenting the Loss of One's Health

Great and gracious Father,

It's precisely because I know you to be great and gracious that I cry out to you today without measuring my words or muting my feelings. Father, I'm so tired of being tired, worn out by being worn out, depressed by being depressed. I'm not sure what hurts the most: the pain of my illness or believers who keep trying to fix me. I'm not as sick as Job, but I've got some of his sick friends dumping their platitudes and formulas on me.

It makes no sense. If I was healthy again, I could serve you like I used to, Lord. My family wouldn't be stressed to the max, and our finances wouldn't keep evaporating.

Father, I hate whiners, and I don't mean to be a whiner, but in your mercy and might, please write a story of redemption in this mess that is my life. I know one day I'll have a resurrected body and perfect health, and if I have to wait till Jesus comes back for that, then give me grace, Lord. You never promised to do all things easy, but you do all things well. I trust you, Lord; deepen, strengthen, sweeten that trust. For your glory and honor I ask it, in Jesus' name. Amen.

Lamenting the Death of a Child

Merciful and mighty God,

I don't have any tears left. The funeral is over, and I'm sitting here stunned, shocked, numb. I ache with heaviness and emptiness. Parents aren't supposed to bury children, Lord. I know, I know, I know what I'm supposed to say. I know the verses, the theological answers, the right things to think and say. But right now, I need to sit in this pain before you, not to grumble but to groan. I want a lot more than relief. I don't need answers right now; I need you, Father.

I hate death. I hate good-byes, especially ones that sabotage the way I think things ought to be. I'm not naïve about life in our broken world, but Father, really . . . a child in a casket? I hate disease and death with a violent and (I pray) holy hatred.

Hold me, Father, but more importantly show me, and our community, how to care for this devastated family. They fought so valiantly; they loved so well; they hurt so deeply. Oh, for the day of no more death and dying, gut-wrenching moans and heart-ripping losses. Even so, Jesus, come soon, please. In your great name I weep and pray. Amen.

Lamenting Betrayal by a Friend

Gracious and loving Jesus,

I'm in shock, Lord. I don't know if I'm more sad or mad. Right now it feels safer to be mad than sad, because I don't know where my tears might take me. I trusted this person with my heart and dreams, my struggles and my community. It's as though someone broke into my home, rummaged through my things, stole what he wanted, and disappeared into the night.

I feel stupid and naïve. Why didn't I see this coming? Why didn't somebody have my back? Why didn't you, Lord?

Jesus, I know better. In fact, being on this side of a betrayal makes me wonder about those I have harmed. I don't want to waste my pain on bitterness or revenge. In the coming hours and days, settle me, Jesus, and center me. Give me wisdom in this mess. Do I confront this person? Do I wait? Out of sight isn't going to be out of mind.

I want to desire for a story of redemption to emerge. Help me to neither lag behind nor run ahead of your will. Thank you, Lord, for your welcome and your grace. Amen.

Lamenting a Personal Failure

Merciful and gracious Father,

Surely there must be a limit to your welcome. How many times can I squander my inheritance, eat the food of pigs, feel sorry for myself, and presume you'll take me back? At what point, instead of running towards me with kisses, will you lock the gate with disgust? I wouldn't blame you one bit. I even hesitate to say I'm sorry for blowing it yet again, because my words feel hollow and meaningless even to me.

Father, my tears and hope are gone. I still believe in you, but how could you possibly still believe in me? I don't even have the energy to throw myself on Jesus; I'll just collapse on him right here, right now. Be gracious to me, a sinner, for Jesus' sake. Amen.

7

Short and Simple Prayers

Sometimes the best prayer we can pray is simply one word: "Help!" Accordingly, the following collection of prayers is offered to once again "prime the pump" for a lifestyle of praying without ceasing. God cares about every moment and every situation in which we find ourselves during the day. Rather than wasting disappointments and joys, crises and crucibles on a self-centered monologue, learn to constantly be pouring your heart out to your Father, as in these examples.

Confused

Lord Jesus, I don't know what's going on inside my heart in this moment. Please center and settle me. I feel confused, weary, and anxious. I hate not knowing what's next, what to do, and when things might change. Be my peace, take my hand, and lead the way forward.

Conflicted

Father of mercies and God of all comfort, please be both of those to me in the coming hours. I don't know what to do; I'm not sure if I'm more sad or mad. My fears are stronger than my faith. Help me, Lord.

Facing a Decision

Lord, I have to make a decision sooner than I had hoped. I feel more uncertain than ever about what's best. Please open a door I cannot shut and shut doors I cannot open. Guide my steps.

Children

Jesus, grab the hearts of my children. Make your grace irresistible to them. More than anything else, I want my kids to know you, love you, and serve you.

Marriage

Father, please intervene in our marriage. I feel lonely, mad, and hopeless. I want to run away, but I choose to run to you. Please help us. Humble me, gentle me, grace me.

Gratitude

Dear Jesus, thank you for the sound of waves, the aroma of coffee, the texture of cheesecake, the color blue, the giggle of a toddler, and the gift of conversation. Please continue to quicken my senses to see your beauty in the gospel and everywhere else.

Insomnia

Father, help my sleepless friends—those who battle with insomnia or stresses that make it nearly impossible to fall asleep. I will never take the gift of sleep for granted again. Thank you, Lord.

Temptation

Father, I'm tempted to do something stupid right now. I feel so alone, hurt, and forgotten. I feel too weak to resist. All I know to do is collapse on Jesus right now. Receive me and strengthen me. Save me from me.

Failure

God, I did it again, and for the ten thousandth time, I ask you to forgive me. I'm not asking for a second chance but for more of Jesus. I'm so tired of fighting this same battle. Do what you must to change and free me.

My Husband

Dear Jesus, my husband is overwhelmed at work. I hate to see him under so much stress. Help me know how to encourage him. Give me the right words. Please make yourself very real to him in this season. Thank you, Lord.

Boundaries

Father, help me to know what good boundaries look like with my adult children. It's hard to watch them make bad choices and not say something, but they resent my unsolicited suggestions. Grant me grace, Lord. Help me to trust you with their lives.

Thankfulness

God, what an awesome afternoon it's been. I love these low humidity, deep blue sky days. Forgive me when I take beauty and creature comforts for granted. Intensify my gratitude for all of your good gifts. Thank you, Father.

Darkness

Father, a veil of fear has fallen over my heart, and I'm having a hard time seeing your hand in my circumstances. I feel out of control and alone. Please meet me in this dark hole. I love you. I trust you. I need you, Lord.

Neighbor Love

Jesus, I saw you at work today in a visit with my neighbor. I still don't know what she thinks about you, but thank you that we met in our brokenness and shared weakness. Please reveal yourself to my friend. Draw her to yourself. Help me to love her well.

Forgiving

God, I don't want to forgive. I don't want to let go of the hurt and anger. I still want the satisfaction of revenge. I'm not proud of any of this; I simply want to acknowledge what you already know. Help me, Lord. I won't make promises I have no plan to keep. I feel like I have emotional cancer. Help me, Father.

Renewal

Holy Spirit, fill me with a fresh love for Jesus, quicker repentances before my family, and a willingness to trust God with important decisions in front of me. I'm fearful and yet at the same time excited.

Repentance

Father, forgive me for indulging such a bad attitude today. I've been irritated and critical, and I even tried to convince myself it was justified. It's not. I know you love me and that you're in control. Thank you for your kindness even when I'm a mess.

Pained Heart

Jesus, my heart hurts. A good friend just moved away, and I'm tired of transitions and changes in my life. I long for the day of no more good-byes. Hasten that day, Lord; make it sooner rather than later.

Struggling at Work

Lord, I'm tired of being overworked and underappreciated. I know I have a lot to be grateful for, but at what point should I start looking for a different position? I get home with no emotional reserves left in my tank for my family. I don't feel like I can do this much longer. Show me the way forward. Grant me wisdom and grace, Father. Thank you, in Jesus' name.

Sickness

God, I'm sick of being sick. It makes me sad for my family. No one is complaining but me, but it's just not right. How long, O Lord? I'm not shaking my fists at you; I just want some relief. Please heal me to whatever degree possible, or at least give me some of Paul's sufficient grace. In Jesus' name I pray.

Prodigal Child

Father, please bring my prodigal daughter (or son) back home. I hate the thought of her being completely broken, but if that's what it takes to bring her to you, do whatever you must. I see and grieve my self-righteousness and controlling ways, and I'm sure I made it easier for her to run away. Help both of us, Lord. In Jesus' name I pray.

Marriages of Friends

Lord, help me fight for the marriages of my friends. It can be so confusing and discouraging. The only side I want to take is yours. It's obvious that Satan hates our marriages as much as he hates you. Give me wisdom beyond my own, compassion, courage, and tenacity. We need your resurrection power. In Jesus' name I pray.

My Wife

Jesus, I don't know how to get close to my wife right now. She feels angry, depressed, and hopeless. Grant me grace to be present in the storm. Free me from every impulse to try to "fix her." Give me a nonanxious spirit, because I'm feeling just the opposite. Help me listen with my heart and wait upon you. I can't do this without you, Jesus.

Feeling "Done"

Father, I'm done with church, Christians, and trying to be spiritual. I just want to go away, be left alone, and find some kind of relief. Why bother? I don't really see change in my life. I'm not trying to tempt you; I just want you to know how much my heart hurts right now. I'm a mess, Father. My only hope is that you love messes.

8

Prayers for Married Couples to Pray Together

Dear heavenly Father, we bring our marriage to the throne of grace today, confident of your welcome, mindful of our needs, thankful for your provision. More than anything else, we want you to be honored in our relationship. We want our marriage to reveal the wonders of your love, the joy of your heart, and the beauty of the gospel.

So we humble ourselves before you, Father, trusting you for sufficient grace and daily mercies. Protect us from our enemy, who has come to steal, kill, and destroy. Help us to be quick with our repentances, regular with our encouragement, and loving in our conflicts. And by your Spirit, teach us what to pray for one another. Grant us fresh grace and joy, that we might serve one another to your glory. In Jesus' wonderful and merciful name we pray. Amen.

Dear heavenly Father, we are grateful for the promise of your steadfast love and daily mercies, for we need both today. Only your love is better than life; only your love will never let go of us; only your love is enough to fill the void in our hearts and redeem the brokenness of our stories. Help us to love each other as you love us in Jesus.

As you are merciful with us, Father, help us extend your mercy to one another. We acknowledge our impatience, lack of forbearance, and judgmentalism. Forgive us and free us, and grant us a relationship in which repenting is easy, quick, and sincere. We want our marriage to be filled with the kindness and encouragement we have found in Christ. Thank you, Father. We make our prayer in Jesus' name. Amen.

Dear heavenly Father, we praise, bless, and adore you for making peace with us in Christ and for reconciling us to yourself. You are with us and you are for us, and nothing will ever separate us from your love. We believe the amazingly good news of the gospel; free us even more from the chains of our unbelief.

May your peacemaking love help us in our disagreements, Father. Teach us how to face conflict redemptively. Show us how faith expresses itself in love when we see things differently, even much differently. Help us to be quick to listen to each other, slow to get irritated and angry, and quick to speak words that are helpful and kind. When we lose sight of the issue and treat each other with disrespect, grant us quick repentances toward each other. May we grow in humility and grace. In Jesus' name we pray. Amen.

Dear heavenly Father, for your steadfast love and daily mercies, we worship and adore you. There is no God like you—so patient, forbearing, and forgiving. Today we bring you our longing to be better forgivers in our marriage. As Jesus has forgiven us, so we want to forgive each other; as Jesus loves us, so we want to love one another.

May your Holy Spirit convict us quickly and free us to humble ourselves in our relationship. Help us to listen from our hearts, understand each other's perspective, and honor each other's longings. Father, may your kindness matter more to us than our rightness. Grant us thick skin and big hearts, as we share life together. In Jesus' tender and triumphant name we pray. Amen.

Dear Lord Jesus, you alone are the perfect Spouse—the spouse we always wanted. You gave your life to make us your Bride, and you have clothed us with the wedding garment of your grace. Our friends in heaven are more alive to your love than we are, but they are not more loved or cherished. We praise, bless, and adore you.

May your relationship with us shape and beautify our marriage, Jesus. May we find great joy in serving one another, even as you delight to serve us. Free us from having too lofty of expectations of one another and for having too low of expectations of you. Forgive us for looking to each other for the life, joy, and fulfillment only you can give us. We offer our prayer in your tender and faithful name. Amen.

Dear Lord Jesus, we are in a stressful season in our relationship. We humble ourselves before you, asking for mercy, grace, and wisdom. Mercy, because we don't want to hold on to unkind thoughts or speak hurtful words. Grace, because we don't have the resources within ourselves that we need right now. Wisdom, because we lack it and you freely give it.

Jesus, it is your kindness that leads us to repentance, your prayers that give us real hope, and your Spirit that gives us courage to stay engaged and move forward together. Help us define the real issues, honor one another, and wait upon you expectantly. Humbly we pray in your wonderful and merciful name. Amen.

Dear Lord Jesus, we bring our physical relationship to you—thankful for your welcome, kindness, and grace. No aspect of our marriage has given us greater moments of intimacy, joy, and pleasure; and yet, at the same time, no part of our marriage has more fully exposed our brokenness, fueled our vulnerability, and stirred up our longings for heaven.

Grant us grace to be kind and unselfish lovers, Jesus. Help us to find great joy in serving one another—with patience, tenderness, and passion. We covenant to keep our marriage bed beautiful, holy, and a celebration of your unbridled affection for us. Grant us grace for the different seasons in our sexual relationship, Jesus. When interest wanes or illness comes, temptation arises or brokenness surfaces, our trust and hope are in you, Jesus. We pray in your loving and powerful name. Amen.

Dear Lord Jesus, you are the God from whom all blessings flow—the source of little pleasures and the fountain of eternal delights. What do we have that we have not received from you? Thank you for freely giving us all things to enjoy. We bless you for our clothing, food, and shelter, and we pray to be content with these great gifts. We also thank you for the privilege of work and for the gift of employment.

Jesus, free us to be good stewards of everything you entrust to us—whether we're in a season of praying for daily bread or have an abundance we never anticipated. Continue to show us the difference between need and greed, between fearful hoarding and good planning, and between foolish spending and gospel generosity. Help us to stay free from the love of money but intensify our love for you. Make us like yourself—cheerful givers. We make our prayer in your merciful and mighty name. Amen.

Dear Lord Jesus, thank you for writing us into your big story of redemption and restoration. All of history is bound up with your commitment to redeem your Bride from the nations and ultimately to make all things new. Great is your mercy; measureless is your grace; limitless is your power. We worship and adore you.

Jesus, help us to find our place in your story and to resist the temptation just to give you bit parts in our marriage story. We don't want an ingrown, status quo, self-absorbed marriage. Help us to live and love missionally. Show us how to be good neighbors, servants in our community, and engaged with your mission in the world. Give us wisdom about lifestyle issues—the use of our time, talents, and treasure. May our marriage make the gospel beautiful and believable. We pray in your holy and loving name. Amen.

Dear Lord Jesus, you are truly a wonderful, merciful Savior— a friend of sinners, familiar with grief—the suffering Servant who loves us more than anyone else. Bruised reeds and smoldering wicks love your appearing. The weak find you welcoming, and the broken find you beautiful. We too run to your throne of grace today with our hurts, weariness, and suffering. You never promised us a pain-free life, but you have promised us rest and peace, and we praise you.

Jesus, grant us grace to enter into each other's brokenness and sorrows. Our issues may differ, but our need is the same—your welcome, acceptance, and comfort. Help us to give each other the gift of a nonanxious presence and nonjudgmental spirit. You have called us not to fix each other but to love and serve one another. Help us to listen from our hearts, encourage with our eyes, and heal with our words. May our marriage be a safe place to hurt and a real place to hope. We offer our hearts and prayers, in your tender and triumphant name. Amen.

9

What Does Jesus Pray for Us?

A Ten-Day Prayer Journey
through the High Priestly Prayer of Jesus

Hebrews 7:25 tells us, "Therefore he [Jesus] is able, once and forever, to save those who come to God through him. He lives forever to intercede with God on their behalf" (NLT).

This one verse of Scripture is jam-packed and crammed to overflowing with God's glory and his grace for us in Jesus. The writer of Hebrews wants us to understand (and experience) the good news that Jesus completely and forever saves anyone who comes to him and that he is always advocating and interceding for his beloved lambs. Since our wonderful, merciful Savior is always praying for us, doesn't it stand to reason we should explore what the Bible reveals about the focus of Jesus' prayers?

For of this we can be sure: any prayer Jesus offers on our behalf will be answered affirmatively. So where might we look to discover some of the petitions Jesus offers on our behalf? In one of the most profound moments recorded for us in God's Word, we are given the awe-producing privilege of overhearing Jesus as he prays for us.

John 17 is often referred to as the High Priestly Prayer of Jesus. Within hours of praying this prayer, Jesus died on the cross, paying the full price for our complete redemption. Three days later, he was raised from the dead, and he ascended to the right hand of the Father, where he presides today as our advocate and great high priest.

To connect with the richness of Jesus' prayer life for us, I want you to join me in meditating your way very slowly through the whole of John 17. Then, over the course of the next ten days (or longer), use the daily meditation I've written, based on one of Jesus' petitions found in John 17, as a springboard for a rich season of fellowshiping with our God.

I've provided you with many opened-ended prayer sentences for launching your heart heavenward in worship, thanksgiving, confession, and intercession. But don't feel constrained by words. Add to them and create your own. Though it's not essential, I recommend you use a prayer journal for this exercise, writing out your prayers each day. This will slow you down a bit and enable you to linger before the gaze of the God of all grace.

Begin now by slowly reading and meditating through John 17.

Day 1: Glorying in the Finished Work of Jesus

I have brought you glory on earth by finishing the work you gave me to do. And now, Father, glorify me in your presence with the glory I had with you before the world began. I have revealed you to those whom you gave me out of the world. They were yours; you gave them to me. (John 17:4–6)

Dear friends, we can never hear this declaration too often or too boldly: "It is finished!" Before returning to be with our heavenly Father, Jesus accomplished everything required for the salvation of our souls and for the renewal of the cosmos. *Nothing* was left undone. Indeed, Jesus came not to give us a second chance but to be the second Adam—to be our substitute to trust, before he is our model to follow. We are forgiven in Jesus, righteous in him, and beloved in him. Rejoice, receive, and rest in this Good News. Let us cease from our strivings and doubts, beloved.

Through the gospel, we have been brought into the fellowship Jesus has forever enjoyed with the Father and Spirit. Incredible! And as Jesus stated in his prayer, he considers us a gift to him from the Father. Astonishing! Though the saints in heaven are more joyful than we are, they are not more secure or cherished.

And one day, not far from this one, we will be united with our brothers and sisters in Christ from every nation and every generation. In that day, we will discover that the Garden of Eden was just a preview of coming attractions. Our life in the new heaven and new earth—this very world, restored and renewed by Jesus—will be the fullest expression of what Jesus meant by his bold declaration, "It is finished!"

Our eyes have never beheld such beauty, our ears aren't capable of entertaining the sonic splendor, and our imagination is simply too small to conceive of the things the Triune God has prepared for us. But we *will* see; we *will* hear; we *will* enjoy these things forever.

Spend a season in adoration and thanksgiving today, not asking one thing from God. Here are a few thoughts to prompt your gratitude and fuel your worship. Don't limit yourself just to a few words, as these aren't "fill in the blank" sentences. Linger in the riches of grace and enjoy communion with our God. Where might the Spirit take your mind and heart? Don't get in a hurry.

Dear Lord Jesus, as I consider your finished work on my behalf, I am . . .

Knowing you paid the full price for my sins and that the Father now counts me righteous in you makes me want to . . .

Father, for presenting me as a gift to Jesus—as hard as that is for me to believe—in response to such great grace and lavish love, I say to you today . . .

Father, I believe; help my unbelief. Spending time with you today, I realize I still have a hard time believing the gospel is really true—or at least true for me. As I quiet my heart before you, please speak to me. Why do I struggle to believe you love me as much as you say you do? Why do I remain allergic to your grace?

Day 2: Resting in God's Commitment to Protect Us

Holy Father, protect them by the power of your name. (John 17:11)

How encouraging and freeing—Jesus steadfastly prays for our protection. What a Savior, what a friend. But how are we to understand this priceless petition? What is implied? As we read the whole testimony of Scripture, we can easily discern that Jesus isn't praying that we will experience a pain-free life, devoid of difficulties, suffering, or sorrows. For Jesus has told us to expect troubles in this world. The day of no more death, mourning, crying, or pain is coming, but that day is not yet.

Rather, Jesus prays that we will be protected from the lies of the devil, who ever lives to tempt, seduce, and condemn us; and from the power of the world, which seeks to squeeze us into its mold and win our hearts away from our ultimate Spouse, Jesus.

Jesus also prays, no doubt, that we will be protected from our limited understanding of the ways of God and the small-ness of our faith and trust. Presently, we know only in part, but one day we will loudly declare with all our brothers and sisters, "My God has done all things well."

When Jesus prayed that we would be protected by the power of God's name, he was asking God to marshal everything God has and is on our behalf—a formidable supply, to say the least. Today, after acknowledging our own need, let's especially think of friends and family members who are in harm's way.

Dear holy and loving Father, thank you for your commitment to protect me from the schemes of the devil, the seduction of the world, and the foolishness of my own weak flesh. In particular, I find myself struggling with . . .

But today, I am especially mindful of these family members, friends, and situations. To your occupied throne of grace I bring:

The persecuted church and Christian leaders under attack around the world.

My church, her leaders, and other congregations in our community—especially those dealing with duress.

My friends and family members who are struggling to believe you are good and can be trusted.

The hearts of our children and grandchildren.

Marriages that are in crisis mode or barely holding on.

The prodigals you've placed in my life.

The self-righteous elder brother types in my life.

The city where I live and the neighborhoods around our church.

Day 3: Growing in the Fullness of Jesus' Joy

I am coming to you now, but I say these things while I am still in the world, so that they may have the full measure of my joy within them. (John 17:13)

Notice that Jesus prays not just for us to experience joy but that God would grant us the full measure of *Jesus'* joy. This prayer will be completely fulfilled only when our salvation is brought to completion at the second coming of Jesus. For it will require our glorified heart and resurrected body to contain the fullness of Jesus' joy.

And yet it is clear that Jesus intends for our joy to grow exponentially while we wait and long for the day of his return. Why do we need joy? Because the joy of the Lord is our strength (Neh. 8:10), and we need all the strength God is pleased to give us as we worship him and serve him in the world.

What is joy? Unlike happiness, joy isn't dependent on circumstances, and neither is joy to be equated with the absence of sadness and tears. For Jesus was a man of sorrows and very familiar with our grief (Isa. 53:3), while at the same time being anointed with the oil of joy (Heb. 1:9). Rather, joy is a settled disposition of peace and delight—a core of certainty that our God loves us in Christ, that he is sovereign over everything, and that he does all things well, even when he doesn't do all things easy. Therefore, joy is far more an expression of knowing God well than having feelings of felicity.

Today I invite you to talk to Jesus about your joy and then battle for the joy of those you love.

Dear Lord Jesus, first of all, when I consider your prayer and passion for me to be filled with your joy, I am so . . .

If I were to compile a list of things that keep me from experiencing more of your joy, it would probably include . . .

Since your joy is my strength, here are the areas of my life in which I'm feeling particularly weak and weary right now . . .

Lord Jesus, I also gladly do battle today for the joy of others. My confidence is in knowing that I join you in this prayer. To your throne of grace, I bring these brothers and sisters who, like me, are weary . . .

Jesus, you tell us to rejoice, above all things, that our names are written in the Lamb's book of life (Luke 10:20; Rev. 21:27).

Here are some friends for whom I ask fresh gospel-astonishment and restoration of the joy of their salvation. Please renew . . .

Day 4: Finding Our Place in God's Work in the World

My prayer is not that you take them out of the world but that you protect them from the evil one. (John 17:15)

As followers of Jesus, we're not to segregate ourselves from the world but to separate ourselves unto Jesus. We who share eternal union with him are called into robust communion with him. Jesus has called us to go with him into the world—to participate in his commitment to redeem his Bride from the nations and to restore our broken world. The future of God's creation isn't annihilation but restoration (Rev. 21:1–22:5). The new heaven and new earth is coming to us, we're not going to it. Indeed, Jesus is making all things new, not all new things. One day our earth will be covered with the knowledge of the glory of God, as the waters cover the sea (Hab. 2:14).

Of course we will experience opposition—even persecution, and some of us, martyrdom. But the gates of hell will not prevail against the church as we move forward into God's story. Jesus came to destroy the works of the devil, and he has succeeded (1 John 3:8), yet he who has been roundly defeated still remains to be thoroughly eradicated. Satan knows his time is short, and he is filled with fury (see Rev. 12:12)—all the more reason to take this petition of Jesus seriously and with great encouragement.

Our labors in the Lord are never in vain (1 Cor. 15:58). Indeed, our prayerful attitude should be more of laboring *in* the Lord, not *for* the Lord. Jesus is very much in the world through the presence of his Holy Spirit. Therefore, let's pray today for the advancing of God's kingdom with faith, not fear—as worshipers, not worriers.

Heavenly Father, I long for the day when your glory will cover the earth as the waters cover the sea. This great hope moves me to worship you as the God of . . .

Father, I am so thankful Jesus is coming back to our world to finish making all things new. As I think about our coming life in the new heaven and new earth, I'm most looking forward to . . .

But as I look at our broken world and the presence of so much darkness and evil, I confess, Father, that sometimes I feel . . .

Lord Jesus, knowing you have defeated Satan, I pray with great joy and confidence, but realizing the devil remains a roaring lion seeking to devour many, I pray with earnestness for the following missionaries and ministries . . .

Jesus, I join you in praying for our church family, knowing how much Satan would love to create havoc in our midst. In particular, I pray that you will . . .

Day 5: God's Grace-Full Commitment to Make Us Like Jesus

Sanctify them by the truth; your word is truth. (John 17:17)

There are two main reasons this prayer of Jesus should be a source of tremendous encouragement. First of all, it underscores the fact that *God uses his Word* to transform us. We don't worship the Bible; we worship the God of the Bible, who uniquely reveals himself in and through the Bible. We cannot thank God too much for the Scriptures—for God's Word is truth. We're not floating haplessly on the sea of relativism, public opinion, or the whims of our druthers.

And we cannot know the Scriptures too well. For the better we know the Bible, the more we will come to experience it as one big unfolding story in many parts. From Genesis through Revelation, the Bible tells a progressive but unified story about God's generous commitment to redeem an everynation family for himself and to restore his broken creation through his Son Jesus. In fact, Jesus emerges as the main character and only trustworthy hero in the entire Bible. So if we want more Jesus, let's spend more time, not less, in the Scriptures.

Second, this prayer is encouraging because it highlights the good news that *God transforms us* through his Word. In other words, we cannot save and change ourselves, though we foolishly try. God must justify us (forgive us and grant us righteousness), sanctify us (transform us into Christlikeness), and glorify us (bring our salvation to a glorious completion at Christ's return). Salvation is *of* and *by* the Lord, from beginning to end. It is all of grace. The most important contribution we make to our salvation is our need for salvation. It's not that we are entirely passive but that we are entirely dependent on God for every aspect of our salvation.

Let's now spend a season of reflection and prayer in response to this bold petition of Jesus. Today let us gladly assume an attitude of confession as we come before our gracious God.

Lord Jesus, I am grateful beyond measure that you are my righteousness before the Father and that when I sin, you advocate for me. You have completely met the demands of the law for me and have exhausted its judgment against me. The more I come alive to this good news, the more I'm compelled to . . .

Jesus, thank you for persistently asking the Father to sanctify me—to make me more like you, because I cannot change myself. God must complete the good work he began in me. In particular, here's where I know I need more of your transforming grace . . .

Gracious Father, I'm struggling to love well in these particular relationships . . .

When I forget the gospel and my heart isn't alive to your grace, I'm most easily tempted to . . .

Father, as far as I can tell, the main idols of my heart, to which I often turn when I feel you're not enough, include . . .

The truth is, Father, only you know my heart. As I quiet myself before you, please reveal to me my core sins and brokenness—things for which Jesus died and from which you intend to free me. Bring your Word, Spirit, and grace to bear upon my conscience. (Take the time to sit still before your Father, with a humble and listening heart.)

Father, thank you for convicting me without condemning me and for humbling me without shaming me. In response to your great love and grace, I say . . .

Day 6: Participating in God's Commitment to Redeem His Big Family

My prayer is not for them alone. I pray also for those who will believe in me through their message. (John 17:20)

We all matter, but none of us is the point in God's story. The gospel comes to us that it might run through us. Indeed, we are to live as pipelines of God's grace, not as holding ponds. In this petition, Jesus underscores one of the central promises God has made—an über-generous covenant that unfolds in the Bible and shapes all of history.

God grabbed hold of a pagan man named Abram and made promises to this Chaldean that he (God) alone could possibly keep (Gen. 12–17). God renamed Abram as Abraham, because he was to become the father of many nations. Abraham was instructed to count the stars, sand, and dust (as if that was possible), for that was how big a family God was going to redeem through the work of the Messiah who, in the fullness of time, would come from Abraham's family—the nation of Israel.

As followers of Jesus, we need to celebrate the Great Commission as God's commitment to be an every-nation Redeemer (Matt. 28:16–20). Indeed, the Great Commission isn't a job we are to get done but a story in which we are to participate. God *will* redeem his family from the nations—no matter what—but he has chosen to do so through us as we share and demonstrate the gospel of his grace.

Note Jesus' emphasis: "I pray for those who *will* believe in me through their message." There's no chance the Great Commission won't be fulfilled. So today, let's focus our prayers on God's generosity in the gospel and his commitment to use *us* to bring many people to new life in Jesus.

245

Gracious Father, thank you for your inviolate commitment to redeem a family from every race, tribe, tongue, and people group. Because in your sovereign mercy you chose to include me in your forever family, I say to you . . .

Because all of history is bound up with your commitment to redeem an every-nation Bride for Jesus, I worship you as the God of . . .

And now, hear my prayers for the advancing of the gospel among the nations and in our community.

I bring these missionaries to your throne of grace . . .

I pray for these local churches, pastors, and parachurch ministries committed to sharing the gospel in our community . . .

Father, I ask you to grant a saving knowledge of Jesus to these members of my family . . .

And here are the names of some of my friends, Father, who I'm not really sure believe the gospel yet. Please draw to Christ . . .

Lastly, Father, grant me grace to be a good neighbor, loving friend, and servant to the members of my family. Show me how to make the gospel more beautiful and believable to all the people for whom I'm praying.

Day 7: Enjoying Greater Intimacy with Jesus and Our Father

That all of them may be one, Father, just as you are in me and I am in you. May they also be in us so that the world may believe that you have sent me. (John 17:21)

What an astonishing image and request—in this part of his prayer, Jesus asks our Father to bring us into a greater experience of the intimacy they have enjoyed with one another throughout eternity. And notice that Jesus isn't just praying about the life we will enjoy with God in heaven but about this life as well. God's relationship with us, and our relationship with him, is meant to impact the way the world thinks about who Jesus is and why he came into the world.

What makes this all the more profound is to remember that God didn't create us out of any sense of lack or loneliness. God has never been bored or lonely. Out of sheer generosity, the Father, Son, and Holy Spirit determined to share with us the beauty, passion, and delights of the life of God. This explains our deep ache for relationships. As image bearers of God, we will be restless, empty, and foolish until we connect with God the way he intends.

As Jesus offers this prayer, the cross looms in front of him. He is on the cusp of paying the supreme price for the fulfillment of this petition. Apart from the finished work of Jesus, there is no reason (or basis) to think we could ever enjoy the relationship with God described in these words. Accordingly, let's express our worship, gratitude, and longings to the Lord.

Lord Jesus, first of all, I confess how hard it is to believe that you desire this degree of intimacy with me, and here's why . . .

I know I crave deep, fulfilling relationship, because I look for it in people. I thank you for the gift of friendship, connection, and intimacy I've experienced in life. In particular, here are a few of the relationships which have given me a taste of heaven . . .

I also realize that no person or relationship can fill the place in my heart reserved for you and my heavenly Father. When I forget this, I can over-expect people to fill me up and

meet needs you alone can meet. These people and relationships come to mind . . .

Jesus, forgive me for my idolatry of people and free me from
living for the approval of man. Help me take back the power
I've given some people to either shame me or make me. My
heart belongs to you. I cannot love anyone well that I over-need.
I will not love anyone well when I under-believe the gospel.
Free me from the depth and stranglehold of my unbelief.

Day 8: Daring to Believe God Loves Us Just as Much as He Loves Jesus

I in them and you in me—so that they may be brought to complete unity. Then the world will know that you sent me and have
loved them even as you have loved me. (John 17:23)

What wondrous love is this, indeed! Though this petition
begins with Jesus praying for our unity, it ends with his longing for us to know that God loves us just as much as he loves
Jesus himself. How astonishing, staggering, and liberating
this request is. We dare not miss, minimize, or marginalize
it. Jesus isn't simply praying that we accept the fact of God's
love, but that we grasp the degree of his love for us.

The apostle Paul certainly understood the grandeur and
greatness of Jesus' petition in this way, for he framed a similar prayer in Ephesians 3. Paul asked our Father to grant us
"strength to comprehend with all the saints what is the breadth
and length and height and depth, and to know the love of
Christ that surpasses knowledge" (Eph. 3:18–19 ESV). The love
between our Father and Jesus is so great, so multifaceted, so

"beyond knowing" that it requires the power of the Holy Spirit for us to comprehend it—and that is what God intends for us.

Dear friends, the language of Scripture must not be reduced to metaphor or treated as poetic hyperbole. Jesus' "It is finished" segues into the "It is now" of the riches of grace for us. God greatly delights in us, quiets us with his love, and rejoices over us with singing (Zeph. 3:17), all because of what Jesus has accomplished for us. And the consistent testimony of Scripture is that there is no more compelling, liberating, or transforming power than the love of God—a love he has lavished on us in the gospel (1 John 3:1–3). How then shall we worship and pray?

Lord Jesus, once again I cry, "I believe; help my unbelief." This isn't just a game changer; it's an everything changer. If the Father loves me as much as he loves you, this means I don't have to . . .

And if the Father loves me as much as he loves you, Jesus, then I'm now free to . . .

Jesus, the biggest obstacles to my believing God loves me just as much as he loves you include . . .

Jesus, as I look back over my spiritual journey, I was taught God would love me more when I . . .

I was also taught that God would love me less when I . . .

Lord Jesus, free me from all distortions of the gospel, and free me from under-believing the true gospel. By the power of the Holy Spirit, grant me faith to believe and to receive the answer to this prayer. I want to experience God's delight in me. I crave being quieted and transformed by his love. Give me ears to hear the Father singing over me with great rejoicing.

Day 9: Igniting Our Longings for Heaven

Father, I want those you have given me to be with me where I am, and to see my glory, the glory you have given me because you loved me before the creation of the world. (John 17:24)

This petition answers the deepest craving in our hearts—the longing to be welcomed and included, desired and enjoyed. Our happiest moments in life, and our most painful ones, are related to our yearning for relational fulfillment—not mere circumstantial pleasure. It's certainly a wonderful thing (and a God thing) to experience seasons of rich connection with people. But the biggest relational hole and vacuum in our hearts is God-shaped, and until that place is filled with Jesus, we will continue to look to people to be to us what God alone can be to us.

Indeed, Jesus' prayer invites us to understand that heaven isn't primarily about getting out of the mess of our world and onto the "streets of gold" in paradise. No, heaven is about the perfection of intimacy between God and us. Jesus wants us to be with him and the Father—to see and enjoy the glory they have shared throughout eternity.

As Christians, we get to experience a grand measure of the answer to this prayer when we die, for to be absent from the body is to be present with the Lord. But this prayer will only be fully answered when Jesus returns to finish making all things new. Our destiny is life in the new heaven and new earth. As surely as our bodies will be resurrected and united with our souls, so our broken world awaits renewal and restoration (Rev. 21:1–22:5).

Lord Jesus, when I think about heaven, these images usually come to mind . . .

As much as I understand about heaven, here's what I'm most looking forward to . . .

What will it be like to see you as you actually are, Jesus? As far as my faith will take me, here's what I think I'm going to feel when I stand before you, face to face . . .

When I think about the life we will enjoy in the new heaven and new earth—with the whole perfected family of God, redeemed from every nation throughout history—here's what thrills me . . .

Jesus, teach me how to live like heaven is a real place. Since you're going to make all things new (not make all new things), help me to engage with my culture and community with hope. Give me a love for all people, not just those of my tribe, club, and clique. Help me to live like no one is beyond the reach of God's grace and no one is beyond the need of God's grace—starting with me. Jesus, I long for you to return and finish making all things new. Until that day, free me to live and to love to your glory.

Day 10: Learning to Love Others as Jesus Loves Us

I have made you known to them, and will continue to make you known in order that the love you have for me may be in them and that I myself may be in them. (John 17:26)

This amazing prayer concludes with Jesus asking the Father to fill us with the same love that has been shared within the Trinity throughout eternity—a love unlike any other love the world has ever witnessed. Overwhelming, right? Earlier in the evening, the disciples were given a profound taste of this love when Jesus disrobed and washed the dirty feet of his soon-to-scatter disciples (John 13). This act of servile humility so shocked the apostle Peter that he initially refused to let Jesus serve him in this way.

John described that holy moment in this way: "Having loved his own who were in the world, he now showed them the full extent of his love" (John 13:1 NIV 1984). Little did the disciples realize that the love Jesus showed them in washing their feet was just a hint and whisper of the exponentially greater love he was about to lavish on them. Dirty feet only need a basin of water and a towel; dirty hearts require the washing that comes through the death of God's Son as God's Lamb. There is no greater love.

Right after washing their feet, Jesus charged these beloved and broken men with the New Commandment: "A new commandment I give to you, that you love one another: just as I have loved you, you also are to love one another. By this all people will know that you are my disciples, if you have love for one another" (John 13:34–35 ESV).

What then is the essence of life as a disciple of Jesus? Our lives are to be increasingly filled with the love the Father has for Jesus, and now for us as his children, and the love Jesus has for us as his disciples—a love measured by the cross and extended by grace.

Jesus, thank you for your ongoing commitment to reveal the Father to me, for I am a slow learner and quick forgetter. But as I think about Abba's love for me, here's what I treasure the most—that he . . .

When I try to imagine the love that is shared within the Trinity actually increasing in my life, it makes me want to . . .

Jesus, I need your daily mercies and fresh grace to love others as you love me. In particular, these are the relationships in which I'm struggling to love well . . .

I know that healthy relationships must work in both directions. Jesus, sometimes it's easier for me to love and serve others than to let other people love and serve me. I know this isn't a good thing. When I think about the main reasons I have a hard time letting people get real close to me or serve me, I think it's because . . .

Jesus, my obedience to the New Commandment is only going to happen and deepen as I live in the reality of that phrase, "as I have loved you." For the rest of my life, take me "further up and further in." Please answer Paul's prayer in my life: "And may you have the power to understand, as all God's people should, how wide, how long, how high, and how deep his love is. May you experience the love of Christ, though it is too great to understand fully. Then you will be made complete with all the fullness of life and power that comes from God" (Eph. 3:18–19 NLT).

10

Prayers of Confession

Acknowledging Our Needs and God's Grace

I wrote the following prayers of confession with congregational worship in mind, but I also wrote them for family and personal use. Simply change the pronouns to fit your particular context and need. I hope you will freely use them for your services of worship.

In my estimation, a good prayer of confession will accomplish two things. First and foremost, it will acknowledge the glory and grace of our God—the one to whom confession is made. Second, it will affirm the reality and depth of our need. It's critical to realize that when we confess our sins, we never inform or shock God. In fact, the Greek word for confession, *homologeo*, literally means "to say the same thing as"—that is, when we confess our sins, we are simply agreeing with what God already knows.

In fact, God knows that the condition of our hearts is far worse than we realize. I've often said that Jesus didn't just die for the 4 percent of our sins we're aware of, but for the other 96 percent as well. How freeing is that! This is also why I have made sure that along with confessing specific sins, we also confess a sufficient gospel. The better our grasp of the gospel, the more honest our confession of sin will be.

Dear heavenly Father, we enter your gates with thanksgiving and praise, because you have redeemed our lives by your mercy and grace. For so great a salvation, we worship you; and for ongoing grace, we trust you. Hear our confession, Father.

Forgive us for under-believing the gospel and over-believing our worries.

Forgive us for listening too lightly and judging too quickly.

Forgive us for wasting our disappointments on blaming and resentment.

Have mercy on us, Lord; have mercy on me. In Jesus' name we pray. Amen.

Heavenly Father, the gospel is a waterfall of everlasting grace. Before the creation of time, you loved us and chose us for yourself. In the fullness of time, you sent Jesus to be our Redeemer and righteousness. At just the right time, you revealed our need and gave us mercy and grace. We praise and adore you for so great a salvation.

We humble ourselves before you today and offer our confession.

Forgive us for minimizing the demands of your law, thus marginalizing our ongoing need for your grace. Forgive us for being quicker to whine than to worship and quicker to make excuses than offer apologies. Forgive us for holding on to grudges tightly and trusting in your promises lightly. Forgive us for giving up too soon and coming to you so late. Forgive us for living as though the gospel is just too good to be true. We make our prayer in the grace-full and loving name of Jesus. Amen.

Dear heavenly Father, we love you because you first loved us and gave Jesus as a sacrifice for our sins. We humble ourselves before you today because of your promise to complete your work in our lives. We praise you for your loving welcome, daily mercies, and sufficient grace.

Forgive us for treasuring the pleasures of the world more than the riches of grace.

Forgive us for dwelling too much on our fears and too little on your beauty.

Forgive us for rehearsing the failings of others more than the truths of the gospel.

Forgive us for being quick to whine and slow to worship.

We offer our confession in Jesus' name and for your glory. Amen.

Father of mercies and God of all comfort, our boast is in Christ and our hope is in you. Forgive us, for our sins are many. Free us, for you alone are able.

We confess our love for money. Have mercy on us, Lord.

We confess our misuse of words. Have mercy on us, Lord.

We confess putting our jobs above our relationships. Have mercy on us, Lord.

We confess making excuses quicker than we offer apologies. Have mercy on us, Lord.

We confess our pettiness, our selfishness, and our unforgiveness. Have mercy on us, Lord.

For the glory of your name, forgive and change us, in Jesus' name we pray. Amen.

Dear heavenly Father, for your joyful welcome and heart of mercy, we give you praise. For your patience and forbearance, we worship and adore you. Apart from our standing in grace, we could not stand before you. In humility and hope, we offer our confession.

Forgive us for being selfish with our money and your grace.

Forgive us for indulging our fantasies and nursing our grudges.

Forgive us for being slow to listen and quick to complain.

Forgive us for using your grace to excuse our sin and using your law to control others.

In Jesus' name and for your glory, we pray. Amen.

God of all hope and Father of mercies, we come boldly to the throne of grace today, trusting in Christ's righteousness and confessing our sins.

Forgive us for lingering in our bad attitudes.

Forgive us for grumbling over petty things.

Forgive us for writing people off too easily.

Forgive us for not following through on our promises.

Forgive us for too easily neglecting time with you.

Our priorities, schedules, and busyness rebuke us, Lord. We humble ourselves and offer our prayer in Jesus' name. Amen.

Heavenly Father, for your steadfast love, we bless you. For your patience and kindness, we praise you. For your daily mercies, we trust you.

Forgive our sins, for they are real and many.

We confess loving relief from our pain more than change in our hearts.

We confess thinking too often of ourselves and too seldom of you.

We confess that it's easier to be cynical than hopeful.

We confess under-trusting the gospel and over-honoring our fears.

We confess seeking our fiefdoms first and your kingdom last.

Have mercy on us, Lord; have mercy on me.

In Jesus' name and for his glory, we offer our prayer and ask for forgiveness. Amen.

Dear heavenly Father, we come boldly to your throne of grace today—thankful it is an occupied throne and rejoicing that it is a throne of grace.

We confess that we often take you and your good gifts for granted. Forgive us for indulging a spirit of entitlement, presumption, and ingratitude.

We confess that we take ourselves too seriously. Forgive us for being too easily offended, too easily irritated, and too easily angered.

We confess that we don't take the needs of others seriously enough. Forgive us for being too preoccupied to notice, too busy to engage, and too selfish to serve.

Have mercy on us, Lord; have mercy on me. In Jesus' name, we pray. Amen.

Heavenly Father, for our life in Christ and citizenship in heaven, we praise and worship you. For your promise of daily mercies and sufficient grace, we trust you. By your grace and for your glory . . .

Forgive us for heeding the opinions of others more than the declarations of the gospel.

Forgive us for being quicker to judge hearts than wash feet.

Forgive us for keeping our burdens, heartaches, and struggles from our friends.

Forgive us for trying to justify our busyness, grumpiness, and emptiness.

We turn once again to you, Father, in humble dependence and expectant faith. In Jesus' loving name, we trust and pray. Amen.

Dear heavenly Father, when we were dead in our sins and trespasses, you raised us to new life in Christ. We praise you for so great a salvation, so glorious a hope, and so firm a standing in grace. We humble ourselves before you today, in gratitude and repentance.

Forgive us for our attitudes that deny your grace.

Forgive us for our words that violate peace.

Forgive us for our habits that sabotage beauty.

Forgive us for our passivity that accepts the unacceptable.

Forgive us for our greed that fuels our idolatry.
Forgive us for our pettiness that robs people we love.
Forgive us for our unbelief that robs you of glory.
Have mercy on us, Lord; have mercy on me. In Jesus' strong and loving name. Amen.

Holy and loving Father, it's because you declared us righteous in Christ that we declare ourselves in need of your grace. You abound in mercy, overflow with compassion, and remain steadfast in your love. We humbly confess our sins of thought, word, and deed.

Father, for entertaining thoughts of lust and greed, envy and revenge, forgive us and cleanse us. Father, for using our words vainly, painfully, and foolishly, forgive and change us. Father, for doing things that misrepresent you and contradict the gospel, forgive and cleanse us. Father, for breaking confidences and sharing gossip, forgive and change us. We offer our prayer in Jesus' name and for his glory. Amen.

Father of mercies and God of all comfort, we praise and bless you for the great salvation you have freely given us in the gospel. We find great peace in the finished work of Jesus. We find great joy in the ongoing work of your Spirit. We find great hope in the future blessings of heaven. As your beloved daughters and sons, we confess our sins, longing for the day we will be made perfect in love.

Forgive us for being more irritable than charitable; quicker to rush to judgment than to run into your presence; and far more inclined to pout than to pray. Forgive us for demanding too much of others and expecting too little from you.

Forgive us for doubting that you really love us as much as you say you do. Forgive us and free us, in Jesus' name, we humbly pray. Amen.

Dear heavenly Father, we praise you for being the God from whom all blessings flow; the Judge who declared us righteous in Christ; and the Lord now working in all things for our good. In response to such incredible grace and love, we gladly take the low place of humility and confession.

Forgive us for caring more about people's approval than cherishing your acceptance.

Forgive us for being quick to judge others and slow to forgive them.

Forgive us for scheduling ourselves into exhaustion and bad attitudes.

Father, teach us how to live and love at the pace of grace.

In Christ's name, we confess our sins and offer our prayer. Amen.

Dear heavenly Father, we praise you for your daily mercies and steadfast love. We bless you for your providential care and everlasting kindness. We worship you for the forgiveness of our sins and the gift of Christ's righteousness. Hear our confession and grant us your grace, Lord.

Forgive us for living too busy, too noisy, and too cluttered of lives.

Forgive us for being quicker to react in anger than repent in humility.

Forgive us for maximizing our disappointments and minimizing your goodness.

Forgive us for living more by fear than by faith—for over-believing our culture and under-trusting your promises. Have mercy on us, Lord; have mercy on me, for Christ's sake and your glory. Amen.

Dear heavenly Father, you are heavenly, because you inhabit eternity and there is no father like you. We dare call you Father, for you have justified us in Christ and adopted us to be your beloved children. We praise, bless, and worship you for our standing in grace and assurance of your love. Even as we confess your greatness and goodness, we confess *our* weakness and our neediness.

We confess our sins of thought, word, and deed. For thinking wrongly and too seldom of you, and too often and too selfishly of ourselves, have mercy on us, O Lord. For withholding words of life and speaking words that harm, forgive us, O Lord. For doing things that contradict your grace and for not doing the things you command, have mercy on us, O Lord—have mercy on me. Forgive us, and grant us your grace. We humbly pray, in Jesus' name. Amen.

Heavenly Father, most loving Jesus, ever-present Holy Spirit, we come into your presence today with joyful hearts and deep gratitude, for we are no longer under the law but are standing in grace. We are no longer condemned for our sins but are righteous in Christ. We are no longer slaves who fear but are children who trust. Because this gospel is true, we own our brokenness and our weakness before you.

For the ways we loved poorly this week, forgive and cleanse us.

262

For being more offended by the sins of others than our own, forgive and cleanse us.

For coveting a different story, home, or spouse, forgive and cleanse us.

For acting as though Jesus isn't enough, grace isn't sufficient, and you aren't really faithful, forgive and cleanse us. In Jesus' name and for his glory, we make our prayer. Amen.

Great and gracious Father, we declare that your love for us is beyond measure and your goodness to us is beyond question. Jesus' empty tomb fuels our humility and intensifies our joy today. We turn once again to you for the manna of grace, the renewing of our hearts, and the regaining of perspective.

Forgive us for not loving you as you deserve to be loved; for not trusting you as your faithfulness commends; and for not obeying you as the gospel commands. Forgive us for living lives marked more by busyness than kindness. Forgive us for fueling resentment rather than forgiving offenses. Forgive us for pampering ourselves into mediocrity while ignoring the poor. We offer our confession, trusting in Jesus' finished work and your promise of grace. Amen.

Dear heavenly Father, our sins are too heavy to carry, too real to hide, and too deep to undo. We praise you for your welcoming heart, daily mercies, and gospel riches.

Forgive what our lips struggle to name, what our hearts can no longer hide, and what our hands cannot change. Set us free from the lingering shame from our past; meet us in the present reality of our need; and grant us hope in the future you have secured.

We trust in the finished work of your Son and the ongoing work of your Spirit. In Jesus' name we make our prayer. Amen.

Dear heavenly Father, we come humbly into your welcoming presence today, thankful for your grace, for our sins are real and many.

We confess how easily we ignore your pursuit of us and your will for us.

We confess the pain, worry, and sorrow we have caused those we love.

We confess holding on to grudges tighter than we hold on to your promises.

We confess thinking about how to get more rather than give more.

We confess downplaying our sin and marginalizing your grace.

We confess being selective in our obedience and casual with our repentance.

Lord, have mercy and forgive us, through Jesus Christ, our Savior and Lord. Amen.

Heavenly Father, you made us for your glory, redeemed us by your Son, and sealed us with your Spirit. We praise, bless, and adore you. By the gospel, we have been set free from the fear of judgment and death. By your grace, we now love and revere you.

We joyfully confess Jesus as our righteousness, and we humbly confess our sins as our foolishness.

Forgive us for sinning against you in thought, word, and deed. Forgive us for living for the approval of men more than for the glory of your name. Forgive us for ignoring the convicting work of your Spirit and for heeding the seductive voice of our lusts. Forgive us and free us from our ingratitude, discontent, and demandingness. In Jesus' name, we humbly offer our prayer. Amen.

Dear heavenly Father, for calling us to life in Christ, sealing us with your Spirit, and making us your beloved children, we love and adore you. Because the gospel is true, our standing in grace is irreversible; the riches of our inheritance are incomparable; the glories of our future are inconceivable. In gratitude and humility, we confess our sins to you.

We grieve the many expressions of our self-centeredness.

Forgive us for the ease with which we complain and grumble.

Forgive us for overspending on ourselves and under-sharing with others.

Forgive us for being generous with criticism and miserly with forgiveness.

Forgive us for crying "victim" more readily than we cry "Abba."

Forgive us for preferring control over contrition.

Have mercy on us, Lord; have mercy on me. In Jesus' name, we make our prayer. Amen.

Dear heavenly Father, because the work of the cross is complete and the tomb of Jesus is empty, we don't have to pretend about our true condition or feign heart contrition. Hear our confession, grant us grace, and deepen our repentance.

For the ways this past week we lived more out of fear and pride than faith and humility, forgive us, Father. For giving the approval of people more power over our hearts than the truth of the gospel, forgive us, Father. For using anger to get our way, flattery to manipulate others, and shame to control our children, forgive us, Father. For doubting your love, avoiding your grace, and withholding your mercy, forgive us, Father. We pray with humble and grateful hearts, in Jesus' name. Amen.

Dear heavenly Father, we come boldly to your throne of grace today because Jesus went gladly to the cross of Calvary for us. We praise, bless, and worship you for so great a salvation and so loving a Savior. Even as we confess Christ today, so we also confess our sins and rebellion.

Forgive us for attitudes and actions that sabotage beauty and intimacy.

Forgive us for speaking words that have labeled, shamed, and harmed others.

Forgive us for covering our sins while exposing the sins of others.

Forgive us for wasting our pain in self-pity and our fears on worry.

Forgive us for spending more time making a name for ourselves than relishing the new names you've given us: "Forgiven, Beloved, Mine."

We offer our prayers, humbly and gratefully, in Jesus' name. Amen.

Dear heavenly Father, our greatest freedom is found in Christ, and our most treasured liberties come from the gospel. We praise you for your great love lavished on us in Jesus. It is your kindness that leads us to repentance today.

Forgive us for being more preoccupied with our temporary fiefdoms than engaged with your eternal kingdom. Forgive us for hoarding our time, talent, and treasure and for living more like selfish owners than grateful stewards. Forgive us for being quicker to judge than to forgive, quicker to make excuses than offer apologies, and quicker to worry than to pray. Forgive us for not believing you are as good and gracious as your Word and gospel declare. In Jesus' name we humble ourselves and offer our prayer. Amen.

Dear heavenly Father, if we say that we have no sin, then we deceive ourselves, and the truth is not in us; so we humbly confess our sins today. We confess that we have sinned against you in our thoughts, by our words, and with our choices. Father, we have not loved you as you deserve—with all of our heart, soul, mind, and strength. We have set up idols in our hearts and have nurtured those idols. Forgive us. Free us. Deepen our sorrow for the wrong we have done and the good that we have left undone. Our comfort is found in knowing that you are full of compassion and daily mercies, slow to anger and abounding in grace. We trust boldly in Christ—our righteousness and only hope. In Jesus' name we pray. Amen.

Dear heavenly Father, we come into your presence this morning only because your mercies are new every morning. We stand before you in this place only because we stand firmly in your grace. We dare call you Abba Father only because you have made us your beloved sons and daughters. We freely confess our sins to you only because you fully gave Jesus for us.

For the ways we loved poorly this past week—in our families, at our vocations, and among our neighbors, forgive us. From the foolish idols to which we cling, the broken cisterns from which we drink, and the false lovers to which we turn, free us. For not believing Jesus is enough and your grace is sufficient, and for not trusting you to be really sovereign and really good, have mercy on us. Our hope rests alone in Jesus' finished work and your steadfast love. Amen.

Most holy and merciful Father, through the freedom of the gospel, we confess our sins to you today. We haven't loved you with our whole heart and mind and strength.

We haven't loved one another as Jesus loves us. We haven't loved our neighbors as ourselves. We have condemned the sins of others but have ignored our own.

We have thought too highly or too lowly of ourselves, instead of believing what you say is true of us in Christ. We have chosen the values of the world over the treasures of Christ. Forgive us, we pray, most merciful Father, and free us from our sin. Renew in us the grace of Jesus. In the power of your Holy Spirit and in Christ's name we make our prayer. Amen.

Dear heavenly Father, with our eyes fixed on Jesus—the Author and Perfecter of our faith—we ask you to forgive our sins. Forgive us for hurting people we love by our impatience and irritation and by our lack of listening and our unkept promises.

Forgive us for thinking of ourselves more proudly than we ought and thinking of others less compassionately than they deserve. Forgive us for giving more power to what others say about us in public than what you say about us in heaven. Forgive us for being too busy to behold your beauty in your Word, meditate on your mercies in Christ, and hear you sing to us in the gospel. Have mercy on us, Lord; have mercy on me. Our hope is built on nothing less, nothing more, and nothing other than Jesus' blood and righteousness. In Jesus' name we make our prayer. Amen.

Dear heavenly Father, for seeking us and finding us, we praise and bless you. For declaring us righteous in Christ and adopting us as your children, we worship and adore you. It is because of this great salvation that we freely confess our sins to you today.

Forgive us for choosing our pride and selfishness over your glory and honor.

Forgive us for minimizing your commands and marginalizing your grace.

Forgive us for giving people power over our hearts they do not deserve.

Forgive us for taking on more debt and showing little concern for the poor.

Forgive us for huddling with friends while we ignore the friendless.

Have mercy on us, Lord; have mercy on me. In Jesus' name we pray. Amen.

Dear heavenly Father, you alone are worthy of our mind's attention, our heart's affection, and our soul's adoration. There is no God as merciful and mighty as you; no God more holy and welcoming, powerful and present, compassionate and caring as you.

Because the gospel is true, we fear you with deep affection and love you with expectant hope. Hear our confession.

We grieve the ways we loved poorly this past week. We were often too busy to listen, too hasty in our judgments, and too preoccupied to care. We grieve the ways we blamed others for our discontent, the ways we didn't humble ourselves before you, the ways we didn't avail ourselves of your grace. Father, forgive us of our sins. Our hope is built on nothing more, nothing less, and nothing other than Jesus' blood and righteousness. In Christ's name we pray. Amen.

Most gracious God and loving Father, we praise and bless you for the great salvation you have freely given us in the gospel. We find great peace in the finished work of Jesus. We find great joy in the ongoing work of your Spirit. We find great hope in the future blessings of heaven. As your beloved daughters and sons, we confess our sins, longing for the day we will be made perfect in love.

Forgive us for being more irritable than charitable and more inclined to fret than to pray. Forgive us for demanding too much of others and expecting too little from you. Forgive us for choosing the power of our anger over the risk of forgiving. Forgive us for doubting that you love us as much as you say you do. Forgive us and free us, in Jesus' name, we humbly pray. Amen.

Almighty and merciful God, for your welcome, we bless you; for your kindness, we praise you; and for your gospel, we worship you. We humble ourselves before you today, in gratitude and repentance.

Forgive us for our attitudes that contradict grace.

Forgive us for our words that violate peace.

Forgive us for our habits that sabotage beauty.

Forgive us for our passivity that accepts the unacceptable.

Forgive us for our greed that fuels our idolatry.

Forgive us for our pettiness that robs people we love.

Forgive us for our unbelief that robs you of glory.

Have mercy on us, Lord; have mercy on me. In Jesus' grace-full name. Amen.

Dear heavenly Father—you are the God from whom all mercy flows, by whom all grace is given, and for whom all things exist. We acknowledge we have more than sufficient reasons to overflow with gratitude and thanksgiving. For the free gift of salvation in Jesus, we adore you. For the secure gift of citizenship in heaven, we worship you. For the multiplied gifts of providence and relationships, we bless you.

Yet too easily we complain, murmur, and grumble. We grieve our attitudes of presumption, entitlement, and selfishness. Have mercy on us, Lord; have mercy on me.

We mourn our habits of prayerlessness, criticism, and gossip. By grace, we repent and ask you to forgive and change us, Father. In Jesus' name and for his glory we pray. Amen.

Dear heavenly Father, we come boldly to your throne of grace today, trusting in the gift of Christ's righteousness and owning the depth of our need. It is your provision and not our promises in which we trust. Your welcoming heart is our refuge, your unlimited patience is our shelter, and your steadfast love is our home.

Forgive our failures to love well—for being too busy to engage, too proud to be vulnerable, and too selfish to care. Forgive our failure to seek you—for letting almost anything crowd you out, for ignoring your desire to fellowship with us, and for trying to do life in our own strength. Have mercy on us, Lord; have mercy on me. In Christ's merciful and mighty name we pray. Amen.

Most holy and gracious Father, for your irrepressible love, we adore you; for your unlimited patience, we bless you; for your inexhaustible kindness we worship you. Because you have forgiven us and declared us to be righteous in Christ, we freely own our brokenness and confess our sins.

Father, for misusing our time, talents, and treasure, forgive us. For indulging anger, irritation, and resentment, have mercy on us, Lord. From being quicker to judge than listen; more prone to hoard than to share; and more likely to complain than to pray, change us, Lord. We humbly offer our prayer in Jesus' great and gracious name. Amen.

Dear heavenly Father, for calling us to life in Christ, sealing us forever by your Spirit, and making us your beloved sons and daughters, we love and adore you. Our standing in grace is irreversible, the riches of our inheritance are incomparable, and the glories of our future are inconceivable. How can we not bow in humility, gratitude, and repentance before you?

Forgive the many expressions of our selfishness and pettiness—have mercy on us, Lord. For the ease with which we complain and grumble, whine and resent—have mercy on us, Lord. For our overspending and under-sharing—have mercy on us, Lord. For being generous with criticism and miserly with forgiveness—have mercy on us, Lord. Please, Lord, have mercy on us and have mercy on me. In Jesus' name and for his glory, we pray. Amen.

Holy and loving Father, it's because you have declared us to be eternally righteous in Christ that we declare ourselves to be presently in need of your grace. What a kindhearted God you are—abounding in mercy, rich in compassion, and steadfast in love.

We confess our sins of thought, word, and deed. Father, for entertaining thoughts of lust and greed, envy and revenge, fantasy and foolishness, forgive us and cleanse us. For using our words to manipulate, rather than to minister; to whine, rather than to worship; and to gossip, rather than to pray, forgive and cleanse us. Father, for doing things that sabotage grace and not doing things that promote your glory, forgive and cleanse us. We humbly offer our prayer in Jesus' name. Amen.

O great and gracious God, your love for us in Jesus is beyond measure, and your goodness to us in life is beyond question. Your sovereign rule over all things fuels our humility and intensifies our joy. We turn once again to you for the manna of grace, the renewing of our hearts, and the regaining of perspective.

Forgive us for not loving you as you deserve to be loved; for not trusting you as your faithfulness commends; and for not obeying you as the gospel commands. Forgive us for living lives marked more by busyness than kindness, for nursing grudges rather than forgiving offenses, and for thinking too highly and too often of ourselves. We offer our confession by the convicting work of your Spirit and in the great hope of the gospel. In Jesus' name we pray. Amen.

Heavenly Father, we come before you today not groveling but through grace; not in penitent fear but in repentant faith; not to make promises but trusting in your promises.

Our hope is built on nothing less, nothing more, and nothing other than Jesus' finished work on our behalf and his righteousness that you have made ours. Because you have raised us up in Christ, we now humble ourselves before you.

We confess the ways we have loved poorly this week: as spouses and parents, friends and neighbors. We confess the ways we have been proud this week: in our attempts to live autonomous lives, believing the lie of self-sufficiency and giving ourselves to performance-based acceptability. We confess the ways we have avoided Jesus this week: by treasuring other things more than you and your kingdom and by refusing to humble ourselves that we might receive grace. Have mercy on me, Lord. In Jesus' name we pray. Amen.

Heavenly Father, for your sovereign rule over all things, we worship you. Lord Jesus, for your steadfast love and constant advocacy, we adore you. Holy Spirit, for your ongoing work in our hearts to make us like Jesus, we praise you. There is no God like you. There is no God but you. Our cry is for mercy, and our hope is in the gospel of your grace.

You are so patient with us, but we have been impatient with others—especially members of our families. Forgive us and free us. You are so generous with us, but we have been selfish with our money, time, and forgiveness. Forgive us and free us. You overlook so much in our lives, but we get irritated easily and notice others' mistakes and failures too often. Forgive us and free us. In Jesus' name and for his glory we pray. Amen.

A Prayer of Confession for Thanksgiving Week

Dear heavenly Father, at the beginning of this Thanksgiving week, our hearts are filled with praise as we consider the many good gifts you have given us.

We praise you for our salvation—so rich and free in Christ. We praise you for our families and friends—for the gift of relationships. We praise you for our homes and jobs, for our food and clothing. We praise you for many other creature comforts and joys we have in life, all traceable to your heart and hand.

Father, we take none of these blessings for granted. Indeed, it's your kindness that leads us to repentance today. Forgive our grumbling and complaining, for you have been so good to us. Forgive our aggravation and irritability, for you are so patient with us. Forgive our critical and judgmental attitudes, for you are so merciful towards us. We offer our confession and make our prayer in Jesus' name. Amen.

Prayers of Confession for Advent

Dear heavenly Father, as we begin the season of Advent, we rejoice in the gift of your Son, Jesus—Immanuel, God with us and God for us. Even as we trust in his finished work, we long for the fullness of Jesus' kingdom. Until that day . . .

Grant us power to grow in the love of Christ. For we are weak and foolishly prone to look to people, places, and things to fill us up. Grant us grace to mature in the likeness of Jesus. For we are broken, and we cannot change our hearts, left to our own resources. Grant us joy in living to the praise of your glory. For we are deceived, and we spend too much energy living for comfort and the approval of people. Have mercy on us, O Lord; have mercy on me. In Jesus' loving and trustworthy name we pray. Amen.

Almighty and most merciful Father, we begin the season of Advent with the brokenness of the world in our eyes, the cries of our neighbors in our ears, and the reality of our sin in our hearts. Thus, we look to Jesus—the Author and Perfecter of our faith, sacrifice and priest of our salvation, Lord and restorer of all things. By your grace and for your glory, forgive our sins and renew our hearts. Help us to move through a worldly holiday of excess into a worshipful Advent and Christmas. Help us to love as you love us, forgive as we've been forgiven, and freely give as we have freely received. In Jesus' name we pray. Amen.

Dear heavenly Father, with the angels we shout loud praises over the birth of Jesus; with the shepherds, we respond with joy for the gift of a Savior; with Mary, we treasure and ponder this good news in our hearts. You have been faithful to fulfill ancient prophecies and your covenant promises. Because of Jesus' finished work, we now live in your perpetual favor, and because of the Spirit's ongoing work, we now humble ourselves before you.

We confess our sins to you. Forgive us for attitudes and actions that misrepresent you, contradict your grace, and sabotage love. Forgive us for speaking words that brought harm and shame and for withholding words that bring healing and hope. Forgive us for spending so much time and energy on ourselves and trifles and so little time with you and on the things that matter the most. We offer our prayer humbly in Jesus' name. Amen.

A Prayer of Confession for Palm Sunday

Father of mercies and God of all hope, we come before you this Palm Sunday with the faith and gratitude of children. Thank you for sending Jesus to us and for us. We sing the hosannas of those who need your mercy and cling to your grace.

As your beloved daughters and sons, we confess our sins, longing for the day we will be made perfect in love. Forgive us for being quicker to criticize others than grieve our own sins. Forgive us for remembering the ways people hurt us better than we remember the gospel that saved us. Forgive us for making more time for the things we crave than for the God we love. During this Passion Week, humble us and convict us, Father. Encourage us and gladden us as we survey the wondrous cross of our Lord. We offer our confession and prayer in Jesus' loving name. Amen.

A Prayer of Confession for Easter Sunday

Dear heavenly Father, on this Easter Sunday, our hearts burst with joy and our lips declare your praise! Jesus has risen; he has risen indeed! We praise, bless, and adore you for so great a salvation and so liberating a hope.

As you have freely given Jesus for us, so we freely confess our need of him today. Forgive what our lips struggle to voice, what our hearts can no longer deny, and what our hands cannot undo. We have sinned in our thoughts, with our words, and by our deeds. We haven't loved each other as Jesus loves us. We haven't served our neighbors as ourselves. We haven't taken the gospel to the nations as you command. Have mercy on us, Father; have mercy on me. In Jesus' great and gracious name we pray. Amen.

A Prayer of Confession for the New Year

Dear heavenly Father, we praise you for your constant care and great faithfulness in this past year. Your mercies were new every morning, your steadfast love sustained and encouraged us, and your grace was sufficient when our days grew long and hard. As we prepare to begin the new year together, we now humble ourselves before you. We will trust not in our new resolutions but in your Son's great redemption.

We confess our need of the gospel for all of our relationships. Help us to love others in the upcoming year as Jesus loves us. We confess we will need your Spirit for challenges unseen. Keep us free from the myth of self-sufficiency and from posing and pretending. We confess how much we need your grace to change us, for we cannot change ourselves. Free us to boast in our weaknesses by boasting more fully in our Savior. We make our prayer humbly and gladly in Jesus' name. Amen.

11

Prayers for the Season of Advent

A Prayer for the First Sunday of Advent

You who bring good news to Jerusalem, lift up your voice with a shout, lift it up, do not be afraid; say to the towns of Judah, "Here is your God!" See, the Sovereign LORD comes with power, and he rules with a mighty arm. See, his reward is with him, and his recompense accompanies him. He tends his flock like a shepherd: He gathers the lambs in his arms and carries them close to his heart; he gently leads those that have young. (Isa. 40:9–11)

Dear heavenly Father, on this first Sunday of Advent, we praise and bless you for a season in which we get to celebrate your great faithfulness and your immeasurable generosity. You have sent Jesus to us, and you have given Jesus for us.

Promises you make are *always* promises you keep, and we are so very grateful.

Enflame our hearts, Father. Help us to engage with the story of Jesus' birth with childlike wonder and renewed hope. Bring familiar Scriptures alive in fresh and transforming ways. Reshape how we do Christmas this year by the truth and grace of the gospel.

I'm so encouraged by Isaiah's picture of your "Advent arms." The promise of the Messiah carries with it the promise of the embrace we all need but barely believe. In Jesus, you come near to us as the sovereign Lord, with your sleeves rolled up as the great ruler. Your arm rules over all history and heartaches, over all kings and crises. Nothing and no one can alter, subvert, or change the story you are telling in Jesus and the kingdom you are advancing through Jesus.

In Jesus, you come near to us as the compassionate Shepherd, gathering and carrying your lambs in your arms. This image and hope are settling and liberating. To be tended as a helpless lamb, to be held close to your heart, to be gently led—what more could we possibly desire?

These aren't mere metaphors, Father, for metaphors cannot save us, only inspire us. You really are this involved in our lives, and you really are this grace-full. The coming of Jesus puts all nations on notice: there is only one true King, and he is Jesus. And the coming of Jesus puts us, your people, facedown in adoring love. Over the next several weeks, show us yet again how Jesus is a most wonderful, merciful Savior— Immanuel, the God who is very much with us and so very for us. We pray with Advent longings in Jesus' matchless and merciful name. Amen.

A Prayer for Orienting Our Hearts during Advent

Concerning this salvation, the prophets, who spoke of the grace that was to come to you, searched intently and with the greatest care, trying to find out the time and circumstances to which the Spirit of Christ in them was pointing when he predicted the sufferings of the Messiah and the glories that would follow. It was revealed to them that they were not serving themselves but you, when they spoke of the things that have now been told you by those who have preached the gospel to you by the Holy Spirit sent from heaven. Even angels long to look into these things. (1 Pet. 1:10–12)

Dear Lord Jesus, Advent has just begun, and I am praying it will be a season marked more by hush than rush. If I'm going to be busy with anything, may it be with quieting my heart, focusing my gaze, and setting my affection on things above—especially *on you*—the Author and Perfecter of my faith; the source and Lord of my salvation; the fountain and fullness of all grace.

Grant me the same intensity and care the prophets invested in searching out the promises of your coming. May old Scriptures come alive in profoundly new ways during this Advent season. Jesus, show me more of yourself throughout the Bible. Humble and gladden my heart with the realization that the prophets were serving me—even me—when they spoke of your coming, your sufferings, and the glories that would follow.

And if angels were on tiptoes with joy as they pondered your coming, so renew my awe and joy as well. I will never cease giving you thanks for those you sent into my life to preach the gospel to me by the power of the Holy Spirit. I will ever praise and worship you, Lord Jesus, for granting me the knowledge of my need and a love for yourself. Apart from the new birth, I would forever be a prisoner to my old life. O come, O come, Immanuel, and bring even greater freedom to my heart and glory to yourself. I pray, in the wonders of your love and the trustworthiness of your name. Amen.

A Prayer for Filling Our Hearts with Jesus, the Lord of Advent

For to us a child is born, to us a son is given, and the government will be on his shoulders. And he will be called Wonderful Counselor, Mighty God, Everlasting Father, Prince of Peace. Of the greatness of his government and peace there will be no end. He will reign on David's throne and over his kingdom, establishing and upholding it with justice and righteousness from that time on and forever. The zeal of the LORD Almighty will accomplish this. (Isa. 9:6–7)

Dear Lord Jesus, knowing that it's possible to "do Christmas" and miss Advent, today I want to fill my heart as full as possible with you. You are the One who has come and is coming again. Isaiah's words fuel my worship and shrink my worries. Hallelujah, so many times over!

Knowing the government of the whole world already rests on your shoulders fills me with a joy second only to knowing your shoulders fully bore the sin of the world, including mine. As this day begins, I gladly surrender to your reign of grace.

You are Wonderful Counselor—our righteousness, holiness, and redemption (1 Cor. 1:30). In you are hidden all the treasures of wisdom and knowledge (Col. 2:3). I look to you for knowledge of great mysteries but also for wisdom about handling fresh disappointments, old hurts, and unfulfilled longings. You care so tenderly for your lambs.

You are Mighty God, Creator and sustainer of the entire universe—the One for whom all things have been made and in whom all things are being summed up (see Eph. 1:10 NASB).

Lord Jesus, to see you is to see the Father and to know you is to know the Father; in this sense you are Everlasting Father. We would never be able to cry, "Abba Father," if you had not first cried, "Father, into your hands I commit my spirit" (Luke 23:46).

Indeed, you paid the price of our peace and so deserve the title Prince of Peace. Thank you for the wonder of your reconciling grace and power. Thank you for destroying hostilities and for securing the day of no more broken relationships, racism, or war of any kind. I long for the fullness of your peace, in my heart and in our world.

For your broad shoulders, big heart, and coming kingdom, I honor, praise and adore you, O blessed Messiah and Redeemer, Jesus. In your matchless and merciful name I pray. Amen.

An Advent Prayer about Joy in the Presence of Jesus

At that time Mary got ready and hurried to a town in the hill country of Judea, where she entered Zechariah's home and greeted Elizabeth. When Elizabeth heard Mary's greeting, the baby leaped in her womb, and Elizabeth was filled with the Holy Spirit. In a loud voice she exclaimed: "Blessed are you among women, and blessed is the child you will bear! But why am I so favored, that the mother of my Lord should come to me? As soon as the sound of your greeting reached my ears, the baby in my womb leaped for joy. Blessed is she who has believed that the Lord would fulfill his promises to her!" (Luke 1:39–45)

Dear Lord Jesus, too easily have I raced by this part of your nativity story—but what encouragement it brings me today. The image of John the Baptist leaping for joy in Elizabeth's womb—just because he was in close proximity to you while you were in Mary's womb—reminds me of another part of your story, thirty-three years later. On the night of your betrayal and arrest, just before going to the cross, you asked the Father to grant us "the fullness of your joy" (see John 17:13). My only response to that is thank you, thank you, thank you, and let it be to me according to your prayer.

I am so grateful to know that nothing has to change in my world and nobody has to be any different for this prayer to be answered. I don't need a different story, less suffering, or more guarantees; I don't have to have a different personality, cooler church, or better health; I don't need to live in a different era or even in a different neighborhood. The joy you give transcends (and transforms) tears, circumstances, and heartaches.

Jesus, throughout Advent, I want to give you more worship than whining and more gratitude than grumbling. Just knowing you, or rather being known and loved by you, makes me a man of incalculable riches. For "I am always with you; you hold me by my right hand. You guide me with your counsel, and afterward you will take me into glory. Whom do I have in heaven but you? And earth has nothing I desire besides you. My flesh and my heart may fail, but [you] are the strength of my heart and my portion forever" (Ps.

73:23–26, emphasis added). I pray in your compassionate and trustworthy name. Amen.

An Advent Prayer about Waiting and Repenting of Impatience

Dear brothers and sisters, be patient as you wait for the Lord's return. Consider the farmers who patiently wait for the rains in the fall and in the spring. They eagerly look for the valuable harvest to ripen. You, too, must be patient. Take courage, for the coming of the Lord is near. (James 5:7–8 NLT)

The Lord is not slow in keeping his promise, as some understand slowness. (2 Pet. 3:9)

Therefore the Lord waits to be gracious to you, and therefore he exalts himself to show mercy to you. For the Lord is a God of justice; blessed are all those who wait for him. (Isa. 30:18 ESV)

Dear heavenly Father, the Advent theme of waiting confronts me in every context of life. Why am I in such a hurry? Why the rush? At just the right time, you sent Jesus. Not a day too early, not a day too late. But as for me, cars in front of me cannot move fast enough; FedEx, UPS, and mail can't get to my house quick enough; restaurants can't bring food to my table soon enough; and Wi-Fi cannot be speedy enough.

Worse is how my impatience plays out in relationships. I finish people's sentences; I fidget instead of linger; I launch instead of listen. Instead of being a nonanxious presence, I often give the impression, "Speak quick, 'cause I'm moving on."

Father, I repent. Have mercy on my busy, cluttered, in-too-much-of-a-hurry self. According to you, the only thing that counts is faith expressing itself in love (Gal. 5:6), not meeting deadlines with time left over. People are forever; stuff is for the ash heap.

Father, thank you for not being in a hurry; thank you for waiting to be gracious to us; thank you for not being slow about your promises. Thank you for being patient with my impatience. I lament my busyness and repent of my hurriedness. Help me recalibrate so that I might live and love at the pace of grace. I want to be the farmer who waits patiently for the harvest—the harvest guaranteed by the life, death, and resurrection of Jesus.

I won't make promises I cannot keep, but I simply collapse on Christ as this day begins. For sufficient grace, I give you praise. In Jesus' merciful and mighty name I pray. Amen.

An Advent Prayer about Bringing Our Fears to Jesus

And there were shepherds living out in the fields nearby, keeping watch over their flocks at night. An angel of the Lord appeared to them, and the glory of the Lord shone around them, and they were terrified. But the angel said to them, "Do not be afraid. I bring you good news that will cause great joy for all the people. Today in the town of David a Savior has been born to you; he is the Messiah, the Lord. This will be a sign to you: You will find a baby wrapped in cloths and lying in a manger." (Luke 2:8–12)

Dear Lord Jesus, like bookends of grace, the heart-settling command "Do not be afraid" accompanies your birth and resurrection (Luke 2:10; Matt. 28:5). Ever since our first parents sinned, fear and hiding have been part and parcel of life, and I've helped keep the family tradition alive. At times, fear has more power over my life than your love does, and though I already know myself to be clothed in your righteousness, I still reach into my closet for fig leaves.

I join shepherds in hurrying to come to you, Jesus, for you alone bring the Good News of great joy for which my heart longs every day. You alone can charm my fears and set this prisoner more fully free.

Because the gospel is true, I'll tell you what you already know. My fears aren't all that noble. I'm not really afraid of angelic hosts, and I'm not afraid to die. I'm not even afraid of facing the final judgment, for your cross was my Judgment Day. You've exhausted God's judgment against all my sins—past, present, and future. Hallelujah!

So for what fears do I need to obey the command "Do not be afraid"? I'll start with "the fear of man." At times, some people's praise and disdain have more in-the-moment power over my heart than the gospel does. It hurts to say it, but it's true.

Then there's the fear of redundancy—the fear of disappearing into a cloud of not mattering anymore. Jesus, even as I acknowledge this fear, I praise you for your noncondemning gaze. It's not easy to confess such weakness. May the joy of being used by you never supersede the much greater joy of being known and loved by you.

Jesus, I have other fears which also need "gospel charming." I bring these to you today with joy, for though you were once a baby wrapped in cloths and lying in a manger, now you're a Savior outside an empty tomb. Thank you, thank you, thank you. I pray in your loving and liberating name. Amen.

An Advent Prayer about Abiding
in God's Full and Permanent Favor

Suddenly a great company of the heavenly host appeared with the angel, praising God and saying, "Glory to God in the highest heaven, and on earth peace to those on whom his favor rests." (Luke 2:13–14)

Dear heavenly Father, there's no way to calculate the riches of this declaration. It's more than we could ever hope or imagine, yet that for which we deeply long. You are at peace with us. We are your beloved children, upon whom your full and permanent favor rests. All of this is true because the gospel is true.

Father, if unredeemed angels were in awe of such good news, how much more should we be staggered and astonished, humbled and grateful, liberated and transformed? By your Holy Spirit, enflame our hearts, stir our affections, and restore to us the joy of so great a salvation.

We invest much of our lives in seeking favor—wanting to be wanted, longing to be celebrated, and seeking to be acceptable. We look to spouses and kids, education and exercise, vocations and vacations—even to spiritual disciplines and ministry—to give us what you alone give us so freely and fully in Jesus.

And what a paradox, Father: the more we come alive to the riches of the gospel, the less we obsess about our own lives. We won't end up thinking more of ourselves or less of ourselves. We just think of ourselves less often. How liberating!

Lord Jesus, may this old host of angels drive us into new worship of you this Advent season. O come, let us adore you, indeed, for you have lived and died in our place—now raised for our justification, you will return for our glorification. Hallelujah, what a Savior! Hallelujah, what a salvation! We pray in your holy and loving name. Amen.

A Prayer for the Second Sunday of Advent about the Day of No More Harm

The wolf will live with the lamb, the leopard will lie down with the goat, the calf and the lion and the yearling together; and a little child will lead them. The cow will feed with the bear, their young will lie down together, and the lion will eat straw like the ox. The infant will play near the cobra's den, and the young child will put its hand into the viper's nest. They will neither harm nor destroy on all my holy mountain, for the earth will be filled with the knowledge of the LORD as the waters cover the sea. (Isa. 11:6–9)

Dear Lord Jesus, since every promise God has made finds its "yes" in you, we worship and adore you for securing the day Isaiah describes in this heart-palpitating passage. And we express our intense longings for the arrival of that day.

Oh, for the day when all "tooth and claw" violence gives way to wolves frolicking with lambs; leopards and goats napping together; calves, lions, and young horses strolling through the new heaven and new earth as friends; cows and bears lunching together rather than having one another for lunch—the day when serpents will be pets rather than pests.

As much as we love the vision of shalom in the animal kingdom, a gazillion times over we long for the day when we, the two-legged image-bearers of the living God, no longer harm one another in any way. No more marginalizing or minimizing one another; no more demeaning or dismissing, vilifying or idolizing one another; no more hating or hurting, ignoring or igniting one another in any way.

Hasten the day when God's glory will cover the earth like waters cover the sea (Hab. 2:14); the day when knowing the Lord won't be something we do but who we are; the day when we will finally and fully love one another as you love us, Lord Jesus.

Until that day, keep us groaning and growing in grace. Grant us quick repentances when we love poorly. May the world recognize us as your disciples by the way we love one another. We pray in your powerful and patient name. Amen.

An Advent Prayer about God's Generosity and Our Stubbornness

"Ask a sign of the Lord your God; let it be deep as Sheol or high as heaven." But Ahaz said, "I will not ask, and I will not put the Lord to the test." Then he said, "Hear then, O house of David! Is it too little for you to weary men, that you weary my God also? Therefore the Lord himself will give you a sign. Behold, the virgin shall conceive and bear a son, and shall call his name Immanuel." (Isa. 7:11–14 ESV)

Dear heavenly Father, what an outrageously generous God you are. This Scripture contrasts the beauty of your love with the ugliness of our stubbornness. I praise you for your relentless commitment to bless the most unworthy, unbelieving, ungrateful people, like me. Truly, Advent is the arrival of irrepressible grace.

It was a time of local and international crisis, and King Ahaz had every opportunity to repent and rely on you. You sent Isaiah with words of wisdom and hope. But he refused. Feigning piety, King Ahaz remained addicted to his illusion of control and self-sufficiency.

Father, as I read this story, I realize how much I'm like King Ahaz. Often I acknowledge you with my lips, but on the inside, I trust more in my Cub Scout kit of self-sufficiency. So I won't throw any stones today at this wicked king. Rather, I grieve the illusion of control and competency.

That's why the promise of Immanuel is so precious to me. Father, you've proven yourself to be a God who is not only with me in Jesus but also so very much for me in Jesus. Your love for us in the gospel isn't just unconditional; it's contraconditional, for you've met every condition necessary to redeem us and restore creation. Mercy without measure and grace without limit; love beyond imagining and peace surpassing understanding.

Though I don't have the Assyrian army outside my door threatening my existence, there are a few real challenges before me this Advent season. Father, by faith through grace, I purpose to rely on you for wisdom from above and grace for the moment. That you are with me and for me is enough. In the trustworthy and triumphant name of Jesus I pray. Amen.

An Advent Prayer
for When Things Seem Impossible

"How will this be," Mary asked the angel, "since I am a virgin?" The angel answered, "The Holy Spirit will come on you, and the power of the Most High will overshadow you. So the holy one to be born will be called the Son of God. Even Elizabeth your relative is going to have a child in her old age, and she who was said to be unable to conceive is in her sixth month. For no word from God will ever fail." "I am the Lord's servant," Mary answered. "May your word to me be fulfilled." Then the angel left her. (Luke 1:34–38)

Dear heavenly Father, the one thing I share in common with Mary is incredulity over the mind-boggling, heart-encouraging promises you have made in connection with the birth of Jesus. I too say, "How will this be?" And I hear you answer back, from the Scriptures and the history of redemption, "*Nothing is impossible with God.*"

Everything you've promised, with regard to Jesus, will come to pass, including the redeeming of Jesus' bride from every nation, tribe, people, and language and the renewal of this broken world into the new heaven and new earth. But, hallelujah, it also includes your plans for each of your children. Just as surely as you placed the life of Jesus in Mary, you have done the same for us. Though in an entirely different way than Mary, we too are "pregnant with glory" (see Rom. 8:18–27).

One day I will love perfectly, with the kindness and compassion of Jesus. I will only think and see with the wisdom and eyes of heaven. I will fully embrace your will as my favorite bread and utter delight.

One day I will never be selfish, petty, or defensive again. I will never get my feelings hurt, insist on being right, or demand more. I will think of others more highly and more often than myself. I won't keep a record of anybody's wrongs and will only and forever be an encourager. I will be free, so very free and whole.

To all of these promises, I find myself saying, "How will this be, since I'm still so very much not like Jesus?" And you answer back so grace-fully, "Things impossible with man are possible with God." To which I say and pray, "May it be as you have promised in the gospel, holy and faithful Father. I am yours and your servant." I pray in Jesus' exalted name. Amen.

An Advent Prayer about Trusting God with Our Children and Grandchildren

And you, child, will be called the prophet of the Most High; for you will go before the Lord to prepare his ways, to give knowledge of salvation to his people in the forgiveness of their sins, because of the tender mercy of our God, whereby the sunrise shall visit us from on high to give light to those who sit in darkness and in the shadow of death, to guide our feet into the way of peace. (Luke 1:76–79 ESV)

Dear heavenly Father, it's easy to forget the other child of promise you sent as an important part of the Advent story— John the Baptist, the forerunner of the Messiah and friend of the Bridegroom. His birth and life are such a testimony to the way, the gospel.

Grant us John's joy of growing small in the world's eye, that Jesus might be greater in the world's gaze. And grant us the joy of John's parents, Elizabeth and Zechariah, who only wanted what you wanted for their son. May the same be true as we consider the lives of our children and our grandchildren.

What more could we want for our kids than for them to love Jesus more than anything or anyone else in the world? What other story would we write for them than a story of serving you with everything they have and are?

Father, we lift our children and grandchildren to you. For those who don't know you, please bring them to a saving knowledge of Jesus. Make the gospel beautiful and irresistible to them. For those who do know you, take them into even greater intimacy with you. Don't let their affection for Jesus grow cool or their passion for your kingdom grow weak.

Our prayer for our children and grandchildren is the same one we offer for ourselves: Father, guide our hearts deeper into the habits of the gospel and guide our feet more surely onto paths of peace. Free us to live and love well between the two Advents of Jesus—loving mercy, doing justice, and walking humbly with you. We pray in Jesus' holy and loving name. Amen.

An Advent Prayer about Knowing and Treasuring Jesus

They hurried to the village and found Mary and Joseph. And there was the baby, lying in the manger. After seeing him, the shepherds told everyone what had happened and what the angel had said to them about this child. All who heard the shepherds' story were astonished, but Mary kept all these things in her heart and thought about them often. (Luke 2:16–19 NLT)

Dear Lord Jesus, this Scripture is crammed so full of holy mystery and immeasurable grace. You, the very God who created and sustains all things, who feeds birds and clothes the fields—you drew nourishment from a young maiden's breast. And Mary "treasured up all these things and pondered them in her heart"—as well she should.

But "hurrying off" like a shepherd to tell others about you has always been easier for me than sitting still and letting you tell me about yourself. It's always been easier for me to talk than to listen, to stay busy than to relax, to be "productive" than to be meditative. I confess this as sin, Jesus, for knowing about you isn't the same as knowing you intimately. An informed mind is not the same thing as an enflamed heart.

Lord Jesus, to know you is eternal life, and I do know you, but I want to know you so much better. Thank you for everything you've already accomplished for us through your life, death, and resurrection and for everything you're presently doing as the King of Kings and Lord of Lords, our constant intercessor and loving advocate, and thank you for everything you will be to us in the new heaven and new earth—Bridegroom to Bride. There's so much to treasure—so much to ponder.

May the gospel totally rearrange all the price tags in my life, Jesus. May the gospel slow me, settle me, and center me, that I might exclaim with Paul, "To live is Christ, and to die is gain. . . . indeed, I consider all things as rubbish compared to the surpassing excellency of knowing Christ Jesus my Lord" (see Phil 1:21; 3:8–9). I pray in your peerless and praise-worthy name. Amen.

An Advent Prayer about How the Good Shepherd Tenderly Cares for Us

But you, Bethlehem Ephrathah, though you are small among the clans of Judah, out of you will come for me one who will be ruler over Israel, whose origins are from of old, from ancient times. . . . He will stand and shepherd his flock in the strength of the LORD, in the majesty of the name of the LORD his God. And they will live securely, for then his greatness will reach to the ends of the earth. And he will be our peace. (Mic. 5:2, 4–5)

The LORD is my shepherd; I have all that I need. (Ps. 23:1 NLT)

Dear Lord Jesus, Micah's prophecy of your coming simply adds to the long list of reasons we love and adore you. Today, I'm especially moved to worship you for being the Shepherd-Savior that you are. Having laid down your life as the Lamb of God, you've risen and are now the *Standing Shepherd*—relentlessly caring, vigilantly protecting, and faithfully providing for us. You never sleep or slumber, because you are always interceding for us. "Good Shepherd" seems like a profoundly understated title for you, Lord Jesus.

Because of your great love for us, we lack nothing that we need. We don't get all our wants, but we do have everything we need for life and godliness. I praise you that it's green pastures and quiet waters to which you are leading us—all for the restoring of our often tired and weary, broken and rebellious souls.

For your glory and our good, you guide us along paths of righteousness and goodness, truth and grace. And even as that journey involves traversing places marked by decay and death, you are with us—and that's all we really need to know. We don't have to be afraid of anything or anyone.

When enemies are close by and threatening, you are even closer. The nearer we live to you, the stronger the fragrance we emit of your goodness and love. Even in the new heaven and new earth, you will be our Shepherd, leading us to springs of living water (Rev. 7:17). Your greatness, Jesus, will reach to the ends of the earth, and we will always live securely, for you are our peace—now and forever. In your great and gracious name I pray. Amen.

An Advent Prayer
about the Blessings of Immanuel

And we know that for those who love God all things work together for good, for those who are called according to his purpose. For those whom he foreknew he also predestined to be conformed to the image of his Son, in order that he might be the firstborn among many brothers. And those whom he predestined he also called, and those whom he called he also justified, and those whom he justified he also glorified. What then shall we say to these things? If God is for us, who can be against us? He who did not spare his own Son but gave him up for us all, how will he not also with him graciously give us all things? (Rom. 8:28–32 ESV)

Dear Lord Jesus—Immanuel, God with us and God so very much for us—I cannot read this favorite Scripture without thinking about Advent, and why you have come, and why you are coming again. The hopes and hurts, fears and tears of all my years are met right here in this passage. You are all we need, and way beyond all we can imagine.

Lord Jesus, oh, the peace I have that comes from knowing you are presently at work in all things for your glory and for our good—in the obvious and when I'm oblivious; in my laughter and in my losses; in the things I "get" and in the things which vex me; when I'm "feeling the love" and

298

when I'm feeling very lonely; when the gospel is my greatest reality, and when I'm tempted to say with John the Baptist, "Are you the Messiah, or should we be looking for another?" (see Matt. 11:3).

There is no other Messiah, Savior, or Lord but you, Jesus; and absolutely nothing will separate me from your love, for I've been called according to the Father's purpose—which will never fail or falter. He "foreknew" me and set his affection upon me before the world began, and he will continue to provide everything necessary to complete the work of the gospel in my life, in the whole family of God, and in the entire creation. Joy to the world, and to me, indeed! I pray, in your merciful and mighty name. Amen.

A Prayer for the Third Sunday of Advent

The Word became flesh and made his dwelling among us. We have seen his glory, the glory of the one and only Son, who came from the Father, full of grace and truth. (John testified concerning him. He cried out, saying, "This is the one I spoke about when I said, 'He who comes after me has surpassed me because he was before me.'") Out of his fullness we have all received grace in place of grace already given. (John 1:14–16)

Dear Lord Jesus, though there's no Mary or manger, shepherds or angels in John's account of your birth, there is most definitely *you*. You are the only star on the horizon in this nativity scene, and how you shine.

We praise you for becoming flesh and "tabernacling" among us in the fullness of time. Though equal to yet distinct from the Father, you didn't consider your glory something to be tightly grasped or held on to selfishly. Rather, you emptied yourself by becoming a man—not just any ordinary man but a servant-man, the servant of the Lord, the second Adam—our Savior.

In your thirty-three years of incarnate life, you accomplished everything necessary for the redemption of your beloved Bride and the restoration of the world you love. We magnify and adore, worship and love you, Lord Jesus. What a wonderful, merciful Savior you are. You are so mighty to save and quick to redeem.

We should sing, "Joy to the World" year round, for you are presently ruling the world with your grace and truth—the grace and truth of which you are full. You are making the nations prove the wonders of your love, as the gospel runs from heart to heart and nation to nation.

From the fullness of your grace we keep receiving one blessing after another and one blessing on top of another: the gift of your imputed righteousness, the perpetual favor of God, your steadfast intercession and advocacy, citizenship in heaven, the work of the Spirit in our lives—the assurance that one day we will see you as you are and we will be made like you. Hallelujah, many times over! Joy to the world, indeed! We pray in your near and exalted name. Amen.

An Advent Prayer about Making Music to Jesus in Our Hearts

Mary responded, "Oh, how my soul praises the Lord. How my spirit rejoices in God my Savior! For he took notice of his lowly servant girl, and from now on all generations will call me blessed.

For the Mighty One is holy, and he has done great things for me. He shows mercy from generation to generation to all who fear him." (Luke 1:46–50 NLT)

Dear Lord Jesus, I woke up today extremely thankful for the gift of music, especially the songs of Advent, and it's a no-brainer why. Every Advent hymn, carol, and chorus—from your Word, in my hymnal, or on my iPod—fuels my hope and liberates my longings. I praise you for igniting my heart to sing your praise. I praise you for giving me a reason to sing, Lord Jesus. I praise you for songwriters who capture what I feel and give me the vehicle for expressing what I long to say to you.

Mary's story is quite different from mine, and yet I join her Advent refrain today. I can sing her song. I'm compelled to sing her song, for you've been mindful of my humble, broken, sinful state too. I have nothing to boast in but you, Lord Jesus. You came to me when I wasn't seeking you, and you're being formed in me as surely as you entered the world through Mary's womb.

I'm a blessed man because you've done great things for me and you continue to do so. Holy is your name, Lord Jesus. I have no concern for what any generation may say about me. It's enough to know what you say about me: that I'm yours—forgiven, declared righteous, desired, enjoyed, and as already loved as I will be in the new heaven and new earth.

Your mercy has been extended to my generation and to me personally. Therefore, my soul glorifies you, Lord Jesus, and my spirit rejoices in you, my God and my Savior. As the gospel goes deeper into my heart, free me from all fears, except the fear of the Lord. Indeed, I want to be filled with and freed by affectionate reverence for you—an awe so compelling I will live and love to your glory, with great joy. In your most glorious and grace-full name I sing and pray. Amen.

An Advent Prayer about How Jesus Is the King We Always Wanted

> Of the increase of his government and of peace there will be no end, on the throne of David and over his kingdom, to establish it and to uphold it with justice and with righteousness from this time forth and forevermore. The zeal of the LORD of hosts will do this. (Isa. 9:7 ESV)

Dear Lord Jesus, your righteousness is our surety and your sovereignty is our sanity. Hallelujah, many times over! How could we have possibly imagined that your humble Advent entrance through a stable would lead to the stabilization of the universe and that your cradle would eventually rock our peaceless world?

Truly, there's only one government and one peace sufficient to meet the needs of our sinful hearts and broken world. You are already installed as "the ruler of kings on earth" (Rev. 1:5 ESV) and of everything else. King David's throne has become a throne of grace, from which you are actively ruling the world with your truth and grace. Joy to the world, indeed!

Truly, you are zealously working all things together after the counsel of your will. You—the Lamb of God, the Lord of Lords, and the Lamp of the New Jerusalem—are working in all things, for your glory and for our good. No one and nothing can derail, deter, or distract you from bringing to completion your good work of redemption and restoration.

You don't promise to do all things easy, but you are always doing all things well. Forgive me when I get impatient with your timing, don't enjoy all your providences, and second-guess your involvement. I've lived long enough to know you do some of your "best work" when I am actually feeling the absence of your presence.

As the gospel of your kingdom continues its transforming work in my life, may it advance through my life. Give me more joy than I've ever had before in loving and serving people. Intensify my hope in the day you will return and finish making all things new. I pray in your mighty and merciful name. Amen.

An Advent Prayer about a Christmas As Big As the New Heaven and New Earth

Look! I am creating new heavens and a new earth, and no one will even think about the old ones anymore. Be glad; rejoice forever in my creation! And look! I will create Jerusalem as a place of happiness. Her people will be a source of joy. I will rejoice over Jerusalem and delight in my people. And the sound of weeping and crying will be heard in it no more. (Isa. 65:17–19 NLT)

Dear heavenly Father, I love meditating through the servant songs of Isaiah during Advent, because they remind me that the birth of Jesus wasn't a "merry little" event. Christmas represents the fulfillment of promises of immeasurable, irrepressible, indescribable proportions and delight. I praise you that every Christmas is colossal—irrespective of the economy or our discretionary spending.

With the first coming of Jesus, you inaugurated your plan to create a new heaven and new earth from the stuff of this very broken world—a new creation world in which you will find great delight. Though it will take the second Advent of Jesus, your kingdom has come, and it will come in fullness. I praise you for your generosity, tenacity, and felicity in doing all that you do, mighty and merciful Father.

You've promised to redeem a people from every race, tribe, tongue, and people group to populate that eternal world of peace and joy—a people in whom you find great delight and over whom you will rejoice forever. The gospel really is that big and that good. You've used stars, sand, and dust to describe the mathematics of your mercy. Free me from my unbelief, grace-full and loving Father.

Because you have sent Jesus to us and for us, we live with the blessed assurance that all of our sins have been wiped away and the glorious hope that all of our tears, likewise, will one day be wiped away. Until that day, free us to engage in your commitment to make all things new, wherever you have placed us and wherever you might send us. I pray with great joy and freshly fueled hope, in Jesus' exalted name. Amen.

An Advent Prayer about the Weakness, Paradox, and Glory of Jesus' Birth

The Spirit of the Sovereign LORD is upon me, for the LORD has anointed me to bring good news to the poor. He has sent me to comfort the brokenhearted and to proclaim that captives will be released and prisoners will be freed. He has sent me to tell those who mourn that the time of the LORD's favor has come and with it, the day of God's anger against their enemies. To all who mourn in Israel, he will give a crown of beauty for ashes, a joyous blessing instead of mourning, festive praise instead of despair. In their righteousness, they will be like great oaks that the LORD has planted for his own glory. (Isa. 61:1–3 NLT)

Dear Lord Jesus, I am so thankful you came to fulfill everything mentioned in these hope-saturated words from Isaiah, and I'm in awe once again as I reflect on your humble entrance into our world. The contrast between your birthing and calling is staggering.

Though Mary nursed you, she depended on you for her next breath and her eternal salvation. Though vulnerable and needing her comfort as a newborn, you came to comfort all who mourn. O holy and profound mystery—a newborn child has come to make all things new!

Even when you were a babe, the Spirit of the Sovereign Lord was on you—for you are the Sovereign Lord, the King of Kings and Lord of Lords, the one by whom all oppression will be stopped, all chains will be broken, all injustice will give way to justice. We praise, bless, and adore you, Lord Jesus.

By you, mourning is transformed into gladness, broken hearts become whole hearts, despairing hearts become delight-filled hearts—we, the disfavored, become the favored of the Lord. Who possibly could've seen, known, and believed such a thing, given the circumstances of your birth?

But the meekness of your birth was a sure hint of the weakness of your death. As surely as you were placed in an unlikely crib, you were nailed to an undeserved cross. Hail the incarnate deity—born that we no more may die, died that we may truly live! We worship you, O glorious and grace-full Lord Jesus. Use us—use me—today as a conduit of your tender mercies and eternal encouragement. In your merciful and mighty name I pray. Amen.

An Advent Prayer
about Worship Replacing Whining

> But when the fullness of time had come, God sent forth his Son, born of woman, born under the law, to redeem those who were under the law, so that we might receive adoption as sons. And because you are sons, God has sent the Spirit of his Son into our hearts, crying, "Abba! Father!" So you are no longer a slave, but a son, and if a son, then an heir through God. (Gal. 4:4–7 ESV)

Dear Lord Jesus, though the immediate circumstances surrounding your birthing experience were less than ideal, *everything* happened just as you, our Father, and the Holy Spirit planned. "Doing all things well" didn't just start happening after your resurrection.

"When the time had fully come" you came, not a day early and not a day late. As humbling as it was to be born under the ceiling of a stable, being born under the weight of the law was an incomparably greater burden. Yet that's exactly why you came into the world—to fulfill every demand of the law for us by your life of perfect obedience and to exhaust its judgment against us by your death for us upon the cross. You are our substitute to trust long before you are our model to follow. Hallelujah, so many times over!

Because you lived and died in our place, we're no longer slaves but daughters and sons of the living and loving God, with the full rights thereof. We've been perfectly forgiven and robed in your righteousness, sealed with the Spirit and given a new family; prayed for every moment and destined to inherit the earth. And one day, one blessed day, we will see you as you are, and we will be made like you. No abacus, group of accountants, or room full of computers can possibly calculate the riches of grace that we've been given in you.

Forgive us when our whining trumps our worship, when our grumbling is more pronounced than our gratitude, when our awareness of what we don't have in the world is more compelling than what we do have in you. During the remainder of Advent, free us to love as we are loved and forgive as we've been forgiven, and to welcome the outsider and serve our families with your servant love. We pray in your tender and triumphant name. Amen.

An Advent Prayer
for When Our Inner Ache Intensifies

His mighty arm has done tremendous things! He has scattered the proud and haughty ones. He has brought down princes from their thrones and exalted the humble. He has filled the hungry with good things and sent the rich away with empty hands. He has helped his servant Israel and remembered to be merciful. For he made this promise to our ancestors, to Abraham and his children forever. (Luke 1:51–55 NLT)

Dear heavenly Father, I awoke today with a deep ache in my heart—an ache that makes Mary's prayer timely and encouraging. I am grateful beyond measure that you are a God who remembers to be merciful. With the gift of Jesus, you remembered all the promises you made to Abraham and to his descendants, which includes me. I'm humbled and overwhelmed.

You promised Abraham you'd take him to a land of your choosing to make of him a nation for great blessing. Israel became the "national womb" for the Messiah—through whom you are redeeming a family from every race, tribe, tongue, and people group (Gen. 12–17). No one can fulfill these promises but you.

Like Mary, Abraham could not have begun to imagine how all of this would play out. But the promises you made to Abraham and the prayer the Spirit prayed through Mary all find their fulfillment in your Son, Jesus. I praise you for your memory and your mercy, Father. Both of these answer the deep ache in my heart today.

Father, thank you for remembering your promise to complete your good work in me and in your world. I am so ready to be made completely like Jesus. I am so ready to live in a world of no more brokenness, sin, and death; no more mourning, crying, and pain; no more fractured relationships and unfulfilled longings; no more "not yet and not enough"; no more tensions, conflicts, and stress.

Until that day, thank you for being the Father of mercies and God of all comfort. Thank you for promising, and delivering, new mercies every morning, including this one. I pray with the faith of Abraham and the humility of Mary, in Jesus' loving name. Amen.

A Prayer for the Fourth Sunday of Advent

When they [the Magi] saw the star, they rejoiced exceedingly with great joy. And going into the house they saw the child with Mary his mother, and they fell down and worshiped him. Then, opening their treasures, they offered him gifts, gold and frankincense and myrrh. (Matt. 2:10–11 ESV)

Dear Lord Jesus, whether they were magicians or kings, astrologers or otherwise, and whether there were three, seven, or twelve of them, it makes zero difference. The Magi were wise men, and they show us the way of true wisdom, because they lead us to the incarnation of wisdom itself—to you, Lord Jesus.

It would take an eternity of eternities to begin to show you the worship you deserve for becoming wisdom from God for us—that is, our "righteousness and sanctification and redemption" (1 Cor. 1:30 ESV). Because of you, we are alive, forgiven, and free. Because of you, we are welcome, wanted, and enjoyed by the three times holy God of eternity.

Though the Magi came to you, you are the real seeker in the story. Promises of your coming and an irrepressible calling; a providential star and a Spirit-generated joy—how we praise you for drawing men and women to yourself from every period of history, every family of humanity, and every segment of society. Come Herod or high water, those you've come to save will come to you, Lord Jesus.

On this fourth Sunday of Advent, we declare our awe of you and our love for you, Lord Jesus. Open the eyes of our hearts to behold even more of your beauty; expand the chambers of our hearts to make room for even more of your grace and glory. Free us to be generous and joyful as the Magi. Free us to love as you love us, to forgive as you have forgiven us, and to pursue others as you so faithfully seek us. We pray in your trustworthy and worship-worthy name. Amen.

An Advent Prayer
about the Sacrificial Tenderness of Jesus

Who has believed what he has heard from us? And to whom has the arm of the Lord been revealed? For he grew up before him like a young plant, and like a root out of dry ground; he had no form or majesty that we should look at him, and no beauty that we should desire him. He was despised and rejected by men; a man of sorrows, and acquainted with grief; and as one from whom men hide their faces he was despised, and we esteemed him not. Surely he has borne our griefs and carried our sorrows; yet we esteemed him stricken, smitten by God, and afflicted. (Isa. 53:1–4 ESV)

Dear Lord Jesus, your manger was a veritable garden of grace, for there the Father planted you as the tender shoot of Isaiah's vision. Hallelujah, you are the root of life that has broken through the dry ground of our fallen world and hearts.

I am truly in awe this morning at the sacrificial tenderness of your incarnation. You created beauty, yet you became the one with "no beauty," for us. You took the vileness and ugliness of my sin, that I might become pure and beautiful in you. O holy, merciful mystery! Though you have always enjoyed the delight of the Godhead, you became the despised one, the rejected one, for us, for me. What wondrous love is this, indeed?

You, the fountain of pleasures, whose laughter fills heaven, whose joy is our strength, you became the man of suffering and sorrows for us—for me. And though you didn't remain a "tender shoot," you have retained all tenderness. In taking up your cross, you took up our infirmities and carried our sorrows; you bore our guilt and exhausted our judgment—once and for all. What a wonderful, merciful, tender Savior you are.

Oh, to esteem and love you as you deserve, Lord Jesus. May your tenderness grow in my heart and be real to my family. In your beautiful and grace-full name I pray. Amen.

An Advent Prayer for When Holidays Are Hard

> And the Word became flesh and dwelt among us, and we have seen his glory, glory as of the only Son from the Father, full of grace and truth. (John bore witness about him, and cried out, "This was he of whom I said, 'He who comes after me ranks before me, because he was before me.'") For from his fullness we have all received, grace upon grace. For the law was given through Moses; grace and truth came through Jesus Christ. No one has ever seen God; the only God, who is at the Father's side, he has made him known. (John 1:14–18 ESV)

Dear Lord Jesus, I'm always thankful you give grace upon grace, but holidays make me even more grateful for this Good News. I woke up today feeling the *weight* of many friends and the *wait* of deep longing. Thank you for your heart-engaging, burden-bearing, peace-instilling love.

I pray for friends who are facing their first Christmas on this side of committing a loved one to eternity. Death is a thief whose robbery is profoundly felt during holidays. Grant grace upon grace for those families, perhaps still raw with the loss and grief. No one is as compassionate as you, Lord Jesus; bring your tenderness and nearness to bear. Thank you for coming into our world to defeat sin and death—which you have magnificently done. The next time we see you, you will eradicate sin and death—once and for all. Hasten that day of eternal delight and dancing.

I also pray for friends bracing to endure Christmas Day, Lord Jesus. Old wounds can be easily triggered; messy relationships make it difficult not to pretend but also painful that we have to pretend. Grant grace upon grace in those complex scenarios and difficult stories. The world into which you were born was filled with madness and sadness. You shy away from neither. Surprise us with your centering, healing, liberating presence. May endearing moments actually trump the moments that must be endured. Sweeten the bitter waters of our brokenness with the new wine of your kindness.

Grant grace upon grace to all of us, Lord Jesus. As we lift our hands to praise you, so we offload our burdens on you. You care for us, you love us, and you enjoy us, and that is enough. Hallelujah, what a Savior! Hallelujah, what a salvation! We pray in your tender and triumphant name. Amen.

A Prayer for Christmas Eve

In those days Caesar Augustus issued a decree that a census should be taken of the entire Roman world. (This was the first census that took place while Quirinius was governor of Syria.) And everyone went to their own town to register. So Joseph also went up from the town of Nazareth in Galilee to Judea, to Bethlehem the town of David, because he belonged to the house and line of David. He went there to register with Mary, who was pledged to be married to him and was expecting a child. While they were there, the time came for the baby to be born, and she gave birth to her firstborn, a son. She wrapped him in cloths and placed him in a manger, because there was no guest room available for them. (Luke 2:1–7)

Dear Lord Jesus, whether or not you entered our world anywhere close to our December 25 is irrelevant. *That* you were born—that you actually came from eternity into time and space, not as a metaphor or myth, fable or tale, but as our Savior—*that's* what matters.

We sing to you on this day with all the humility and felicity we can muster, "Mild he lays his glory by, born that man no more may die. Born to raise the sons of earth, born to give them second birth." We praise, bless, and adore you.

Luke took great care to detail the history of your birth, but it's the quietness of your birth that is noteworthy. Any other king would've come with great fanfare and a royal entourage. But you came into our world in utter stillness and profound weakness. "No room in the inn" wasn't an insult to you; it was your choice, your plan, the way of the gospel.

For you didn't consider your equality with God something to be protected or hoarded. Rather, you made yourself "nothing," becoming one of us—tabernacling among us as God in the flesh, the Servant of the Lord. And with measureless humility and joy, you died in our place upon the cross.

"Veiled in flesh, the Godhead see! Hail, the incarnate deity! Pleased, as man, with men to dwell, Jesus, our Emmanuel!" "Peace on earth and mercy mild, God and sinners reconciled!" Hallelujah, so many times over!

We long for the day when every knee will bow and every tongue confess that you are Lord, to the glory of God the Father. It's going to be a loud and large day, but on this Christmas Eve, we humble ourselves in quietness and stillness, gratefulness and peace. Thank you for coming to us,

Lord Jesus—thank you for saving us from our sins. We pray in your great and gracious name. Amen.

A Prayer for Christmas Day

The Savior—yes, the Messiah, the Lord—has been born today in Bethlehem, the city of David! (Luke 2:11 NLT)

Dear Lord Jesus, we *joyfully* celebrate the day angels "harked," shepherds ran, and Mary treasured. You have come *to* us and *for* us. For God so loved the world, he gave you—blessed Savior, Christ and Lord.

We praise you for being born in Bethlehem, which means "house of bread." We were a famished people—filling ourselves at empty buffets, spending money "for that which is not bread" (Isa. 55:2 ESV). But you came as the Bread of Life, and now we freely dine at the banqueting table of your welcome and grace. Our hearts are filled with unfettered gratitude.

Indeed, how fitting that you entered our world in the city of David—Israel's beloved shepherd-king. For what King David could never be, you've become for us—the Good Shepherd who laid down his life for his sheep. And now you perpetually care for us with relentless tenderness and unwavering kindness. There is no other Savior like you; there is no other Savior but you.

We worship you with irrepressible delight, for you are the long-time promised and much-longed-for Christ, the Messiah. Every promise God has made finds its fulfillment—its unequivocal and irrevocable "Yes!"—in you. You are the resolve for all our fears and the answer to all our hopes.

We bow before you in joyful adoration, for you are the Lord of Lords, very God of very God, presently reigning over everything and working in all things for our good. You are the ruler of the kings of the earth, setting them up and sitting them down at your sovereign discretion. Only your kingdom is unshakable and everlasting. Of the increase of your government and peace, there will be no end.

As we celebrate your first Advent, our passion for your second Advent is intensified. Oh, for the day when every knee will bow and every tongue confess that you are indeed Lord, to the glory of God the Father! Oh, for the day when every tear will be wiped away and everything sad will come untrue. Oh, for the day when all things broken will be all things new. We pray in your magnificent and merciful name. Amen.

A Prayer for the Day after Christmas

And the shepherds returned, glorifying and praising God for all they had heard and seen, as it had been told them. (Luke 2:20 ESV)

Dear heavenly Father, it's the day after Christmas, and many of us are overstuffed, underslept, and flat-out exhausted. But above all, we're grateful for the gift of Jesus, for our best Christmases and our most difficult ones all need your grace. The "after Christmas sale" ads began a week before the actual day, clearly signaling that we're always yearning for a little more.

For those of us for whom the day was nearly perfect, we worship you as the God from whom all blessings flow. For those of us for whom the day was a constant reminder of how much we long for the day of all things new, we worship you as the God who has secured that very day through Jesus.

When the shepherds left Jesus' manger, they were still shepherds. They still couldn't worship at the temple; they still couldn't give testimony in a court of law; and they were still "profiled" as untrustworthy members of the community. And a five-star inn didn't open up for Mary and Joseph the next morning in Bethlehem, with angels serving as round-the-clock nurses.

Father, thank you that as followers of Jesus, we don't have to pretend about anything. Jesus came into a broken world for broken people, and we all qualify. You call us to believe, not to make believe; to delight in you, not to deny reality. Should we remain "shepherds" the rest of our lives in this world, you promise to give us all the grace we will need. Just keep showing us more and more of Jesus, and it will be enough.

Help us to live these next few days at the pace of grace. Keep us from getting in too big of a hurry to clean up the messes, put away decorations, and figure out what we're going to do for New Year's Eve. Free us to enjoy one another, to listen to one another's hearts, to linger in the presence of family and friends alike. Indeed, Father, teach us how to live and love at the pace of grace. In Jesus' wonderful and merciful name we pray. Amen.

12

Prayers for the Season of Lent and Passion Week

A Prayer for a Gospel-Inundated, Grace-Soaked Lenten Season

And when you fast, do not look gloomy like the hypocrites, for they disfigure their faces that their fasting may be seen by others. Truly, I say to you, they have received their reward. But when you fast, anoint your head and wash your face, that your fasting may not be seen by others but by your Father who is in secret. And your Father who sees in secret will reward you. (Matt. 6:16–18 ESV)

Let us rejoice and be glad and give him glory! For the wedding of the Lamb has come, and his bride has made herself ready. (Rev. 19:7)

Dear Jesus, it's Ash Wednesday, the beginning of the season of Lent. For the next forty days we have the privilege of fixing our gaze on you—the Author and Perfecter of our faith. For your glory and our growth, we ask you to overwhelm us with fresh mercies and irrepressible grace in the coming weeks.

Don't let this be a typical Lenten season, Jesus. Saturate and empower it with the gospel. It's all about you, Jesus. It is all about your finished work—not our constant failings and vain promises of doing better and doing more. Whatever fasting we may choose to practice, may it be as a betrothed Bride, not as gloomy hypocrites. Our deepest repentance is always born out of seeing more of your beauty, more of the gospel, more of you, Jesus.

Indeed, Jesus, we begin Lent today anticipating our wedding, not our funeral. The law has been fulfilled and judgment is complete; the dowry has been paid in full and our wedding dress is your righteousness; the invitations have been sent out and the date has been secured. We praise, bless, and adore you.

Over these next forty days, intensify our hunger and fuel our hope. Break us that you might beautify us. Increase our love for holiness as you supersize our love for your glory. Free us from our idols as you reveal their emptiness and silliness in comparison with your beauty and bounty. We pray in your exalted and worship-worthy name. Amen.

A Prayer for Palm Sunday

Rejoice greatly, O daughter of Zion! Shout aloud, O daughter of Jerusalem! Behold, your king is coming to you; righteous and having salvation is he, humble and mounted on a donkey, on a colt, the foal of a donkey. I will cut off the chariot from Ephraim and the war horse from Jerusalem; and the battle bow shall be cut off, and he shall speak peace to the nations; his rule shall be from sea to sea, and from the River to the ends of the earth. As for you also, because of the blood of my covenant with you, I will set your prisoners free from the waterless pit. Return to your stronghold, O prisoners of hope; today I declare that I will restore to you double. (Zech. 9:9–12 ESV)

Dear Lord Jesus, we'll exhaust the glory of this passage when the Amazon River flows backwards, the sun turns into a snow cone, and yellowfin tuna yodel. Who is it that fulfills Zechariah's magnificent vision? It is you, King Jesus, and we welcome you and rejoice in you on this Palm Sunday.

No other king could vanquish warhorses and warriors, riding the foal of a donkey. No other king could break the battle bow and backbone of warfare by the brokenness of the cross. No other king could replace the dominion of darkness and the tyranny of evil with an eternal reign of grace and peace.

No other king would give his life and death for the redemption of rebels and idolaters like us. No other king can possibly make slaves of sin into prisoners of hope.

Lord Jesus, you are that King—the King of Glory, the Monarch of Mercy, the Governor of Grace, the Prince of Peace—the King of Kings and Lord of Lords! Great is our rejoicing, because grace is our salvation! You have come to us and for us, righteous and victorious, loving and sovereign.

By the riches of your grace, continue to free us from waterless pits, broken cisterns, and worthless idols. By the power of the gospel, enable us to live as prisoners of hope and agents of redemption, until the day you return to finish making all things new. We pray in your holy and matchless name. Amen.

A Prayer for Monday of Holy Week

"Now my soul is deeply troubled. Should I pray, 'Father, save me from this hour'? But this is the very reason I came! Father, bring glory to your name." Then a voice spoke from heaven, saying, "I have already brought glory to my name, and I will do so again." When the crowd heard the voice, some thought it was thunder, while others declared an angel had spoken to him. Then Jesus told them, "The voice was for your benefit, not mine. The time for judging this world has come, when Satan, the ruler of this world, will be cast out. And when I am lifted up from the earth, I will draw everyone to myself." (John 12:27–32 NLT)

Dear Lord Jesus, as the events of Holy Week began to unfold, the exuberant "Hosannas" gave way to the great disturbance in your soul—no hesitation, but profound consternation. No surprises awaited you, just an overwhelming assignment, which you helped plan before the world began (Eph. 1:3–14). Within days, you would take the judgment we deserve to give us the grace we can never earn. At the end of the week, your "bruised heel" (see Gen. 3:15) would crush the head of the "ruler of this world" and cast him down in defeat, once and for all (John 12:31 ESV).

At the end of the week, you would gladly pay the price for the salvation of God's immense covenant family—children of grace redeemed from every nation, tribe, people, and language; daughters and sons of mercy as numerous as the stars in the sky, the sand of the beaches, and the dust of the earth (Gen. 12–17).

It was for this purpose you came from eternity into time and space. For this very reason you emptied yourself of your glory by taking the form of a servant-man, the Lord's Servant;

to this end you became obedient, even obedient to death on the cross (Phil. 2:5–11). Understandably so, Lord Jesus, your heart was overwhelmed.

As the events of our week now unfold, grant us grace to slow our pace and quiet our hearts, that we might survey the wonders of your sacrifice and love for us. May our boasting in your cross grow exponentially, demonstratively, joyfully. In your holy and grace-full name we pray. Amen.

A Prayer for Tuesday of Holy Week

As he [Jesus] approached Jerusalem and saw the city, he wept over it and said, "If you, even you, had only known on this day what would bring you peace—but now it is hidden from your eyes." (Luke 19:41–42)

Dear Lord Jesus, long before the day when you will wipe away our tears, you wept many of your own, and we praise, bless, and adore you for doing so. The tears you shed coming into a broken and rebellious Jerusalem underscore the mercy and magnificence of these words from the apostle Paul: "You see, at just the right time, when we were still powerless, Christ died for the ungodly. Very rarely will anyone die for a righteous person, though for a good person someone might possibly dare to die. But God demonstrates his own love for us in this: While we were still sinners, Christ died for us" (Rom. 5:6–8).

Jesus, I humbly and gladly acknowledge Paul was writing about me in that Scripture. I am one of the powerless, ungodly sinners for whom you gave your life—demonstrating God's lavish love for the undeserving. I wasn't an impassioned

321

seeker or a misguided God-fearer; I was an indifferent rebel when I received the gift of reconciliation (Rom. 5:10). The only reason I have peace with God is because God made peace with me through you.

I would still be looking for peace elsewhere, if you hadn't opened my eyes to see my need and your grace. I have no claim to salvation—no boast or hope, no assurance of sins forgiven or of righteousness received—apart from God's sovereign grace.

Jesus, I long for the Day when I will no longer even be tempted to look for peace anywhere else but in you. Until that day, show me more of your incomparable beauty and the bounty of the gospel. I pray in your tenacious and tender name. Amen.

A Prayer for Wednesday of Holy Week

Then, surrounded by the Pharisees, Jesus asked them a question: "What do you think about the Messiah?" (Matt. 22:41–42 NLT)

Dear Lord Jesus, we praise, bless, and adore you for the unparalleled privilege of knowing you, and there's so much more to know. That's why the question you put to Pharisees on the day before your arrest remains the most important question for *us* to answer.

What do I think about you, Jesus, today? You are everlasting God, and I am a mere man. I would despair if you were less, and I am weary of pretending to be more. You are the Creator, Sustainer, and Restorer of all things. You are the Alpha and the Omega and everything in between. Angels worship you and birds depend on you.

You are the Second Adam—our substitute in life and in death. You lived a life of perfect obedience for us and exhausted God's judgment against us. By you, we've been completely forgiven, and in you, we're declared perfectly righteous. You are our impassioned Bridegroom, and we are your beloved Bride. You cannot love us more, and you'll never love us less. We believe; help our unbelief, Lord.

You are the reigning and returning King, sovereign over days and dominions, over our joys and our sufferings. Broken reeds love your appearing and demons tremble in your presence. Lord Jesus, you are all this and so much more. Eternity will be an endless revelation of your glory and grace.

But what stuns me the most as I think about you, Jesus— what compels me to fall down before you in love and worship today—is to realize that you are always thinking about us. Even me. We are in your heart and on your mind, all the time. You know us perfectly and delight in us fully. O blessed truth! There's not a moment you're not praying for us, singing over us, and living in us. Hallelujah, hallelujah, hallelujah! We pray in your holy and grace-full name. Amen.

A Prayer for Thursday of Holy Week: Maundy (Mandate) Thursday

Now before Feast of the Passover, when Jesus knew that his hour had come to depart out of this world to the Father, having loved his own who were in the world, he loved them to the end. (John 13:1 ESV)

So now I am giving you a new commandment: Love each other. Just as I have loved you, you should love each other. Your love for one another will prove to the world that you are my disciples. (John 13:34–35 NLT)

Dear Lord Jesus, it's the day of Holy Week we call Maundy or "Mandate" Thursday, a day crammed full of glory and overflowing with grace. Israel's Passover will soon become the Lord's Supper—*your* supper. The entire old covenant system of perpetual temple sacrifices is about to be fulfilled by the once-and-for-all sacrifice of your life, given as a ransom for us (Heb. 10:12). Behold the Lamb of God, who takes away the sin of the world!

Having shared eternal glory with the Father, you now show measureless grace to your disciples. Having loved this beautiful bunch of broken men well—men who vied for positions of honor a few hours earlier (Mark 10:35–45), men who would soon all scatter and leave you—having loved them so well, you now show them the full extent of your love.

The humility you showed by disrobing to wash their feet was a preview to your being stripped naked, publically shamed, and nailed to the cross, so that you could wash their hearts and ours. What wondrous love is this, indeed—how wide, long, high, and deep (Eph. 3:14–19). "There is no greater love than to lay down one's life for one's friends" (John 15:13 NLT).

How then shall we respond to your unparalleled love for us? "Love one another. As I have loved you, so you must love one another" (John 13:34). This is the new and never-ending command you've given us as your disciples. The most obvious expression of our "getting" the gospel is our loving others as you have loved us. Jesus, forgive our disobedience to so central and essential a command, and free us for a new season of loving well, to your glory. In your holy and loving name we pray. Amen.

A Prayer for Good Friday

And Jesus said, "Father, forgive them, for they know not what they do" (Luke 23:34 ESV)

Jesus cried out with a loud voice, saying, "Eli, Eli, lema sabachthani?" that is, "My God, my God, why have you forsaken me?" (Matt. 27:46 ESV)

It is finished. (John 19:30)

Dear Lord Jesus, for years I struggled with calling the day of your crucifixion "good." How presumptuous on our part. That there had to be a day when you, the eternally glorious Son of God, would be made sin for us is not good at all. But at the same time, that you would freely and gladly give yourself for us on the cross is never-to-be surpassed goodness—quintessential goodness.

Oh, the wonder of it all. From the cross and from your heart came these two impassioned cries: "Father forgive them" (Luke 23:34) and "My God, my God, why have you forsaken me?" (Matt. 27:46 ESV). The first required the second. The second secured the first. Together they humble our hearts and fuel our worship.

And then there's the third cry: "It is finished." Nothing is left undone concerning our salvation and for the transformation of our world. Once and for all, perfectly and fully, we have been reconciled to God. You became sin for us that in you, we might become the righteousness of God (2 Cor. 5:21)—the Just for the unjust, the Beautiful One for the broken ones, the Lamb of God for the rebels from God.

Lord Jesus, a million years into our life in the new heaven and new earth, we will still be stunned with awe, worship, and gratitude for the greatness of your sacrifice and love for us. Because you were fully forsaken, we are forever forgiven. Because you exhausted God's judgment against our number-less sins, we now live by the gift of your perfect righteousness. Bow our heads in humility and raise our hands in praise. We pray in your all-glorious, all-grace-full name. Amen.

A Prayer for Holy Saturday

The next day, on the Sabbath, the leading priests and Pharisees went to see Pilate. They told him, "Sir, we remember what that deceiver once said while he was still alive: 'After three days I will rise from the dead.' So we request that you seal the tomb until the third day. This will prevent his disciples from coming and stealing his body and then telling everyone he was raised from the dead! If that happens, we'll be worse off than we were at first." (Matt. 27:62–64 NLT)

Dear Lord Jesus, how could your family and followers have slept the night of Good Friday? I can only imagine the depth of sadness that seized their hearts. And yet others were eu-phoric and relieved that you, "the deceiver," could no longer threaten the status quo of the religious community.

As the sun rose on Saturday, no one understood that the most undeserved death imaginable would yield the greatest return calculable. As you were nailed to the cross, the written code—God's law, with all its regulations and requirements—lost all its condemning power over us. With your last breath, you disarmed the powers of darkness, triumphing over all authorities marshaled against God's kingdom (Col. 2:14–15).

No one realized that your mortal punishment would bring our eternal peace; that your fatal wounding would secure our everlasting healing; that your being crushed under God's judgment would lead to our being cherished by the thrice-holy God (Isa. 53). Though they had the Scriptures, they had no clue.

And yet the chief priests and the Pharisees did remember your promise of resurrection. They weren't sad about your death; they were mad with fear about the possibility of your life. Having planned to put to death a resurrected Lazarus (John 12:10), they weren't about to indulge a resurrected Jesus.

Oh, silly, sinful men—they'd sooner hold back the rising of the sun than the rising of the Son of God. Resurrection Sunday was coming, and there was absolutely nothing they could do about it. The sadness of Saturday would soon be shattered with the shouts of Sunday: "The Lord is risen! He is risen indeed!" In your triumphant and loving name we pray. Amen.

A Prayer for Easter Sunday

Praise be to the God and Father of our Lord Jesus Christ! In his great mercy he has given us new birth into a living hope through the resurrection of Jesus Christ from the dead, and into an inheritance that can never perish, spoil or fade. This inheritance is kept in heaven for you, who through faith are shielded by God's power until the coming of the salvation that is ready to be revealed in the last time. In all this you greatly rejoice. (1 Pet. 1:3–6)

Exalted and resurrected Jesus, we join the apostle Peter's bold declaration of living hope and great joy. For you *have* risen from the dead, and this good news changes *everything.*

Because of your resurrection, we're neither afraid to die nor afraid to live; we're not hapless vagabonds on earth but hope-filled children of God. We're no longer enslaved to our sins; we're now wrapped in your righteousness. Those who have "gone to sleep" in you aren't slumbering in the void; they're rejoicing in your presence. Hallelujah!

Because of your resurrection, we're less to be pitied than anybody and more to be grateful than anybody (1 Cor. 15:14–19). You are the firstfruits and guarantee of a whole new order—the "new creation" dominion of redemption and restoration. Everything sad will come untrue, and all things broken will be made new. How we long for that day!

Because of your resurrection, you are already reigning as King of Kings and Lord of Lords. All evil dominions, wicked authorities, and malevolent powers now stand defeated, and one day they will be fully eradicated. Hallelujah, many times over!

Jesus, your death is the death of death, and your resurrection is the resurrection of all things. You died for our sins and have been raised for our justification. Oh, the wonder, marvel, and gratitude that fills our hearts today. We are forgiven, we are beloved, and we are yours!

In light of this living hope and compelling love, this measureless grace and eternal inheritance, free us for spending the rest of our days living and loving to your glory. We pray, Jesus, in your resurrected and reigning name. Amen.

A Prayer for Easter Monday

And he said to them, "O foolish ones, and slow of heart to believe all that the prophets have spoken! Was it not necessary that the Christ should suffer these things and enter into his glory?" And beginning with Moses and all the Prophets, he interpreted to them in all the Scriptures the things concerning himself. (Luke 24:25–27 ESV)

Dear Lord Jesus, of all your post-resurrection appearances (1 Cor. 15:3–7), my favorite is your visit to forlorn friends on the road to Emmaus, for I have much in common with them (Luke 24:13–35). I too am foolish and slow of heart, in constant need of the Spirit's ministry to free me from my unbelief. I remain deeply grateful for your tenacious tenderness, limitless patience, and steadfast love.

Jesus, continue to do for me what you did for my Emmaus Road brothers. Help me to see you everywhere in the Scriptures—the point and hero of the whole Bible. May Moses' words, especially the law, constantly drive me to you. For you have fulfilled the demands of the law for us and are now fulfilling the beauty of the law in us. Keep me clear and free from all forms of me-centered spirituality. The older I get, the more I want to grow in gospel astonishment.

Jesus, keep convincing me that you are the resounding "Yes!" to every promise God has made through the prophets—not just with respect to your cross, but also to your crown (2 Cor. 1:20). Things in our world are not as they appear. Having risen from the dead, you are now making all things new. You are sovereign over everything. Faith, not fear, is the order of this and every day.

Jesus, give me an incurable case of "redemptive heart-burn," like that which you ignited in the hearts of my Emmaus brothers. Keep showing me more of your glory and grace, that I might give you the adoration and allegiance of which you alone are worthy. In your holy and transforming name I pray. Amen.

Scotty Smith is founding pastor of Christ Community Church (PCA) in Franklin, Tennessee. He is now teacher in residence at West End Community Church (PCA) in Nashville, a daughter church of CCC. Scotty also serves as an adjunct professor at five seminaries, including Covenant, Westminster, Redeemer, RTS Orlando, and Western Seminary in Portland. He is the author of several books including *Everyday Prayers* as well as *Unveiled Hope* with Michael Card and *Speechless* and *Restoring Broken Things* with Steven Curtis Chapman.

CONNECT WITH
SCOTTY SMITH

Scotty Smith planted Christ Community Church in Franklin, Tennessee, and pastored there for twenty-six years. He now serves as Teacher in Residence at West End Community Church in Nashville, a daughter church of CCC. Scotty is also an adjunct professor at five seminaries around the country and blogs daily for The Gospel Coalition.

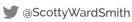 @ScottyWardSmith

 Scotty Smith

To learn more, visit his prayer blog at The Gospel Coalition:
blogs.thegospelcoalition.org/scottysmith

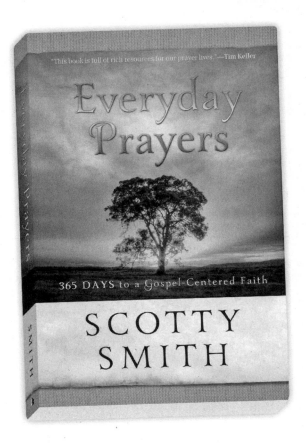

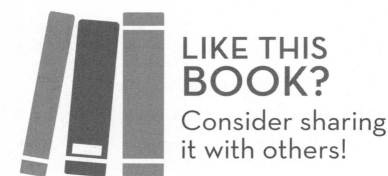

LIKE THIS
BOOK?
Consider sharing
it with others!

- Share or mention the book on your social media platforms. Use the hashtag **#EverySeasonPrayers**.

- Write a book review on your blog or on a retailer site.

- Pick up a copy for friends, family, or strangers! Anyone who you think would enjoy and be challenged by its message.

- Share this message on Twitter or Facebook. **"I loved #EverySeasonPrayers by @ScottyWardSmith @ReadBakerBooks"**

- Recommend this book for your church, workplace, book club, or class.

- Follow Baker Books on social media and tell us what you like.

 Facebook.com/ReadBakerBooks

 @ReadBakerBooks